More Guaranteed Goof-Proof Microwave Cooking

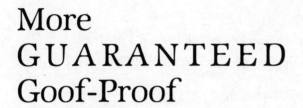

More
GUARANTEED
Goof-Proof

Microwave Cooking

Margie "The Microwhiz®" Kreschollek

BANTAM BOOKS

NEW YORK · TORONTO · LONDON · SYDNEY · AUCKLAND

MORE GUARANTEED GOOF-PROOF MICROWAVE COOKING
A Bantam Book / January 1991

Book design by Ann Gold.

Library of Congress Cataloging-in-Publication Data
Kreschollek, Margie.
   More guaranteed goof-proof microwave cooking / Margie "the
Microwhiz" Kreschollek.
      p.   cm.
   Includes index.
   ISBN 0-553-35201-6
   1. Microwave cookery.   I. Title
TX832.K684 1991
641.5'882—dc20   90-43571
                                                              CIP

Published simultaneously in the United States and Canada

Bantam Books are published by Bantam Books, a division of
Bantam Doubleday Dell Publishing Group, Inc. Its trademark,
consisting of the words "Bantam Books" and the portrayal of
a rooster, is Registered in U.S. Patent and Trademark Office
and in other countries. Marca Registrada. Bantam Books, 666
Fifth Avenue, New York, New York 10103.

PRINTED IN THE UNITED STATES OF AMERICA

BVG 0 9 8 7 6 5 4 3 2 1

To my husband, Willie,
whose LOVE has been constant and continual,
through good food and bad

Contents

Acknowledgments

———————————————•

Richard Sandella has been my editor at the *New Haven Register* since I started my newspaper column there, and his patience and help certainly deserve my biggest thanks. My mom and dad have tested and tasted most of my recipes, and I could not have perfected so many different and tasty ones without them. I hope they both know how much I love and appreciate them.

The folks at Donnkenny, Inc., and Clairol have been so wonderful and helpful, and I want them to know how much they have meant to me.

I also want to thank Rubbermaid, Inc., E-Z Pour, Progresso, Best Brands Corp., and McCormick for allowing me to experiment with their products.

As always, my backup team of Doe Coover, Fran McCullough, Coleen O'Shea, and Joan Shiel have always been there for me—making a book like this possible. Thanks, girls; you deserve a great big cheer!

Introduction

Shortly after *The Guaranteed Goof-Proof Microwave Cookbook* was published, I received a letter from a woman in Africa who wanted to know why the book didn't have more recipes made from scratch (convenience foods were of course completely unavailable to her). To answer her I explained my concept of microwaving, and it occurred to me that all my readers might be interested in this philosophy.

When I was a young girl, my dad's side of the family gathered every Sunday at his mother's. All my aunts, uncles, and cousins visited for the afternoon and then sat down to dinner at a table that took up every available nook and cranny in Grandma's kitchen. I spent most of the day at my aunt Lee's elbow watching and learning, sometimes without even realizing it, the techniques of cooking. As the years passed, my mom was the one who continued my cooking education. It seemed only natural that I was to marry a chef. Trained at the Culinary Institute, my husband, William, taught me many new things, as well as recipes that had been his family's favorites.

After we were married, I wanted a microwave to shorten my time in the kitchen. Finally, after years of pleading, William relented, with the stipulation that I learn to make this very expensive bun warmer *cook*! At the time, I considered myself a very good cook, but that didn't help me one bit with my microwave.

Why? Because all the methods of cooking and recipes I had learned to that point were geared for conventional cooking, and to cook with a microwave oven takes a bit of reeducation in cooking techniques for any cook, regardless of ability.

So I jumped into microwaving using my conventional cooking knowledge, only to find that I ruined a great deal of food. I don't want that to happen to you. So I wrote my first book as a primer: to teach you the basics of microwaving and to make the transition from stove top to microwave as painless as possible. Thus the book uses many frozen, canned, and packaged foods, both for convenience and to teach you how quick and easy microwave cooking can be once you understand its secrets. These kinds of recipes are also helpful for families on the run, single folks, and the elderly who can't shop daily for fresh ingredients.

After years of writing weekly newspaper columns, doing a weekly television segment, and being able to talk directly to folks on my radio program, I feel I know the type of recipes people want. Most cooks, both men and women, either do not have the time or don't want to spend the time with long, complicated recipes that call for vast numbers of ingredients. They want to be able to put together new and interesting-tasting dishes with a minimal amount of preparation.

My second book, *The Guaranteed Goof-Proof Healthy Microwave Cookbook*, offers those healthy-minded cooks the opportunity to prepare both low-cholesterol and low-salt recipes using fresh ingredients with no dependence on packaged cake mixes or canned sauces. This, my third book, incorporates both concepts and offers a choice. There are recipes for those wanting to incorporate fast prepackaged items and recipes from scratch for those with the time and interest.

Please remember that a recipe with many ingredients including lengthy and involved steps of preparation does not necessarily produce a better dish than a simple one. I have spent years researching my recipes and making them over and over again for my family of critical palates to save you the time and trouble. I truly love people, and knowing that I can help them sit down to a home-cooked meal rather than rely on a frozen entrée makes all my work worthwhile. Sharing what I have worked so hard to perfect is my gift to you.

Mastering Your Microwave

I cannot tell you how many microwave recipes I have tried that don't come out exactly right the first time you make them. The directions are usually vague, and they always assume the cook is an experienced microwaver. What I have done with my recipes is take the guesswork out and tell you exactly what to do in each step of the recipe preparation.

Most microwave recipes are tested in 600- to 700-watt microwaves. After writing my first book, I found that there are many microwavers with compact, lower-wattage ovens using them only for heating because cooking times for their ovens are never listed in recipes. So I provide two sets of times for each cooking step in all my recipes. The first set is for those ovens ranging in power from 600 to 700 watts. The second set of times, set off with parentheses and always beginning with the letters *LW* for low-wattage ovens, are for those ovens between 450 and 600 watts of power.

You will notice, too, that the key word in each procedure is in bold print in every recipe to draw your attention to its importance. I take for granted that you welcome information on what utensils to use, how to cover the dish, and the specific techniques needed in every recipe to produce conventional oven-perfect dishes: that is why my recipes are goof-proof. Everything you need to know to reproduce one of my recipes is given to you *in* the recipe, along with troubleshooting tips and suggestions where I feel they will most benefit you.

Also scattered throughout the book are boxes filled with hints and tips to help you become more aware of the various techniques needed to make microwaving as comfortable for you as conventional cooking is.

HOW THE MICROWAVE WORKS

The microwave oven is no longer owned by only the adventurous new gadget seeker; it's now a necessary appliance due to today's fast-paced lifestyle. The days of microwave anxiety are over, but how to produce microwaved food that both looks and tastes like it was cooked conventionally is still a problem. The main reason that many microwaves are still being used only to heat frozen foods, leftovers, and coffee is that these tasks produce a product the user is used to seeing. Reeducation in cooking techniques and experimentation are the keys to utilizing this time-, energy-, and heat-saving appliance.

Every microwave oven has a magnetron tube encased in either the top or bottom of the oven. This tube emits invisible microwaves that spread throughout the inside cavity of the oven. The sides, top, bottom, and door of all microwaves are made of metal, which reflects the emitting microwaves. As the microwaves spread throughout the oven, they bounce away from the metal walls and metal-mesh-covered door and concentrate in the center of the oven.

Microwaves are attracted to molecules of water, sugar, or fat. They penetrate whatever they find in the oven to a depth of not more than one to one-and-a-half inches. They then cause the molecules of water, sugar, or fat to vibrate. This vibration causes heat, and the heat is spread from the outside to the center of the self-cooking food through conduction. Many times I hear people say that the microwaves cook from the center to the outside edges, but this is incorrect. The center of the food is the last place to cook and receives the least amount of heat for the shortest amount of time.

Once the microwaves are stopped, when the oven is shut off or the door is opened, they are no longer in the food, causing the cooking process, and cannot be ingested. However, the molecules are still vibrating, and the food continues to cook for five to 10 minutes after the microwaves are shut off: this is called *standing time*. When you're cooking food in a microwave oven, you must always remember to undercook the food slightly as it continues and finishes cooking during standing time. This principle can be seen when baking a cake. If you were to remove a partially baked cake from a conventional oven, it would fall. However, because the vibrating molecules are still creating heat in a microwaved cake, you can remove it during cooking and it will not fall, as it is still cooking itself.

The microwaves need something to concentrate into, and therefore you must never turn a microwave oven on without having something in it. If you fear that by accident this might happen to you, simply keep a glass of water or a box of baking soda in the oven when it is not in use. The baking soda will also act as a deodorizer and will absorb any excess moisture in the oven when it is not cooking. You will damage your microwave if you allow it to run empty for any length of time, so please be careful.

POWER LEVELS

I was researching an article for *Consumers Digest*, and I had a question about a specific microwave oven. I called the manufacturer and spoke with a gentleman from the company. I asked him some particulars about a certain oven's capabilities and then asked how many power levels that oven offered. Very sheepishly he told me he had this oven in his own kitchen but used only HIGH power and didn't know offhand the other power levels it had. If someone working for a microwave manufacturer doesn't understand power levels, it seems evident to me that many of you may not either.

You certainly would not cook everything on your conventional range on the highest temperature setting, and you should not do that in the microwave either. The best description I can give you of what the power levels will do is to have you picture in your mind a gas burner on a gas range with a full flame. When you use HIGH power on your microwave, it is like cooking over this high flame. Many foods, when placed on that gas flame, need to have the heat reduced to keep them from cooking too fast or burning, and this also applies when microwaving.

Now picture that gas flame turned down to medium-high, or 70 to 80 percent; this is MEDIUM-HIGH power in the microwave. Cooking at this level of heat is quite adequate for some foods, while others may need only a medium flame, or 50 to 60 percent: MEDIUM power in the microwave. Some foods require a low flame, or an equivalent of 30 percent—LOW power in the microwave. If you have no idea what power level to use in the microwave, first remember that gas flame and ask yourself how high a flame you would use and adjust that to the proper power level in your microwave.

If your microwave comes with a DEFROST or REHEAT button, you will find that the power and sometimes even the time are preset for you. Most often a DEFROST button will set only the power level, leaving the time up to the cook, whereas the REHEAT button usually will set both the power and a time of somewhere between 2 and 3 minutes. If after reheating for the preset time your dish is not adequately reheated, push REHEAT again, but watch carefully that you do not overheat or dry out your leftovers. The REHEAT button is not usually recommended for cooking but just for reheating leftovers.

Keep in mind that when you're cooking in the microwave you can always cook something a little longer, but once you have overcooked it there just isn't any way of saving it. When you are not sure what power level to use, but you know HIGH power is too much, start with 50 or 60 percent power. If the food seems to be cooking too slowly, go up to 70 or 80 percent power. It may take a few minutes more to cook, but you will be sure that your dish will not burn or overcook.

EQUIPMENT

Microwave myth number one: I am not going to do much cooking in my microwave, because I have to buy all sorts of expensive cooking containers. You would be surprised by how much of your conventional cooking and serving equipment you can use safely in the microwave. There are some specialty items that cannot be duplicated with conventional dishes, such as a browning dish, microwave pressure cooker, plastic meat racks, covered meat roasting pans, and plastic bundt dishes. And there are many lightweight, easy-to-clean plastic pieces on the market made just for the microwave that you may want to purchase. But you will also find you can use many of the items you have accumulated over the years quite well.

Do you have glass, Pyrex, or Corning Ware dishes in your cabinets? If so, they all work fine. However, some plastics will melt, and some pottery pieces actually gather microwaves because of the materials they are composed of and thus are not considered safe for microwave use. How do you tell what is and what is not safe for use in your microwave? By simply testing it using this easy method.

Place the piece of equipment in question in the microwave along with a glass of water, either inside or outside of it, but be sure it's touching the piece. Microwave on HIGH power for 1 minute. Only the water should be warm. If the test piece is warm, it is not safe for continued microwave use. But you always use your favorite ceramic mug in the microwave to heat your coffee, you say, and you just tested it to find it got warm. Well, you may have noticed that the handle is never really cool when you heat it, but you never considered it unsafe. Time to change mugs.

Safe equipment for microwave use will not melt, crack, or chip from the heat. Except for the browning dish, dishes used in the microwave should get hot only in the areas where the food is sitting and has transferred its heat to that surface. These safeguards are especially important when children or those with handicaps or disabilities are using this equipment. People become very accustomed to putting their hands into the microwave without using pot holders, because they do not expect dishes to be warm.

You will find that most paper products work wonderfully in the microwave, but be careful when using Styrofoam. Unless it specifically says "safe for microwave use," I have found most Styrofoam plates and cups will melt when heated. Wooden products such as toothpicks, skewers, and chopsticks will not give you a problem, and you can quickly reheat rolls in a paper or cloth napkin-lined wooden or straw bread basket with no trouble.

Metal utensils or dishes that have a decorative metal design or border are definitely *out* for the microwave. When the microwaves hit metal, they bounce away. Metal touching metal in the microwave causes arcing. Have you seen arcing in your oven? If you can't recall, then you haven't! It looks just like a Fourth-of-July fireworks display, and believe me, once you see it you will recognize what is happening. If this happens, you are using a utensil with some metal in it or possibly you have left a spoon or fork in the container. If you are defrosting, you may have left a twist tie on the bag or accidentally picked up a foil margarine wrapper on the underside of your cooking container. Should you see arcing, immediately shut off the oven and remove the culprit before continuing.

The one piece of equipment you most assuredly have in your cabinets that will help your microwaved food cook more evenly is a saucer. If you own a piece of equipment made specifically for microwave cooking, take a look at the bottom. You will see that the container sits on a short rim or little legs and the very bottom is slightly concave to allow the microwaves to get underneath and through the bottom as well as through the top and sides. You can accomplish the same thing by placing all of your flat-bottomed cooking containers on an inverted saucer free of any metal decoration.

Turntables are one item that you will not find on your cabinet shelves. Some ovens distribute their microwaves in such a way that the food gets an equal amount of cooking power all around it. However, many ovens do not, and some ovens have what we call a *hot spot*. If you find that everything you place in a particular area of your microwave always overcooks, you have a hot spot. The easy way to solve the hot spot problem is to use a turntable that revolves the food around the available microwaves; you can also manually rotate the dish out of the hot spot area frequently.

Microwave browning dishes actually gather the microwaves rather than letting them pass through and concentrate on the food inside. Browning dishes, similar to the silver trays you find in frozen microwave pizzas and fish, are coated with a material that absorbs the gathered microwaves and gets hot. When you place food on this hot surface, the food sizzles or crisps, as does the crust on pizza. This dish does get hot and must be preheated before adding food, and you should always use pot holders when handling it. There are many types on the market; some are flat like a skillet, and others have sides and a cover for stir-frying or other recipes that incorporate searing or frying meat.

A meat rack is handy not only for cooking meat, but it can be used to elevate bags of microwave popping corn, too. The meat rack makes consistently turning meat unnecessary, as the rack raises the meat off the flat surface of the cooking container, allowing the microwaves to cook from all sides. If you do not have a meat rack, you can substitute a couple of inverted custard cups, a small inverted bowl, or wooden chopsticks in the bottom of a casserole dish to elevate the meat.

As you can see, except for a few specialty items there is no need to spend lots of money on all new cooking utensils and to look for extra cabinet space to hold them. Remember that round containers cook more evenly than square-cornered ones, so check your utensils and try to microwave with your everyday kitchen equipment and use the money you saved to experiment with the new recipes you will find in this book.

COVERING AND VENTING

When you read a recipe that calls for covering the dish, do you know what to cover it with? I get upset when I see microwave recipes written this way. The writer knows what type of covering was used when the recipe was prepared and should always pass this necessary information on to the cook. Most people would assume the writer means to use the lid of the casserole dish, and often that's the wrong choice. You will find that my recipes always tell you what to cover your dish with, because the wrong covering can cause an imperfect finished product. When I describe a method of covering in the beginning of the recipe, you should use the same method throughout the recipe.

There are four basic ways to cover foods for microwave cooking. The lid that comes with many casserole dishes produces the same effect as plastic wrap. It holds in the moisture and allows the food to steam. When you use the lid, it can just be placed snugly on the dish; however, when you use plastic wrap you must pull back one corner to give the steam an avenue of escape to keep the plastic wrap from melting onto the food. In my recipes you'll see that I always tell you to "pull back one corner to vent the steam." If you read a recipe elsewhere that says "prick the plastic wrap," please just pull back one corner. Pricking the plastic wrap for very short periods of cooking may not cause a problem, but if you are cooking for any length of time, I have found that the steam inside the dish can cause the little holes to melt shut and melt the plastic wrap onto the food. Vented plastic wrap is not something you can buy, it is the procedure of pulling back one corner of the plastic wrap covering a dish to vent it.

Wax paper should be used when you want the food in the dish to steam but you don't want to hold in the accumulating moisture. I've had many letters asking if there is a right and wrong side to wax paper and whether the wax will melt onto the food. I've checked with the folks at Reynolds, and they tell me that the wax is bonded onto the paper and will not melt off or in any way come off the paper onto the food, so please don't worry about it. And because it won't melt, venting is not necessary.

If you're concerned only about keeping the spatters inside a dish, then cover it with paper towels. Melting butter or heating liquids that could decorate your oven requires only a layer of paper towel over the top to prevent spattering. Look at your paper towels before using them, however. If they have a printed design on them, the ink used to print the design should be on only one side of the paper. Place the all-white side next to the food to be sure the inks don't transfer color to the food. The only problem I have ever had was in cooking bacon. The green ink on a border-print towel came off on bacon I had placed right on top of the ink. It is the only time I have had this problem, but my motto is better to be safe than sorry.

DEFROSTING

How many times have you forgotten to defrost something for dinner and popped it into the microwave, only to have the edges begin to cook while the center was still brick hard? Many books and charts tell you that meats defrost in a certain number of minutes per pound. These guidelines may be accurate, but what they don't tell you is that the defrosted edges also start to cook during long periods of defrosting. Here are several suggestions for solving this problem.

Begin preparing for microwave defrosting before freezing, if possible. Remove meats from their store wrappings and repackage them in plastic bags or freezer wrap. You'll notice that most meats come packaged from the supermarket with a thin moisture packet underneath them: remove it before freezing. This packet absorbs excess moisture and defrosts in the microwave very quickly. Microwaves are attracted to liquids before ice, and much of the needed defrosting power will be drawn to this quickly defrosted packet and away from the frozen object on top of it.

Elevate frozen foods of all kinds on a meat rack or an inverted saucer to allow the microwave energy to defrost from underneath as well as from the top and sides.

If you're one who consistently forgets to remove twist ties when going from freezer to microwave, substitute the plastic bread closures that can go right from the freezer to the microwave. They come on many different types of bread and can sometimes be found in the produce section of your supermarket to close the plastic bags used for purchasing fresh vegetables.

When you're freezing ground meats, form them into a ball and place the ball in a plastic bag. Make a fist and flatten the meat, forming a hole in the center. The microwaves will then be able to defrost from all sides and in the open center as well. Remove the neck and giblet bag from chickens and turkeys before freezing, as this will also help them defrost more quickly. If you plan to defrost and/or cook your turkey in the microwave, you must remove the metal piece that holds the legs together.

Many microwaves today have a built-in defrost cycle, but if yours doesn't, use 30 percent or LOW power for defrosting. Defrost for short periods of time, 4 to 5 minutes at most. Allow the frozen food to stand for 5 minutes right in the oven and repeat the process. You may have to repeat the process several times, but you will find that the food will defrost far more evenly, with no cooking occurring on the defrosted edges.

WHAT TO LOOK FOR WHEN BUYING A MICROWAVE

Before you go out to purchase a new microwave, determine the size of the oven that will best suit your family. A family of four or more will need a full-size oven if you're going to be doing more than reheating. A mid-size model will suit a family of two or three. For a single person, for those interested in just quick heat-ups, or for use in the office, a compact model will do. If the unit will be used for a large percentage of the daily cooking, and the finished appearance of the food is high on the list of priorities, select a microwave with a browning unit or a microwave/convection combination. Keep in mind that both of these units may require cookware that is safe for both microwaving and conventional cooking.

The available space to house the oven is another consideration when you're selecting oven size. But remember that a microwave can be placed on a rolling cart, mounted on the wall or under a cabinet, or hung in a unit complete with exhaust fan and light that mounts over a conventional stove. Some models vent from the front, while others vent from underneath or the back of the oven. If the oven vents from the back, several inches of back and side clearance must be allowed; make sure the casing is not flush against a wall or cabinet. To be a sensible shopper, prepare yourself with the measurements of the area where the microwave will be placed and take the largest cooking container you're likely to use to the store when selecting a microwave.

The higher the wattage in the oven, the faster it will cook. If time is a premium, select the model that fits the available space, holds the largest cooking container needed, and has the highest wattage available. To ensure maximum energy output, microwave ovens should be plugged into their own separate electric line with an electrical surge protector and not be on a line with other household appliances. If defrosting and reheating are all you require, and time is not a factor, smaller models with lower wattages are available.

Manufacturers are now offering color choices on the exteriors of various model microwaves, and the interiors of the ovens vary from white plastic coating to an easier-to-clean stainless steel. The plastic-coated interiors may get stained if not cleaned frequently, which should not happen with the stainless-steel cavity.

Along with capacity, the method of timing should be considered. Units equipped with electronic touch-control pads are far more accurate and easy to operate than the less expensive dial-control models. Touch-control pads also afford the use of automatic defrost, heat, and preprogrammed cook cycles available on some models. These features, along with temperature probes that allow the food to be cooked by temperature rather than time, and oven racks that add extra space for utilizing more cooking containers, are available extras that may not be necessary for the person just reheating leftovers and popping corn.

Each manufacturer distributes the microwaves differently inside the oven cavity. Either the food must turn around the microwaves or the microwaves must be stirred in a fashion that moves them around the food. Some ovens are equipped with turntables that continually turn the food around the emitting microwaves. The recessed turntable with an exterior on/off switch makes excellent sense because it doesn't limit the size of the dishes that can be used. Other ovens operate only as long as the dish is small enough to fit inside the turntable. Some models allow the turntable to be removed or turned over to accommodate large dishes.

The magnetron tube is as important to the microwave as the picture tube is to the television, so always check to be sure it is covered in the warranty.

Look at the outside of the oven to be sure the programming area is easy to read and that the door opens comfortably to your touch.

Purchasing from a reputable dealer that offers service is a plus as most discount houses do not offer service and independent repair service may be difficult to find. Check warranties carefully, especially if the unit is mounted on the wall as some warranties cover only carry-in repair. The most frequent repair problems occur with door closures and fuses. Slamming, hanging, or pulling on the doors can cause them to close improperly, which knocks the switches they control out of adjustment. Fuses can be a problem if the oven is not plugged into its own electric line with a surge protector. Microwaves must be protected from fluctuations in electric current, from voltage changes or electrical storms.

You will probably own your microwave for at least as long as you own your conventional stove, so be a careful shopper and consider more than just price. Check for features, size, capacity, wattage, the warranty, and available service on the model you select.

CHECKLIST OF IMPORTANT THINGS TO REMEMBER

1. Don't turn your microwave oven on unless something is inside it.

2. Don't operate your microwave if there is a crack in the door or in the glass tray in your oven or if the door does not close properly.

3. Don't use cooking containers unless they are made for the microwave, made of glass, Corning Ware, or paper products (but not newspaper), or have been tested to be sure they are safe for microwave use.

4. Don't leave forks, spoons, or knives in dishes while cooking unless they are made of micro-safe materials.

5. Don't use meat or candy thermometers in the microwave unless they are made for microwave use. To test the temperature with a conventional thermometer, remove the cooking item from the microwave, insert the thermometer, let it stand for a minute or two, read, and remove the thermometer before placing the item back into the microwave oven.

6. Don't try to dry clothing in the microwave oven.

7. Whenever possible, plug the microwave into a circuit that doesn't run any other household appliance.

8. Under any circumstances, don't try to cook or reheat an egg either in its shell or one that is peeled but unsliced. The egg will explode in the oven or in your face when you remove it.

9. Don't turn the microwave on and walk away before first looking inside to be sure you did not leave a metal utensil, a twist

tie, or a foil wrapper inside (say on a box of frozen vegetables) or that you didn't accidentally pick up a foil margarine wrapper on your cooking container. If this should happen—and you will be able to tell by the multicolored sparks that will be given off— immediately shut the oven off, remove the scoundrel, and then continue cooking.

10. Don't allow children to use anything but plastic microwave-safe containers that can neither burn or cut them should they be dropped.

11. Under no circumstances, regardless of what you read in other books, attempt to deep-fry in the microwave. You can be burned and damage plastic-coated oven interiors with the hot grease.

12. Care for your oven gently when cleaning. Don't use harsh abrasives or oven cleaners and never try to scrape off burnt-on spots. Use mild soaps and soft cloths when cleaning.

13. Don't bake two-crust pies in the microwave; the bottom crust will not cook.

14. Don't wedge your microwave into a tight corner if it vents from the rear. You must leave a sufficient amount of clearance around rear-venting machines.

15. Don't use square-cornered dishes when cooking things that cannot be moved out of the corners frequently.

16. Don't use flat-bottomed cooking containers without first elevating them on an inverted saucer free of metal decoration.

17. Don't microwave red meats totally on HIGH power. They will cook so fast there will not be time for tenderizing.

18. Don't cover cooking containers tightly with plastic wrap, as it may very well melt onto the food. Making little slits in tightly covered plastic wrap also will not work, because they may melt shut. Simply pull back one corner to let the steam vent.

19. Don't place food directly on the floor of the microwave. Put two layers of paper towel underneath it to absorb the moisture that will form.

20. Don't try to microwave something that touches the top or sides of the inside of the oven cavity; it is just too big.

21. Don't slam, hang on, or force the door to close. If you feel the door is not operating properly, have a reputable service person look at it.

22. Don't try to repair your microwave yourself. As of this writing, this is not a repair task that can be done by the home mechanic.

23. And especially, don't become nervous when learning to microwave with my recipes! These recipes have been tested repeatedly, and if you follow my instructions the results will be very satisfying to even the most inexperienced microwaver.

24. Communication with my readers is important to me, so *do* please feel free to write to me in care of my publisher with your comments and suggestions. That's the only way I can help you better understand this new art of cooking.

Appetizers

Cheddar Pick-Me-Ups

MAKES 30 APPETIZERS

EQUIPMENT:	10-inch glass pie plate, medium mixing bowl
COOKING TIME:	14 to 18 minutes (Low wattage ovens 16½ to 21 minutes)
STANDING TIME:	10 minutes

½ **cup imitation bacon bits**
1 **8-ounce package shredded Cheddar cheese**
¼ **cup finely chopped scallions**
1 **cup Bisquick**
1 **cup milk**
4 **eggs**
¼ **teaspoon onion powder**
¼ **teaspoon salt**
⅛ **teaspoon pepper**

Sprinkle bacon bits, cheese, and scallions in the bottom of pie plate. In mixing bowl, **whisk** together remaining ingredients until smooth. Carefully pour mixture into pie plate. (If dish is flat-bottomed, **elevate** it on an inverted saucer.) Place on a turntable if available and microwave on 70 percent power or MEDIUM-HIGH for 14 to 18 minutes (LW 16½ to 21 minutes) or until a knife inserted halfway between center and edge comes out clean and mixture seems set. (**Rotate** dish ¼ turn every 4 minutes if not using turntable.)

Let **stand** on a hard heat-proof surface for 10 minutes before cutting into 1½ inch squares.

Troubleshooting: If you have a hot spot in the oven or if one area of the dish seems to be overcooking, rotate the dish more often.

Chicken Canapé Rounds

MAKES 26 TO 28 APPETIZERS

EQUIPMENT:	medium mixing bowl, round dinner plate
COOKING TIME:	3 to 3½ minutes (Low wattage ovens 3½ to 4 minutes)
STANDING TIME:	none required

2 **cups finely chopped cooked chicken**
¼ **cup shredded Cheddar cheese**
¼ **cup finely chopped celery**
¼ **cup mayonnaise**
1 **tablespoon snipped fresh parsley**
¼ **teaspoon paprika**
½ **teaspoon onion salt**
26 **to 28 melba toast rounds**
snipped fresh chives or sliced pitted black olives for garnish

Combine chicken, cheese, celery, mayonnaise, parsley, paprika, and onion salt in medium bowl. Place 1 teaspoon of chicken mixture on each toast round.

Arrange 14 canapés on flat plate **covered** with 2 layers of paper towel. Microwave on 70 percent power or MEDIUM-HIGH for 3 to 3½ minutes (LW 3½ to 4 minutes) or until cheese melts. Repeat procedure with remaining appetizers.

Suggestions: Prepare filling ahead of time and microwave just before serving.

Crabmeat Canapés

I started out to make regular English muffin pizzas one day, and then thought I would get a bit more creative. My husband likes these so much he always has me make extra filling, leaves the muffin halves whole, and tops them with sliced tomatoes for lunch.

MAKES 40 CANAPÉS

EQUIPMENT:	medium bowl, round dinner plate
COOKING TIME:	4¾ to 7 minutes (Low wattage ovens 6 to 8 minutes)
STANDING TIME:	none required

1   **8-ounce package cream cheese**
2   **tablespoons mayonnaise**
2   **tablespoons horseradish sauce**
1   **tablespoon white wine**
¼   **cup chopped pitted black olives**
½   **teaspoon salt**
⅛   **teaspoon pepper**
½   **pound crabmeat, flaked, or imitation crabmeat, chopped**
5   **English muffins, split and quartered**

Remove foil wrapper from cream cheese and place in bowl. Microwave on HIGH for 45 to 60 seconds (LW 55 to 70 seconds) or until soft, checking texture after 45 seconds to be sure the cheese doesn't melt. **Whisk** in mayonnaise, horseradish sauce, and white wine. **Stir** in black olives, salt, pepper, and crabmeat.

Mound 1 teaspoon of crabmeat mixture onto each muffin quarter. Place quarters on dinner plate lined with 2 layers of paper towels. Microwave on 80 percent power or MEDIUM-HIGH for 4 to 6 minutes (LW 5 to 7 minutes) or until hot and bubbly.

Curaçao Caribbean Keshi Jena

This recipe is a unique appetizer that could also be used as a main dish; it's very filling. In Curaçao they call stuffed Gouda cheese *keshi jena*.

SERVES 6

EQUIPMENT: plastic dishwasher-safe colander and casserole dish, medium mixing bowl, round serving dish

COOKING TIME: 10 to 13 minutes (Low wattage ovens 11¾ to 15½ minutes)

STANDING TIME: none required

1   **pound lean ground beef**
1   **small onion, chopped**
1   **teaspoon paprika**
1   **teaspoon drained capers**
¼   **cup chopped pitted black olives**
½   **teaspoon salt**
½   **teaspoon dried oregano**
1   **tablespoon raisins**
2   **Gouda cheeses, 3 to 4 inches in diameter**

Crumble ground beef into colander set into a casserole dish to catch the drippings. Microwave on HIGH for 3 minutes (LW 3½ minutes). **Break up** the meat chunks with a fork and add the onions. Microwave on HIGH for 3 to 4 minutes (LW 3½ to 4¾ minutes) or until the meat loses its pink color. Transfer cooked meat to bowl and add paprika, capers, olives, salt, and oregano, mixing to combine. Microwave on HIGH for 2 minutes (LW 2½ minutes). **Stir** in raisins and set aside.

Carefully **remove** the wax from each cheese, cut the top off, and scoop out the center, leaving a thick shell, reserving top and scooped-out cheese. (Try using a grapefruit spoon for scooping.) Place the shells on a round serving dish and fill each shell with ground beef mixture, mounding if necessary. Top with the reserved cheese, adding the sliced-off top last. Microwave, **uncov-**

ered, on 30 percent power or LOW for 2 to 4 minutes (LW 2¼ to 4¾ minutes) or until cheese shells are warm and soft but not completely melted.

Suggestions: Ground pork may be substituted for ground beef.

Donnkenny Meatballs

My friends at Donnkenny, Inc., really gave me a challenge, and I love challenges. They asked me to come up with a microwave recipe for toothpick appetizers that they could serve their clients in the showroom and use the leftovers in sandwiches for the sales staff lunch. "Make them different and tasty," they said, and so I did my best. This recipe doubles or triples easily; just remember to do the meatballs in batches and use a large casserole dish.

MAKES 35 COCKTAIL MEATBALLS

EQUIPMENT: medium mixing bowl, 10-inch round dinner plate, 4-cup glass measure, 1½-quart round casserole dish

COOKING TIME: 17 to 22 minutes (Low wattage ovens 20¼ to 26 minutes)

STANDING TIME: none required

MEATBALLS
1 **pound lean ground beef**
1 **egg, slightly beaten**
½ **cup plain dry bread crumbs**
¼ **cup grated Parmesan cheese**
⅓ **cup water**
¼ **cup finely chopped onion**
1 **large garlic clove, finely minced**
1 **tablespoon snipped fresh parsley**
½ **teaspoon dried oregano**
1 **teaspoon salt**
¼ **teaspoon pepper**

SAUCE
1 12-ounce jar chili sauce
1 12-ounce jar grape jelly

Combine all meatball ingredients in mixing bowl. Shape mixture into 35 uniformly sized balls and arrange them in circles on dinner plate.

Cover with wax paper. (If dish is flat-bottomed, **elevate** it on an inverted saucer.) Place on turntable if available, and microwave on HIGH for 5 minutes (LW 6 minutes). (**Rotate** dish ½ turn after 3 minutes if not using turntable.)

Drain any liquid and **rearrange** balls, bringing those in the center of the dish to the outside edges and the ones along the edges into the center of the dish. **Cover** again and microwave on HIGH for 3 to 5 minutes (LW 3½ to 6 minutes) or until the centers are no longer pink. (**Rotate** dish ½ turn after 3 minutes if not using turntable.) Remove dish from microwave, **drain** any liquid, tent with foil, and allow to **stand** while preparing sauce.

In glass measure, **whisk** together chili sauce and grape jelly. **Cover** with plastic wrap, pulling back one corner to vent the steam, and microwave on HIGH for 5 to 6 minutes (LW 6 to 7 minutes) or until hot, **whisking** once.

Transfer meatballs to casserole dish and add heated sauce, **stirring** gently to coat. **Cover** with wax paper and microwave on 80 percent power or MEDIUM-HIGH for 4 to 6 minutes (LW 4¾ to 7 minutes) or until hot and bubbly, carefully **stirring** once. **Stir** before serving and serve with toothpicks or cocktail forks or as a sandwich filling.

Troubleshooting: Roll meatballs uniformly in size, because things of the same size cook in the same length of time.

Suggestions: For a variation or if you're in a real hurry, substitute cocktail franks or regular frankfurters cut into 1-inch pieces for the meatballs. Prepare the sauce as directed above, add the franks, **cover** with wax paper, and microwave at 80% on MEDIUM-HIGH for 5 to 7 minutes (LW 6 to 8 minutes) or until franks are cooked and sauce is hot and bubbly.

Ham Bites

SERVES 10 TO 12

EQUIPMENT: 1½-quart round casserole dish, 4-cup glass measure

COOKING TIME: 10 to 14 minutes (Low wattage ovens 11 to 16 minutes)

STANDING TIME: none required

1 to 1½ pounds cooked boneless ham, cut into bite-size cubes
2 cups ketchup
1 tablespoon chili sauce
¼ cup sweet pickle relish
2 teaspoons prepared yellow mustard
3 tablespoons dark brown sugar
2 tablespoons lemon juice
½ cup water

Place ham cubes in casserole dish and set aside.

Place remaining ingredients in glass measure, **whisking** together to blend. **Cover** with plastic wrap, pulling back one corner to vent the steam. Microwave on HIGH for 5 to 7 minutes (LW 6 to 8 minutes) or until hot and bubbly, **stirring** once. Pour sauce over ham cubes, **stir** well to coat, and **cover** with wax paper. Microwave on 80 percent power or MEDIUM-HIGH for 5 to 7 minutes (LW 5 to 8 minutes) or until ham is heated through, **stirring** once. Serve with toothpicks or cocktail forks.

Suggestions: This is a great way to use up leftover baked ham, or you can buy boiled ham at the deli and have it cut into thick slices.

Spinach Squares

MAKES 48 1½-INCH SQUARES

EQUIPMENT:	colander, small and large mixing bowls, 9 × 13-inch baking dish
COOKING TIME:	41 to 49 minutes (Low wattage ovens 47½ to 56½ minutes)
STANDING TIME:	8 minutes

2 **10-ounce paper-covered boxes chopped spinach**
2 **tablespoons butter or margarine, sliced**
½ **cup chopped onion**
1 **large garlic clove, minced**
3 **eggs, slightly beaten**
1 **cup milk**
1 **cup flour**
1 **teaspoon baking powder**
½ **teaspoon salt**
¼ **teaspoon pepper**
1 **cup shredded Monterey Jack cheese**
1 **cup grated Muenster cheese**
3 **tablespoons grated Parmesan cheese**

Place paper-covered boxes of spinach on 2 layers of paper towels on floor of microwave. Microwave on HIGH for 6 minutes (LW 7 minutes). Turn boxes over and rearrange. Microwave on HIGH for 6 minutes (LW 7 minutes). Let **stand** for 3 minutes, then place in colander to drain.

Place butter, onion, and garlic in small bowl. **Cover** with plastic wrap, pulling back one corner to vent the steam, and microwave on HIGH for 3 to 4 minutes (LW 3½ to 4½ minutes) or until crisp-tender. Transfer mixture to large bowl and add eggs, milk, flour, baking powder, salt, and pepper. **Whisk** well and add Monterey Jack and Muenster and well-drained spinach. Pour mixture into baking dish and sprinkle with Parmesan cheese. (If dish is flat-bottomed, **elevate** it on an inverted saucer.)

Microwave, **uncovered,** on 50 percent power or MEDIUM for 26 to 33 minutes (LW 30 to 38 minutes) or until center is set but not dry, **rotating** dish ½ turn every 5 minutes. Let **stand** on a hard heat-proof surface for 5 minutes. Cool before cutting into 1½-inch squares.

Troubleshooting: If your oven has a hot spot or if one area appears to be overcooking, rotate dish more frequently.

Sweet and Sour Turkey Meatballs

MAKES 36 COCKTAIL MEATBALLS

EQUIPMENT:	medium mixing bowl, 10-inch round dinner plate, 2-quart round casserole dish
COOKING TIME:	15 to 20 minutes (Low wattage ovens 17¾ to 23¾ minutes)
STANDING TIME:	none required

MEATBALLS
- **1 pound ground turkey**
- **1 egg, slightly beaten**
- **¼ cup plain dry bread crumbs**
- **2 tablespoons grated Parmesan cheese**
- **¼ cup finely chopped onion**
- **¼ cup finely grated carrot**
- **⅓ cup tomato juice**
- **1 tablespoon snipped fresh parsley**
- **¾ teaspoon dried oregano**
- **½ teaspoon garlic salt**
- **¼ teaspoon pepper**

SAUCE
- **1 12-ounce jar marinara sauce**
- **1 16-ounce can jellied cranberry sauce**

Mix all meatball ingredients together in mixing bowl and shape into 36 uniformly sized balls. Arrange balls on dinner plate in circles and **cover** with wax paper. (If dish is flat-bottomed, **elevate** it on an inverted saucer.) Place on turntable if available and microwave on HIGH for 4 minutes (LW 4¾ minutes). (**Rotate** dish ½ turn every 2 minutes if not using turntable.) **Drain** any liquid and **rearrange** balls, bringing the less cooked ones from the center of the dish to the outside edges and the ones along the edges into the center.

Cover again and microwave on HIGH for 4 to 5 minutes (LW 4¾ to 6 minutes) or until the centers are no longer pink. (**Rotate** dish ½ turn every 2 minutes if not using turntable.) Remove dish from microwave, **drain** any liquid, **cover** with foil, and let **stand** while preparing sauce.

Combine sauce ingredients in casserole dish and **whisk** until well blended. **Cover** with plastic wrap, pulling back one corner to vent the steam, and microwave on HIGH for 4 to 6 minutes (LW 4¾ to 7 minutes) or until hot, **stirring** once.

Add meatballs, **stir** gently to coat, and **cover** with wax paper. Microwave on 80 percent power or MEDIUM-HIGH for 3 to 5 minutes (LW 3½ to 6 minutes) or until heated through, **stirring** once. (**Rotate** dish ½ turn when stirring if not using turntable.) Serve with toothpicks or cocktail forks.

Troubleshooting: Roll meatballs uniformly in size, because things of the same size cook in the same length of time.

Suggestions: Excellent as a filling for hero sandwiches.

Candi's Meatless Meatballs

During my sister Candi's vegetarian days this was one of her favorite recipes. It converted beautifully to the microwave, and you will not be able to tell from looking or tasting these "meatballs" that they do not contain meat of any kind. Serve them as an appetizer in a chafing dish with sweet and sour sauce and toothpicks or combine with your favorite spaghetti sauce and serve over macaroni.

MAKES 24 BALLS

EQUIPMENT:	medium mixing bowl, 10-inch round dinner plate or flat glass dish
COOKING TIME:	10 to 12 minutes (Low wattage ovens 12 to 14 minutes)
STANDING TIME:	5 minutes

1 cup finely ground walnuts
⅔ cup Italian-flavored dry bread crumbs
⅔ cup wheat germ
1 cup shredded Cheddar cheese
½ cup grated Parmesan cheese
2 eggs, slightly beaten
1 5-ounce can evaporated milk
2 teaspoons vegetable oil
½ cup grated onion
¼ cup snipped fresh parsley
1½ teaspoons salt
½ teaspoon pepper

Blend all ingredients together in mixing bowl. Shape into 24 uniformly sized balls and arrange in circles on dinner plate. **Cover** plate with wax paper. (If plate is flat-bottomed, **elevate** it on an inverted saucer.) Place on turntable if available and microwave on HIGH for 10 to 12 minutes (LW 12 to 14 minutes) or until firm. (**Do not** rearrange. As the cheeses melt the balls become too soft to handle, but don't worry; they will firm up as they cook.) (**Rotate** dish ¼ turn every 3 minutes if not using turntable.) Let **stand, covered,** for 5 minutes.

Troubleshooting: Be sure to make balls uniform in size and shape, because things of the same size cook in the same length of time.

SWEET AND SOUR SAUCE

MAKES 3 CUPS

EQUIPMENT: medium mixing bowl, 2-quart round casserole dish
COOKING TIME: 3 to 4 minutes (Low wattage ovens 3½ to 4½ minutes)
STANDING TIME: none required

1   16-ounce can whole-berry cranberry sauce
1   8-ounce can tomato sauce
1   teaspoon finely minced garlic

In mixing bowl, mix ingredients together well. Place cooked balls in casserole dish. Pour blended sauce over balls and **cover** dish with wax paper. (If dish is flat-bottomed, **elevate** it on an inverted saucer.) Microwave on HIGH for 3 to 4 minutes (LW 3½ to 4½ minutes) or until sauce is hot, carefully **stirring** once.

Creamy Bacon Dip.

Serve this dip with assorted raw vegetables: carrot and celery sticks, green pepper strips, cherry tomatoes, and cauliflower and broccoli flowerets.

MAKES 1½ CUPS

EQUIPMENT: medium mixing bowl
COOKING TIME: 2¾ to 3½ minutes (Low wattage ovens 3¼ to 4 minutes)
STANDING TIME: none required

1   8-ounce package cream cheese
½   cup mayonnaise
3   tablespoons milk
2   tablespoons finely chopped onion
3   teaspoons lemon juice
⅛   teaspoon pepper
¼   cup bacon-flavored chips
    chopped pitted black olives for garnish

Remove foil wrapper from cream cheese and place in bowl. Microwave on HIGH for 45 to 60 seconds (LW 55 to 70 seconds) or until soft, checking texture after 45 seconds to be sure the cheese doesn't melt. **Whisk** in mayonnaise, milk, onion, lemon juice, and pepper. **Stir** in bacon chips. (If dish is flat-bottomed, **elevate** it on an inverted saucer.) Microwave on 70 percent power or MEDIUM-HIGH for 2 to 2½ minutes (LW 2¼ to 2¾ minutes) or until warm, **stirring** every minute. Garnish with olives.

Mexican Hot Dip

Serve this dip with corn chips, tortilla chips, or nachos.

MAKES 3 CUPS

EQUIPMENT:	4-cup glass measure or medium mixing bowl
COOKING TIME:	7 to 10 minutes (Low wattage ovens 8¼ to 11¾ minutes)
STANDING TIME:	none required

1   15-ounce can chili without beans
½   cup shredded Colby cheese
½   cup shredded Monterey Jack cheese
12 drops hot cayenne pepper sauce
1   teaspoon hot taco sauce

Place chili and cheeses in glass measure and **stir** well. Microwave on 80 percent power or MEDIUM-HIGH for 5 to 6 minutes (LW 6 to 7 minutes) or until mixture is hot and cheeses have melted, **stirring** every 2 minutes.

Add sauces, **stir** well, and microwave on 80 percent power or MEDIUM-HIGH for 2 to 4 minutes (LW 2¼ to 4¾ minutes) or until heated through.

BARBECUE SAUCES

The biggest frustration I had as a novice cook, from the day we were married, was grilling chicken to the perfect degree of doneness. Always afraid I would overcook it, I usually removed it from the grill still pink—and if there is anything my husband can't tolerate rare, it's chicken.

For years I actually avoided grilling chicken. Then I discovered microwaving and started precooking my chicken parts before grilling. Microwaving first is a great idea; it removes a great deal of the fat that usually causes the coals to flare up and always produces completely cooked barbecue chicken.

To precook 2 to 3 pounds of fryer parts in the microwave for grilling, wash and pat the pieces dry. Arrange the chicken pieces on a meat rack in a circle with the meatiest portions to the outside of the dish. **Cover** with wax paper and microwave on HIGH for 4 to 5 minutes (LW 4½ to 6 minutes) per pound, **rotating** dish ½ turn and rearranging pieces halfway through cooking time. Finish on your barbecue grill, adding barbecue sauce once chicken is on the grill.

Sweet and Sour Sauce

This is an excellent marinating sauce for chicken wings or parts. If used for marinating and basting, it will be sufficient for about 3 pounds of chicken parts. If using only as a basting sauce, it will cover 4 to 5 pounds of poultry.

MAKES 1⅓ CUPS

> EQUIPMENT: 2-cup glass measure
> COOKING TIME: 4 to 6 minutes (Low wattage ovens 4½ to 7 minutes)
> STANDING TIME: none required

½ **cup soy sauce**
½ **cup ketchup**
⅓ **cup honey**
½ **teaspoon ground cinnamon**
2 **tablespoons sugar**
3 **large garlic cloves, minced**

Whisk together all ingredients in glass measure. **Cover** with plastic wrap, pulling back one corner to vent the steam, and microwave on HIGH for 4 to 6 minutes (Low wattage 4½ to 7 minutes) or until hot and bubbly, **stirring** once.

Orange Sauce

Use this delicious sauce to baste chicken parts, ribs, or appetizer-size pork spareribs.

MAKES ½ CUP

> EQUIPMENT: small mixing bowl
> COOKING TIME: 2 to 4 minutes (Low wattage ovens 2½ to 4½ minutes)
> STANDING TIME: 10 minutes

¼ **cup orange marmalade**
¼ **cup French salad dressing**
   dash of chili powder
   dash of cayenne pepper
   dash of onion powder
1 **large garlic clove, minced or crushed**

Whisk together all ingredients in mixing bowl and allow to **stand** for 10 minutes to blend flavors. Microwave on HIGH for 2 to 4 minutes (LW 2½ to 4½ minutes) or until marmalade dissolves, **stirring** once during cooking time.

Ladies' Choice Barbecue Sauce

This sauce is wonderful for chicken, spareribs, or pork chops.

MAKES 1⅔ CUPS

EQUIPMENT:	4-cup glass measure or medium mixing bowl
COOKING TIME:	4 to 6 minutes (Low wattage ovens 4½ to 6½ minutes)
STANDING TIME:	none required

2 4½-ounce jars strained baby food peaches
¼ cup red wine vinegar
¼ cup ketchup
3 teaspoons Worcestershire sauce
1 tablespoon sherry or white wine
1 tablespoon prepared mustard
½ cup brown sugar
1 teaspoon ground cinnamon
½ teaspoon ground ginger
3 large garlic cloves, minced or crushed
½ teaspoon salt
¼ teaspoon pepper

In glass measure or bowl, **whisk** together all ingredients. Microwave on HIGH for 4 to 6 minutes (LW 4½ to 6½ minutes) or until sauce is hot and bubbly, **stirring** once during cooking.

Peach Tree Sparerib Sauce

This excellent sauce is right for chicken and pork chunks as well as spareribs.

MAKES 1½ CUPS

EQUIPMENT:	medium mixing bowl
COOKING TIME:	3 to 5 minutes (Low wattage ovens 3½ to 6 minutes)
STANDING TIME:	none required

1 **cup bottled barbecue sauce**
½ **cup peach preserves**
2 **tablespoons Worcestershire sauce**
¼ **cup chopped scallions**
2 **large garlic gloves, minced**
½ **teaspoon paprika**

Whisk all ingredients in bowl and microwave on HIGH for 3 to 5 minutes (LW 3½ to 6 minutes) or until preserves dissolve and sauce is hot and bubbly, **whisking** once during cooking time.

Troubleshooting: Ingredients will blend better if a whisk is used.

Main-Dish Soups

One-dish meals are perfect for those weekend cooks who want to prepare a week's worth of dinners in advance. The microwave can really save time in soup preparation as long as you are preparing only 2 to 3 quarts at a time. Cooking large batches requires using large micro-safe casserole dishes, which are too big for many ovens.

Be sure to use deep round dishes, preferably with covers. If covers aren't available, use plastic wrap, being sure to pull back one corner to vent the steam, not wax paper—you want soups to steam. Most soup recipes need very few ingredient changes from the conventional to the microwave recipe. Do keep in mind, however, that if you're adding rice or noodles you must allow extra microwaving time for them to cook as well as the soup. And remember that most soups only improve in flavor as they sit on the refrigerator shelf, so make them ahead.

Mushroom Barley Soup

I'll never forget the first time I tasted barley soup; I was still in pigtails. Our entire family had been invited out for dinner. Since my mother had never made barley soup, I remember having no idea what we were eating. The hostess took barley soup for granted, but seeing our puzzled faces, she finally told us what it was. Today I'm not sure whether everyone has tasted barley soup, but if you haven't, be adventurous and try something different; you'll be surprised at how good it is.

SERVES 4

EQUIPMENT: deep 3-quart round casserole dish
COOKING TIME: 50 to 63 minutes (Low wattage ovens 60 to 74 minutes)
STANDING TIME: 5 minutes

2 **tablespoons olive oil**
1 **cup chopped onion**
1 **cup thinly sliced celery**
1 **cup thinly sliced carrot**
3 **13¾-ounce cans chicken broth**
2 **cups hot water**
½ **cup pearl barley**
⅛ **teaspoon lemon pepper**
  dash of cayenne pepper
¼ **teaspoon garlic powder**
2 **cups sliced fresh mushrooms**

Place olive oil, onion, celery, and carrot in casserole dish. **Cover** with lid or plastic wrap, pulling back one corner to vent the steam. (If dish is flat-bottomed, **elevate** it on an inverted saucer.) Place on turntable if available and microwave on HIGH for 5 to 7 minutes (LW 6 to 8 minutes) or until vegetables are crisp-tender, **stirring** once. (**Rotate** dish ½ turn when stirring if not using turntable.)

Add chicken broth, hot water, barley, lemon pepper, cayenne pepper, and garlic powder. **Cover** again and microwave on HIGH for 10 to 14 minutes (LW 12 to 16 minutes) or until boiling.

Stir, cover again, reduce power to 50 percent or MEDIUM, and microwave for 25 to 30 minutes (LW 30 to 36 minutes) or until barley is almost tender, **stirring** every 10 minutes. (**Rotate** dish ½ turn when stirring if not using turntable.)

Add mushrooms, **cover** again, and microwave on 50 percent power or MEDIUM for 10 to 12 minutes (LW 12 to 14 minutes) or until barley is tender, **stirring** every 5 minutes. (**Rotate** dish ½ turn when stirring if not using turntable.) Let **stand, covered,** for 5 minutes before ladling into soup bowls.

BOK CHOY

Bok choy, which means white vegetable, is a sweet, tender Chinese cabbage found in most supermarkets. Its stalks are firm and white with dark green leaves, and it's used widely in Chinese dishes. Like all fresh leafy vegetables, it's best stored in a plastic bag or the vegetable crisper in your refrigerator. It will remain fresh for one week.

Chinese Chicken Noodle Soup

SERVES 4

EQUIPMENT:	deep 2-quart round casserole dish
COOKING TIME:	10 to 14 minutes (Low wattage ovens 12 to 16 minutes)
STANDING TIME:	5 minutes

2 13¾-ounce cans chicken broth
1 cup bok choy leaves, cut into ½-inch strips
1 cup hot cooked fine egg noodles
¼ pound cooked roast pork, shredded
2 tablespoons finely chopped scallions

Place broth and bok choy in deep casserole dish. **Cover** with lid or plastic wrap, pulling back one corner to vent the steam. (If dish is flat-bottomed, **elevate** it on an inverted saucer.) Place on turntable if available and microwave on HIGH for 10 to 14 minutes (LW 12 to 16 minutes) or until cabbage is tender to your taste, **stirring** twice during cooking time. (**Rotate** dish ½ turn when stirring if not using turntable.)

Stir in cooked noodles and pork. Let **stand, covered,** for 5 minutes. Serve in individual bowls and garnish with chopped scallions.

Suggestions: To shred pork, first slice meat, then slice lengthwise into shreds approximately 1½ inches long and ⅛ to ¼ inch wide.

Roast pork can be purchased at many deli counters today. If you buy it already sliced, shredding is much easier.

Creamy Chicken and Vegetable Soup

SERVES 4

EQUIPMENT:	deep 3-quart round casserole dish
COOKING TIME:	22 to 28 minutes (Low wattage ovens 26½ to 33 minutes)
STANDING TIME:	none required

- 1 **10-ounce paper-covered box frozen mixed vegetables**
- ½ **cup chopped onion**
- ½ **cup chopped celery**
- ½ **cup sliced fresh mushrooms**
- 3 **tablespoons butter or margarine, sliced**
- 1 **18¾-ounce can chunky creamy chicken with mushrooms soup**
- 1 **10¾-ounce can condensed cream of celery soup**
- 1 **cup water**
- ½ **teaspoon dried thyme**
- 1 **teaspoon salt**
- ¼ **teaspoon paprika**
- 1 **cup diced cooked chicken**
- 1 **cup half-and-half or milk**

Place paper-covered box of frozen vegetables on 2 layers of paper towel on floor of oven and microwave on HIGH for 7 minutes (LW 8¼ minutes). Set aside.

Place onion, celery, mushrooms, and sliced butter in deep casserole dish. **Cover** dish with lid or plastic wrap, pulling back one corner to vent the steam. (If dish is flat-bottomed, **elevate** it on an inverted saucer.) Place on turntable if available and microwave on HIGH for 5 to 7 minutes (LW 6 to 8¼ minutes) or until vegetables are crisp-tender, **stirring** every 3 minutes. (**Rotate** dish ½ turn when stirring if not using turntable.)

Add cooked mixed vegetables, canned soups, water, thyme, salt, paprika, and diced chicken, **stirring** well. **Cover** again and microwave on HIGH for 6 to 8 minutes (LW 7½ to 9½ minutes) or until boiling point is reached, **stirring** every 3 minutes. (**Rotate** dish ½ turn when stirring if not using turntable.)

Stir in half-and-half, **cover** again, and microwave on HIGH for 4 to 6 minutes (LW 4¾ to 7 minutes), just to reheat, **stirring** every 3 minutes. *(Do not boil.)*

Troubleshooting: If frozen vegetable box is covered with a foil wrapper, be sure to remove it before microwaving or it will arc and could ignite the paper towels.

Suggestions: Top each bowl of soup with croutons.

Double-Corn Chowder

SERVES 4

EQUIPMENT:	deep 2- or 3-quart round casserole dish, blender or food processor
COOKING TIME:	7 to 11 minutes (Low wattage ovens 8¼ to 13 minutes)
STANDING TIME:	none required

½ **cup finely chopped onion**
½ **cup finely chopped celery**
2 **tablespoons butter or margarine, sliced**
2 **chicken-flavor bouillon cubes**
¼ **cup hot water**
1 **16-ounce can cream-style corn**
1 **17-ounce can whole-kernel sweet corn, drained**
¼ **teaspoon salt**
⅛ **teaspoon pepper**
1½ **cups half-and-half**
fresh parsley sprigs for garnish

Combine onion, celery, and butter in deep casserole dish. **Cover** with lid or plastic wrap, pulling back one corner to vent the steam. (If dish is flat-bottomed, **elevate** it on an inverted saucer.) Place on turntable if available and microwave on HIGH for 2 to 4 minutes (LW 2¼ to 4¾ minutes) or until onion and celery are tender, **stirring** every 2 minutes.

Dissolve bouillon cubes in hot water and set aside. In a blender or food processor, puree cream-style corn and ½ the drained kernel corn.

To the onion and celery, add the dissolved bouillon, pureed corn, the remaining whole-kernel corn, salt, pepper, and half-and-half. **Cover** again and microwave on 80 percent power or MEDIUM-HIGH for 5 to 7 minutes (LW 6 to 8¼ minutes) or until heated through, **stirring** every 3 minutes. (**Rotate** dish ½ turn when stirring if not using turntable.) Garnish with parsley.

Ham and Cannellini Soup

SERVES 4

EQUIPMENT:	blender or food processor, deep 3-quart round casserole dish
COOKING TIME:	27 to 31 minutes (Low wattage ovens 32 to 38 minutes)
STANDING TIME:	5 minutes

2 **16-ounce cans cannellini (white kidney beans), drained**
2 **13¾-ounce cans chicken broth**
½ **cup chopped onion**
½ **cup chopped celery**
1 **10-ounce box frozen sliced carrots, defrosted**
½ **cup chopped cooked ham**
½ **teaspoon salt**
¼ **teaspoon pepper**
¼ **cup chopped scallions**

Puree one can of cannellini and one can of broth in blender or food processor and pour into casserole dish. Add remaining can of beans, remaining can of broth, onions, celery, carrots, ham, salt, and pepper, **stirring** together well.

Cover dish with lid or plastic wrap, pulling back one corner to vent the steam (If dish is flat-bottomed, **elevate** it on an inverted saucer.) Place on turntable if available and microwave on HIGH for 12 to 14 minutes (LW 14 to 17 minutes) or until boiling, **stirring** every 5 minutes. (**Rotate** dish ½ turn when stirring if not using turntable.)

Stir, cover again, reduce power to 60 percent or MEDIUM, and microwave for 15 to 17 minutes (LW 18 to 21 minutes) or until vegetables are tender, **stirring** every 5 minutes. (**Rotate** dish ½ turn when stirring if not using turntable.)

Let **stand, covered,** for 5 minutes and serve each bowl of soup with a sprinkling of chopped scallions.

Fiesta Oyster 'n' Corn Chowder Olé

I can't take credit for the idea for this recipe. The annual St. Marys County National Oyster Cook-Off is held every October in Leonard-town, Maryland. The 1988 grand prize was awarded to Shirley DeSantis for this recipe, which I've converted for the microwave.

SERVES 6 TO 8

EQUIPMENT:	deep 3-quart round casserole dish, meat/bacon rack
COOKING TIME:	18½ to 26 minutes (Low wattage ovens 22 to 30¼ minutes)
STANDING TIME:	none required

1 quart milk
1 3-ounce package cream cheese, cubed
1 15- or 16-ounce can cream-style corn
6 bacon strips
1 onion, chopped
4 medium potatoes, cooked, peeled, and diced
1 4-ounce can chopped green chilies, drained
½ teaspoon seasoned salt
⅛ teaspoon cayenne pepper
1 quart shredded Maryland select oysters
½ cup sour cream

Place milk in deep casserole dish and microwave, **uncovered,** on HIGH for 4 to 6 minutes (LW 5 to 7 minutes) or until just boiling, **whisking** every minute. Add cream cheese cubes and corn. Microwave, **uncovered,** on HIGH for 3 to 4 minutes (LW 3½ to 4½ minutes), **whisking** every minute until cream cheese melts. Set aside.

Lay bacon strips on bacon rack and microwave on HIGH for 4½ to 6 minutes (LW 5 to 7 minutes) or until crisp. **Drain** bacon strips on paper towels, discard drippings, and, once cool enough to touch, dice.

Add bacon, onion, and potatoes to milk mixture. Reserve 2 to 3 teaspoons green chilies for topping and add the remaining ones along with the seasoned salt and cayenne to the mixture. Microwave on 80 percent or MEDIUM-HIGH power for 4 to 6 minutes (LW 5 to 7 minutes), **stirring** every minute until heated through.

Drain oysters and add to hot soup. Microwave on 80 percent or MEDIUM-HIGH for 3 to 4 minutes (LW 3½ to 4¾ minutes) or just until edges of oysters curl. Ladle chowder into bowls, top each serving with a dollop of sour cream, scatter reserved chilies over top.

Troubleshooting: Please keep in mind that boiling milk will go foaming over the sides of the pan, so watch this chowder carefully and be sure to whisk or stir according to directions to keep the milk from boiling over.

PUMPKIN

Many of us see the bright orange pumpkin playing only the role of jack-o'-lantern. But once the holiday is over, the pulp can be cooked and turned into delicious soups, cheesecake, muffins, and much more while the shell can be used as a disposable soup tureen.

Freshly cooked pumpkin is more flavorful than the canned version; it's also lighter in color and contains more water than canned. One of the easiest ways to cook fresh pumpkin is in the microwave. Begin by washing the pumpkin well and cutting it crosswise. If the pumpkin halves are large, you will have to microwave them separately by placing them cut side down in a casserole dish large enough to accommodate the section.

Cover the dish and pumpkin with plastic wrap, pulling back one corner to vent the steam, and microwave on HIGH for 6 to 8 minutes (LW 7 to 9 minutes) per pound or until fork-tender. Let the pumpkin half **stand** for 10 minutes, then scrape away the seeds, remove the fibers, and peel. (If you want to toast the seeds, remove them before microwaving the halves.) Place the pumpkin pulp in a food processor or blender and puree or mash thoroughly with a potato masher. The puree will remain fresh for 1 week in your refrigerator or for about 3 months when frozen. Drain it before using in recipes.

Pumpkin Bisque

SERVES 6 TO 8

EQUIPMENT: deep 3-quart round casserole dish, food processor or blender

COOKING TIME: 22 to 28 minutes (Low wattage ovens 25 to 31 minutes)

STANDING TIME: none required

- **1 whole 2- to 3-pound pumpkin**
- **1 potato, peeled and diced**
- **½ cup finely chopped green bell pepper**
- **¼ cup finely chopped onion**
- **1 garlic clove, finely minced**
- **2 tablespoons butter or margarine, sliced**
- **2 tablespoons white wine**
- **1 14-ounce can plum tomatoes, undrained and chopped**
- **2 cups chicken broth**
- **dash of salt and pepper**
- **1½ cups half-and-half**
- **sour cream and fresh parsley for garnish**

Cut top off pumpkin and scoop out seeds and fiber. Using a grapefruit spoon, remove pumpkin flesh from inside shell, leaving a ¼- to ½-inch lining of flesh attached to the shell.

Place pumpkin, potatoes, green pepper, onions, garlic, and butter in deep casserole dish and **cover** with lid or plastic wrap, pulling back one corner to vent the steam. (If dish is flat-bottomed, **elevate** it on an inverted saucer.) Place on turntable if available and microwave on HIGH for 9 to 11 minutes (LW 10 to 12 minutes), **stirring** every 5 minutes. (**Rotate** dish ½ turn when stirring if not using turntable.)

Add wine, tomatoes, broth, salt, and pepper. **Cover** and microwave on HIGH for 9 to 11 minutes (LW 10 to 12 minutes) or until all vegetables are very soft, **stirring** every 5 minutes. (**Rotate** dish ½ turn when stirring if not using turntable.)

Pour hot soup carefully into a food processor or blender and puree until smooth. Pour pureed soup back into the casserole dish and add half-and-half, **stirring** until well combined. **Cover** again and microwave on HIGH for 4 to 6 minutes (LW 5 to 7 minutes) or until hot, not boiling, **stirring** well every 2 minutes. (**Rotate** dish ½ turn when stirring if not using turntable.)

While soup is heating, wash pumpkin shell well and pat dry with paper towels. Pour hot soup into pumpkin shell and garnish with dollops of sour cream and fresh parsley.

Troubleshooting: Be sure soup doesn't boil after adding the half-and-half, because it will foam over the sides of the casserole dish.

Grandma's Russian Cabbage Soup

The seasoning of cabbage soup is hotly debated in Russian households. It should have a slightly sharp sweet-sour flavor. The taste of this soup is definitely improved if cooked a day or 2 before serving.

SERVES 4 TO 6

EQUIPMENT:	deep 3-quart round casserole dish
COOKING TIME:	1 to 1¼ hours (Low wattage ovens 1 hour and 7 minutes to 1 hour and 23 minutes)
STANDING TIME:	10 minutes

- 1 **pound beef short ribs, cut into serving-size pieces**
- 1 **small head of cabbage (about 1 pound), shredded**
- 1 **16-ounce can or jar beets, undrained and cut into julienne strips**
- 1 **large onion, chopped**
- 1 **medium carrot, thinly sliced**
- 1 **28-ounce can peeled tomatoes, undrained and cut up**
- 2 **cups hot water**
- 1 **teaspoon salt**
- ¼ **teaspoon pepper**
- ¼ **cup lemon juice**
- 4 **to 6 tablespoons brown sugar, to taste**

Place all ingredients in deep casserole dish. **Stir** well and **cover** with lid or plastic wrap, pulling back one corner to vent the steam. (If dish is flat-bottomed, **elevate** it on an inverted saucer.) Place on turntable if available and microwave on HIGH for 10 to 15 minutes (LW 12 to 18 minutes) or until boiling.

Reduce power to 70 percent or MEDIUM-HIGH and microwave for 50 to 60 minutes (LW 55 to 65 minutes) or until cabbage and meat are soft, **stirring** every 10 minutes. (**Rotate** dish ¼ turn when stirring if not using turntable.)

Let **stand, covered,** for 10 minutes before ladling into bowls and serving with hot crusty bread.

Troubleshooting: Cut meat and vegetables into uniformly sized pieces, because things of the same size cook in the same length of time.

Chick-Pea and Sausage Soup

SERVES 8

EQUIPMENT:	deep 3-quart round casserole dish
COOKING TIME:	22 to 26 minutes (Low wattage ovens 26 to 30 minutes)
STANDING TIME:	5 minutes

1 **10-ounce paper-covered box frozen french-cut green beans**

¾ **pound Italian sweet or hot sausage, cut into ¼-inch slices**

½ **pound fresh mushrooms, sliced**

1 **cup chopped onion**

2 **large garlic cloves, crushed**

3 **13¾-ounce cans chicken broth**

1 **16-ounce can chick-peas, drained**

¼ **teaspoon pepper**

⅛ **teaspoon powdered saffron**

1 **small bay leaf**

1 **tablespoon snipped fresh parsley**

Place paper-covered box of green beans on 2 layers of paper towel on oven floor and microwave on HIGH for 6 minutes (LW 7 minutes). Set aside.

Place sausage, mushrooms, onions, and garlic in deep casserole dish. **Cover** with lid or plastic wrap, pulling back one corner to vent the steam. (If dish is flat-bottomed, **elevate** it on an inverted saucer.) Place on turntable if available and microwave on HIGH for 6 to 8 minutes (LW 7 to 9 minutes) or until sausage loses its pink color and onion is tender, **stirring** halfway through cooking time. (**Rotate** dish ½ turn when stirring if not using turntable.)

Add green beans and remaining ingredients. **Stir** and **cover** again. Microwave on HIGH for 10 to 12 minutes (LW 12 to 14 minutes) or until heated through, **stirring** halfway through cooking time. (**Rotate** dish ½ turn when stirring if not using turntable.)

Let **stand, covered,** for 5 minutes. Discard bay leaf before ladling into soup bowls.

Troubleshooting: If frozen vegetable box is covered with a foil wrapper, remove before microwaving as it will arc and may cause paper towels to ignite.

Be sure to slice sausage into uniformly sized pieces, because things of the same size cook in the same length of time.

Turkey Sausage Vegetable Soup

SERVES 6 TO 8

EQUIPMENT:	deep 3-quart round casserole dish
COOKING TIME:	34 to 40 minutes (Low wattage ovens 41½ to 47½ minutes)
STANDING TIME:	5 minutes

   3   tablespoons olive oil
   1   cup coarsely chopped onion
   1   cup thinly sliced carrot
   1   cup chopped celery
   2   tablespoons snipped fresh parsley
   2   garlic cloves, minced
   1   46-ounce can chicken broth
   1   10¾-ounce can condensed cream of chicken soup
   2   cups coarsely shredded green cabbage
  ½   pound turkey smoked sausage, sliced into ¼-inch slices and cut in half
   1   small zucchini, cut into julienne strips (1¼ by ¼ inch)
  ½   cup uncooked ditalini macaroni
   1   cup hot water
  ½   teaspoon dried oregano
  ¼   teaspoon paprika
  ¼   teaspoon pepper

Combine olive oil, onion, carrot, celery, parsley, and garlic in casserole dish. **Cover** with lid or plastic wrap, pulling back one corner to vent the steam. (If dish is flat-bottomed, **elevate** it on an inverted saucer.) Place on turntable if available and microwave on HIGH for 6 to 8 minutes (LW 7½ to 9½ minutes) or until vegetables are crisp-tender, **stirring** every 3 minutes. (**Rotate** dish ½ turn when stirring if not using turntable.)

    Stir in remaining ingredients, **cover** again, and microwave on HIGH for 28 to 32 minutes (LW 34 to 38 minutes) or until cabbage is crisp-tender, **stirring** frequently during cooking. (**Rotate** dish ½ turn every 10 minutes if not using turntable.)

    Let **stand, covered,** for 5 minutes before serving.

Troubleshooting: Cut vegetables and sausage into uniformly sized pieces, because things of the same size cook in the same length of time.

Vegetables and Rice

Whiz's Green Beans

SERVES 4

EQUIPMENT: 2-quart round casserole dish, deep 2-quart round casserole dish

COOKING TIME: 17 to 22½ minutes (Low wattage ovens 20¼ to 26½ minutes)

STANDING TIME: 7 minutes

1½ **pounds green beans, cut into 1-inch pieces**
 1 **cup water**
 1 **cup canned french-fried onions**
 1 **16-ounce jar Cheeze Whiz**

Wash, snip ends, and cut beans into uniformly sized 1-inch pieces. Place beans in round casserole dish and add water. **Cover** with lid or plastic wrap, pulling back one corner to vent the steam. (If dish is flat-bottomed, **elevate** it on an inverted saucer.) Place on turntable if available and microwave on HIGH for 10 to 13 minutes (LW 12 to 15½ minutes) or until crisp-tender, bringing the beans from the center of the dish to the outside edges and the ones along the edges into the center every 5 minutes. (**Rotate** dish ½ turn when stirring beans if not using turntable.) Let **stand, covered,** for 5 minutes.

In deep casserole dish, alternate layers of cooked green beans and fried onions. Remove lid from Cheez-Whiz jar and microwave entire jar on HIGH for 2 to 2½ minutes (LW 2¼ to 2¾ minutes) or until cheese is hot and melted, **stirring** every 30 seconds. (Jar will be hot, so use pot holders to remove from microwave.) **Stir** well and pour over green beans and onions.

Cover dish with lid or plastic wrap, pulling back one corner to vent the steam. (If dish is flat-bottomed, **elevate** it on an inverted saucer.) Place on turntable if available and microwave on HIGH for 5 to 7 minutes (LW 6 to 8¼ minutes) or until hot and bubbly. (**Rotate** dish ½ turn after 3 minutes if not using turntable.) Let **stand, covered,** for 2 minutes and serve.

Troubleshooting: Cut beans uniformly in size, because things of the same size cook in the same length of time.

Vegetables cook best in round containers as square-cornered containers tend to overcook the pieces in the corners. If only a square container is available, stir the pieces out of the corners more frequently.

Remove metal lid from Cheez-Whiz jar before heating and remove jar with pot holders as the heat from the melted cheese will make the jar very hot.

Green Bean Bake

SERVES 4

EQUIPMENT:	1- and 2-quart round casserole dishes, small mixing bowl
COOKING TIME:	17 to 22 minutes (Low wattage ovens 20¼ to 26¾ minutes)
STANDING TIME:	none required

1 **pound green beans, cut into 1-inch pieces**
¾ **cup water**
4 **bacon strips**
¼ **cup flavored dry bread crumbs**
½ **can (8-ounce size) french-fried onions**
½ **10¾-ounce can condensed cream of mushroom soup**

Wash, trim, and cut beans into uniformly sized 1-inch pieces. Place beans in 2-quart casserole dish and add water. **Cover** dish with lid or plastic wrap, pulling back one corner to vent the steam. (If dish is flat-bottomed, **elevate** it on an inverted saucer.) Place on turntable if available and microwave on HIGH for 9 to 12 minutes (LW 11 to 15 minutes) or until crisp-tender, bringing the less cooked pieces from the center of the dish to the outside edges and the ones along the edges into the center of the dish every 5 minutes. (**Rotate** dish ½ turn when stirring if not using turntable.)

Lay bacon strips in 1-quart casserole dish and microwave on HIGH for 2 to 3 minutes (LW 2¼ to 3½ minutes). Remove bacon strips, reserving drippings, drain on paper towels, and crumble. Add bread crumbs and drippings to small bowl and **stir**. Microwave on HIGH for 2 minutes (LW 2¼ minutes), **drain** any excess fat, and set aside.

Combine cooked beans, bacon, onion rings, and undiluted soup in 1-quart casserole dish. Mix together well and top with bread crumbs. Microwave on HIGH for 4 to 5 minutes (LW 4¾ to 6 minutes) or until hot and bubbly.

Troubleshooting: Be sure to cut beans uniformly in size, because things of the same size cook in the same length of time.

BLANCHING VEGETABLES FOR THE FREEZER

The microwave is the preserving answer for those with backyard gardens who want to freeze small amounts of fresh vegetables. Unlike the conventional stove, where large pots accommodate many pounds at a time, the microwave requires small batches. Blanching inactivates the enzymes to preserve the vitamin content of vegetables stored in the freezer. Cook green vegetables, such as green beans, only until they change color, while other vegetables should be blanched until pliable but not tender.

Green or wax beans blanch and freeze beautifully as long as you begin with nice, bright beans that have firm, crisp pods. Clean, trim off the ends, and cut into 1½-inch pieces. Place the beans and 1 cup water in a deep 3-quart round casserole dish and **cover** with the lid or plastic wrap, pulling back one corner to vent the steam. (If dish is flat-bottomed, **elevate** it on an inverted saucer.) Microwave on HIGH for 5 to 6 minutes (LW 6 to 7½ minutes), until water comes to a boil, pour into a colander or strainer, and plunge into a bowl of ice water to stop the cooking.

Drain the blanched vegetables on paper towels and package in plastic bags or freezer containers, marking the contents and date. If you want to be able to separate the vegetables easily once frozen, first freeze them in a single layer on a cookie sheet. Once they're frozen, remove and place in freezer containers.

Green and Wax Bean Casserole

SERVES 4 TO 6

EQUIPMENT: 2-quart round casserole dish, 1-quart mixing bowl, 4-cup glass measure, small mixing bowl

COOKING TIME: 18¾ to 26¾ minutes (Low wattage ovens 22¾ to 32 minutes)

STANDING TIME: 5 minutes

½   pound green beans, cut into 1-inch pieces
½   pound wax beans, cut into 1-inch pieces
⅓   cup water
2   tablespoons butter or margarine, sliced
½   cup chopped celery
½   cup chopped onion
1   cup sliced fresh mushrooms
1   10¾-ounce can condensed cream of chicken soup
¼   cup milk
4   bacon strips, microwaved (see box on page 52) and crumbled
1   cup shredded Monterey Jack cheese

TOPPING
2   tablespoons butter or margarine, sliced
½   cup butter flavored cracker crumbs
½   teaspoon paprika
    fresh parsley for garnish

Place green and wax beans and water in round casserole dish. **Cover** with lid or plastic wrap, pulling back one corner to vent the steam. (If dish is flat-bottomed, **elevate** it on an inverted saucer.) Place on turntable if available and microwave on HIGH for 9 to 12 minutes (LW 11 to 15 minutes) or until beans are crisp-tender, bringing the less cooked pieces from the center of the dish to the outside edges and the ones along the edges into the center of the dish every 4 minutes. (**Rotate** dish ½ turn when stirring if not using turntable.) Let **stand, covered,** for 5 minutes, then drain and set aside.

Combine 2 tablespoons butter, celery, onion, and mushrooms in 1-quart bowl. Microwave, **uncovered,** on HIGH for 4 to 6 minutes (LW 5 to 7 minutes) or until vegetables are crisp-tender, **stirring** halfway through cooking.

In glass measure, **whisk** together soup and milk. **Stir** in bacon, cheese, and vegetable mixture. Add to beans and **stir** well.

Place 2 tablespoons butter in small bowl and microwave on HIGH for 40 to 50 seconds (LW 50 to 60 seconds) or until melted. **Stir** in cracker crumbs and paprika. Sprinkle over casserole, **cover** again, and microwave on HIGH for 5 to 8 minutes (LW 6 to 9 minutes) or until heated through. (**Rotate** dish ½ turn every 3 minutes if not using turntable.) Garnish with parsley.

Troubleshooting: If you're using a square-cornered container to cook the beans, be sure to move the beans out of the corners frequently, or they will overcook.

Forgetting to whisk soup and milk may not blend it as completely.

Suggestions: Ritz cracker crumbs may be substituted for topping. Crush whole crackers in food processor or place in a plastic bag and crush with a rolling pin.

STIRRING

You may think you know what stirring means; *Webster's* says it's "to mix as by agitating with a spoon." But in the microwave just whirling a spoon around is not enough. When stirring in the microwave, you must actually move the less cooked food from the center of the dish to the outside edges and bring the food that has had more cooking time along the edges of the dish into the center. Stirring actually means moving the food from one area of the dish to another.

MICROWAVING BACON

There are two methods you can use to microwave bacon. If you want to reserve the drippings for other uses, place a single layer of slices on a meat or bacon rack, **cover** with 2 layers of paper towel, and microwave on HIGH for 30 to 45 seconds per slice of bacon. Let them stand for 2 to 3 minutes and check to be sure they are crisp enough; if not, microwave for 10 to 20 seconds per slice on HIGH, let **stand,** and check again.

If you don't want to reserve drippings, place a single layer of slices on 3 to 4 layers of paper towel, cover with 2 more layers, and pat gently to keep slices flat. Microwave on HIGH as above. For this method I recommend using white paper towels, since I have had the color in printed paper towels come off on the bacon slices. If only printed paper towels are available, turn them over, as most brands have color printed only on one side.

Beans with Cranberry Sauce

This dish is excellent served as an accompaniment to hot dogs or hamburgers or on a buffet table.

SERVES 4 TO 6

EQUIPMENT: 3-quart round casserole dish
COOKING TIME: 22 to 25 minutes (Low wattage ovens 26¼ to 30 minutes)
STANDING TIME: 5 minutes

1 16-ounce can whole-berry cranberry sauce
3 16-ounce cans pork and beans
1 cup finely chopped onion
4 teaspoons dry mustard

Place cranberry sauce in casserole dish and break up with a fork. Add beans, onions, and mustard. **Stir** together and **cover** with lid or plastic wrap, pulling back one corner to vent the steam. (If dish is flat-bottomed, **elevate** it on an inverted saucer.) Place on a turntable if available and microwave on HIGH for 22 to 25 minutes (LW 26¼ to 30 minutes) or until flavors have blended and onions are crisp-tender, **stirring** every 10 minutes. (**Rotate** dish ½ turn when stirring if not on turntable.)

Let **stand, covered,** for 5 minutes.

CABBAGE

Be sure to trim and wash cabbage as you prepare to use it, because wet or damp cabbage can become discolored and moldy. Refrigerate cabbage whole or in large pieces, unwashed, in a plastic bag for no longer than 1 week as small pieces will become dry and wilted. Always select heads that are firm, with undamaged leaves and a fresh-looking color. When shredding cabbage, remember to discard the core.

Swiss Scalloped Cabbage

SERVES 4

EQUIPMENT:	2-quart round baking dish, 6-cup glass measure, small mixing bowl, 2-quart round casserole dish
COOKING TIME:	23½ to 34¾ minutes (Low wattage ovens 28½ to 41 minutes)
STANDING TIME:	3 minutes

5 cups shredded green cabbage
1 large onion, thinly sliced
3 tablespoons butter or margarine, sliced
3 tablespoons water
2 cups milk
2 1-ounce envelopes white sauce mix
1 cup finely shredded Swiss cheese

TOPPING
2 tablespoons butter or margarine, sliced
½ cup crushed vegetable-flavored crackers
2 tablespoons grated Parmesan cheese

Combine cabbage, onion, 3 tablespoons butter, and water in baking dish. **Cover** with lid or plastic wrap, pulling back one corner to vent the steam. (If dish is flat-bottomed, **elevate** it on an inverted saucer.) Place on turntable if available and microwave on HIGH for 9 to 15 minutes (LW 10¾ to 18 minutes) or until vegetables are crisp-tender, **stirring** halfway through the cooking time. (**Rotate** dish ½ turn when stirring if not using turntable.) Let **stand, covered,** for 3 minutes.

Heat milk in glass measure on HIGH for 5 to 7 minutes (LW 6 to 8¼ minutes). **Whisk** in white sauce mix and microwave, **uncovered,** on HIGH for 4 to 5 minutes (LW 5 to 6 minutes) or until smooth and thick, **whisking** every minute. Add shredded cheese and **whisk** until melted.

For topping, place 2 tablespoons margarine in small bowl. Microwave on HIGH for 30 to 45 seconds (LW 40 to 50 seconds) or until melted. **Stir** in cracker crumbs and Parmesan cheese. Place a layer of cooked cabbage in casserole dish. Follow with a layer of cheese sauce. Continue to layer until all the cabbage and all the sauce have been used. Sprinkle top with crumb mixture and microwave, **uncovered,** on HIGH for 5 to 7 minutes (LW 6 to 8 minutes) or until hot and bubbly.

Troubleshooting: When you're boiling vegetables on a conventional stove, many of the vitamins and nutrients are left in the cooking water. In the microwave, to preserve the high vitamin and nutrient content, cook just until tender.

Forgetting to whisk sauce may cause it to be lumpy.

CORN ON THE COB

The fastest and easiest method I know for microwaving corn on the cob is to use a heavy plastic zip-close bag. (I use the Glad freezer weight that turns green when zipped closed.) Husk and butter the corn if you like, but don't salt the ears. Place the thicker ears to the outside and the thinner ears to the center in the bag, which will hold about 6 good-sized ears. If you're not using butter, add 2 tablespoons water and zip the bag two-thirds closed, leaving at least a 2-inch open space for the steam to escape.

Place 2 layers of paper towel on the floor of the microwave with the bag on top. Microwave on HIGH for 2 to 3 minutes (LW 2¼ to 3½ minutes) per ear of corn and then allow the entire batch to **stand** for 5 minutes before serving.

There are new plastic corn holders on the market made for the microwave that can be inserted into each end before cooking. When done, the holder remains cool to the touch and you don't have to burn your fingers trying to insert them into the hot corn.

Remember to use *heavy* (freezer-weight) zip-close plastic bags; the thin economy plastic bags, like sandwich bags, will melt.

Corn Soufflé

SERVES 6 TO 8

EQUIPMENT: 2-quart round casserole dish, medium mixing bowl, custard cup

COOKING TIME: 21¼ to 23½ minutes (Low wattage ovens 25 to 29 minutes)

STANDING TIME: 10 minutes

2 tablespoons butter or margarine, sliced
½ cup chopped scallions
1 tablespoon chopped pimiento
2 eggs
2 tablespoons flour
2 tablespoons sugar
½ teaspoon baking powder
1 cup half-and-half
1 16-ounce can cream-style corn
1 12-ounce can whole-kernel corn, drained
½ teaspoon salt
¼ teaspoon white pepper

TOPPING
1 tablespoon butter or margarine
⅓ cup Swiss cheese-flavored snack cracker crumbs
½ teaspoon paprika

Place 2 tablespoons butter, scallions, and pimiento in round casserole dish. **Cover** with lid or plastic wrap, pulling back one corner to vent the steam. (If dish is flat-bottomed, **elevate** it on an inverted saucer.) Place on turntable if available and microwave on HIGH for 2 minutes (LW 2¼ minutes). Set aside.

Beat eggs in mixing bowl. **Whisk** in flour, sugar, and baking powder until combined. **Whisk** in half-and-half, cream-style corn, whole-kernel corn, salt, and pepper. Pour into casserole dish and blend with scallion mixture. **Cover** again and microwave on HIGH for 17 to 19 minutes (LW 20 to 24 minutes) or until a knife inserted in center comes out clean. (**Rotate** dish ½ turn every 8 minutes if not using turntable.) Let **stand** on a hard heat-proof surface for 10 minutes.

For topping, put 1 tablespoon butter in custard cup and **cover** with a paper towel. Microwave on HIGH for 25 to 35 seconds (LW 30 to 40 seconds) or until melted. Stir in crumbs and paprika and microwave, **uncovered,** on HIGH for 2 minutes (LW 2¼ minutes) or until crumbs are browned. Sprinkle browned crumbs over casserole and serve.

Suggestions: Add 3 slices of cooked and crumbled bacon to casserole if desired.

Any flavor snack cracker of your choice may be substituted for a different taste. Crush crumbs in food processor or place crackers in plastic bag and roll with rolling pin to crush.

BLACK-EYED PEAS

To microwave black-eyed peas, shell about 2 pounds (about 2 cups shelled) just before you're ready to microwave them. Place them in a 2-quart round casserole dish (square-cornered dishes don't cook as evenly). Add 1 cup water and **cover** with wax paper, not plastic wrap. (If dish is flat-bottomed, **elevate** it on an inverted saucer.) Microwave on HIGH for 14 to 18 minutes (LW 16½ to 21 minutes), **stirring** every 4 minutes and **rotating** dish ¼ turn each time you stir. Add additional water as the peas cook if you find them absorbing it and not remaining moist. Once the peas are soft to your taste, let **stand, covered,** for 5 minutes and drain the slightly thickened water. Now they are ready to add to your own favorite recipe or mine.

Saucy Black-Eyed Peas

Black-eyed peas are traditionally served in the South at New Year's to help ensure good luck. These relatively inexpensive legumes are a good source of iron and phosphorus and also contain some protein. If you're using fresh black-eyed peas, be sure to microwave them *before* adding them to a recipe.

SERVES 6

EQUIPMENT: deep 2- or 3-quart round casserole dish
COOKING TIME: 22 to 28 minutes (Low wattage ovens 26¼ to 36¼ minutes)
STANDING TIME: none required

2 **cups fresh black-eyed peas, microwaved (see box on page 57) and drained**
4 **bacon strips**
1 **garlic clove, minced**
1 **medium onion, diced**
2 **celery stalks, diced**
1 **medium green bell pepper, diced**
1 **16-ounce can whole tomatoes, undrained and chopped**
½ **teaspoon seasoned salt**
1 **teaspoon A-1 Steak Sauce**
½ **teaspoon dry mustard**
¼ **teaspoon black pepper**

Slice bacon strips in half and place in deep casserole dish. Microwave on HIGH for 3 to 4 minutes (LW 3½ to 4¾ minutes) or until bacon is crisp. Remove bacon strips and place on several layers of paper towel to drain; set aside.

Add garlic, onion, celery, and green pepper to bacon drippings and stir to coat. (If dish is flat-bottomed, **elevate** it on an inverted saucer.) Microwave on HIGH for 4 to 6 minutes (LW 4¾ to 7½ minutes) or until vegetables are crisp-tender. Add remaining ingredients (except reserved bacon) to vegetables, **stirring** well.

Stir in peas and **cover** dish with lid or plastic wrap, pulling back one corner to vent the steam. Microwave on 50 percent power or MEDIUM for 15 to 18 minutes (LW 18 to 24 minutes) or until flavors blend. Crumble reserved bacon and sprinkle over the dish before serving.

Creamed Onions

This recipe is not only an excellent addition to your holiday menu but also makes a great side dish to accompany meat, fish, or chicken any day of the year. You can, of course, peel fresh onions for this recipe and weep, but once you try this recipe using frozen small whole onions your weeping days will be over.

SERVES 4

EQUIPMENT:	2-quart round casserole dish, 4-cup glass measure
COOKING TIME:	19 to 22 minutes (Low wattage ovens 23 to 26¼ minutes)
STANDING TIME:	5 minutes

1   **16-ounce package frozen small whole peeled white onions**
1   **1.8-ounce envelope white sauce mix**
2   **cups half-and-half**
⅛   **teaspoon white pepper**
⅛   **teaspoon ground nutmeg**

Remove frozen onions from plastic wrapper and place in casserole dish. **Cover** dish with lid or plastic wrap, pulling back one corner to vent the steam. (If dish is flat-bottomed, **elevate** it on an inverted saucer.) Microwave on HIGH for 10 minutes (LW 12 minutes), **stirring** halfway through cooking time. Let **stand, covered,** for 2 minutes on a hard heat-proof surface. **Drain** onions, reserving liquid.

Place white sauce mix, reserved onion liquid, half-and-half, pepper, and nutmeg in glass measure, **whisking** until smooth. Microwave sauce on 80 percent power or MEDIUM-HIGH for 6 to 8 minutes (LW 7 to 9 minutes) or until boiling and thick enough to coat a spoon, **whisking** every minute.

Pour sauce over onions and **stir** well. **Cover** again and microwave on 80 percent power or MEDIUM-HIGH for 3 to 4 minutes (LW 4 to 5 minutes) or until bubbly and onions are heated through. Let **stand, covered,** for 3 minutes.

Troubleshooting: Forgetting to whisk sauce will not produce as smooth a sauce.

POTATOES

The potato was once known as the "earth apple." It was cultivated in South America centuries before Columbus was born. Potatoes are low in calories, contain no fat or cholesterol, are very rich in vitamins and minerals, and are a good source of complex carbohydrates.

Whipped Potato Casserole

SERVES 6 TO 8

EQUIPMENT:	large mixing bowl, electric mixer, 2-quart round casserole dish, custard cup
COOKING TIME:	4¾ to 7 minutes (Low wattage ovens 5¾ to 8 minutes)
STANDING TIME:	5 minutes

6 cups hot mashed potatoes
2 eggs, lightly beaten
1 cup sour cream
¼ cup milk
½ cup shredded Cheddar cheese
¼ cup thinly sliced scallions
1 teaspoon salt
¼ teaspoon pepper
⅛ teaspoon garlic powder
2 tablespoons butter or margarine, sliced
½ cup bread crumbs
¼ cup grated Parmesan cheese
½ teaspoon paprika

Combine potatoes, eggs, sour cream, and milk in large bowl. **Whip** together with electric mixer until well blended. **Stir** in Cheddar cheese, scallions, salt, pepper, and garlic powder. **Stir** well and spoon into casserole dish.

Place sliced butter in a custard cup, **covered** with a paper towel to prevent spattering, and microwave on HIGH for 40 to 50 seconds (LW 50 to 60 seconds) or until melted. **Stir** in crumbs, Parmesan cheese, and paprika. Sprinkle topping over top of potato mixture. (If dish is flat-bottomed, **elevate** it on an inverted saucer). Place on turntable if available and microwave, **uncovered,** on HIGH for 4 to 6 minutes (LW 5 to 7 minutes) or until heated through. (**Rotate** dish ¼ turn every 3 minutes if not using turntable.) Let **stand** for 5 minutes and serve.

Troubleshooting: If an electric mixer is not available, beat eggs, sour cream, and milk together well before mixing in mashed potatoes.

Hash Brown Squares

These potato squares are a real change from baked or mashed potatoes and are especially nice to serve on a buffet table.

SERVES 6 TO 8

EQUIPMENT:	2½- or 3-quart bowl, large mixing bowl, 9 × 13-inch baking dish
COOKING TIME:	16 to 19 minutes (Low wattage ovens 19¼ to 22¾ minutes)
STANDING TIME:	17 to 18 minutes

1	**6-ounce box hash brown potatoes with sweet onions**
1½	**teaspoons salt**
1	**8-ounce container soft cream cheese**
3	**eggs**
½	**cup finely chopped red bell pepper**
½	**cup chopped scallions**
½	**cup half-and-half**
¼	**cup grated Parmesan cheese**
½	**teaspoon garlic salt**
⅛	**teaspoon pepper**
½	**cup shredded Cheddar cheese**
	paprika for garnish

Place potatoes in bowl and cover with very hot water. Stir in salt and let **stand, uncovered,** for 15 minutes. **Drain** thoroughly and set aside.

Completely remove aluminum covering from container of cream cheese and microwave on HIGH power for 1 minute (LW 1¼ minutes) or until cheese is very soft; **stir** well.

Whisk eggs together in mixing bowl. Add cream cheese, red peppers, scallions, and half-and-half. **Stir** in potatoes, Parmesan cheese, garlic salt, and pepper. Spoon mixture into baking dish.

Cover dish with plastic wrap, pulling back one corner to vent the steam. (If dish is flat-bottomed, **elevate** it on an inverted saucer.) Microwave on HIGH for 15 to 18 minutes (LW 18 to 21½ minutes) or until center is set, **rotating** dish ½ turn after 7 minutes. Sprinkle top with Cheddar cheese and let **stand** on a hard heat-proof surface for 2 to 3 minutes or until cheese melts. Sprinkle with paprika and cut into squares before serving.

Troubleshooting: If you find one area of the dish overcooking, you may have a hot spot in the oven and need to rotate the dish more often.

Suggestion: To use up leftovers, ½ cup cooked chopped ham or roast beef may be added with soaked potatoes.

HOT SPOTS

When the microwaves are dispersed from the magnetron tube, sometimes too many concentrate in one particular area of the oven, causing a hot spot. You will know you have one if whatever food is placed in that area of the oven always seems to overcook or cook faster than the rest of the dish. The best solution to this problem is to use a turntable, but if one isn't available, rotate the dish out of the hot spot frequently.

Yellow Squash Soufflé

SERVES 4 TO 6

EQUIPMENT:	6-cup glass measure, 2-quart ring mold or bundt dish
COOKING TIME:	16 to 21½ minutes (Low wattage ovens 19¼ to 25¾ minutes)
STANDING TIME:	5 minutes

4 **scallions, chopped**
2 **tablespoons butter or margarine, sliced**
2 **pounds fresh yellow squash, cooked, mashed, and drained well**
1 **teaspoon salt**
¼ **teaspoon pepper**
2 **eggs, slightly beaten**
¾ **cup (about 1 5-ounce can) evaporated milk**
1 **cup herb-seasoned stuffing mix**
¼ **cup grated Parmesan cheese**

Place scallions and butter in glass measure. Microwave on HIGH for 1 to 1½ minutes (LW 1¼ to 1¾ minutes) or until tender. Stir in remaining ingredients.

Grease ring mold with butter or solid shortening. Pour squash mixture into prepared dish and place on a turntable if available. Microwave, **uncovered,** on HIGH for 15 to 20 minutes (LW 18 to 24 minutes) or until set. (**Rotate** dish ¼ turn every 3 minutes if not using a turntable.)

Let **stand** on a hard heat-proof surface for 5 minutes, then loosen the edges and invert onto serving dish. Tent loosely with foil to keep warm until ready to serve.

Suggestions: Fill open center with fresh or cooked colorful vegetables.

Sunburst of Garden Vegetables

SERVES 4 TO 6

EQUIPMENT:	2-quart round casserole dish, 4-cup glass measure, small mixing bowl
COOKING TIME:	15½ to 20½ minutes (Low wattage ovens 16½ to 24 minutes)
STANDING TIME:	none required

2 tablespoons butter or margarine, sliced
¼ cup hot water
2 cups fresh cauliflower flowerets, cut into 1-inch pieces
1 cup sliced carrots, ¼ inch thick
2 cups fresh broccoli flowerets, cut into 1-inch pieces
1 cup sliced fresh mushrooms

SAUCE
2 10¾-ounce cans condensed cream of potato soup
½ cup milk or water
¼ cup sour cream
2 tablespoons grated Parmesan cheese
2 tablespoons snipped fresh parsley
⅛ teaspoon white pepper

TOPPING
2 tablespoons butter or margarine, sliced
½ cup crushed Saltine cracker crumbs
½ teaspoon paprika

Place 2 tablespoons butter in round casserole dish and microwave on HIGH for 40 to 50 seconds (LW 50 to 60 seconds) or until melted. Add hot water and **stir.** Add cauliflower, carrots, and broccoli, **stirring** well. **Cover** dish with lid or plastic wrap, pulling back one corner to vent the steam. (If dish is flat-bottomed, **elevate** it on an inverted saucer.) Place on turntable if available and microwave on HIGH for 3 to 4 minutes (LW 3 to 5 minutes).

Stir in mushrooms, **cover** again, and microwave on HIGH for 6 to 8 minutes (LW 7 to 9 minutes) or until crisp-tender. (**Rotate** dish ½ turn when stirring if not using turntable.)

Combine all sauce ingredients in glass measure. (Do not whisk, as whisking will mash the potatoes.) Add sauce to vegetables and **stir** gently. Set aside. (If a thinner sauce is desired, add an additional ¼ cup sour cream.)

Place 2 tablespoons butter in small bowl and microwave on HIGH for 40 to 50 seconds (LW 50 to 60 seconds) or until melted. **Stir** in crumbs and paprika. Sprinkle crumb topping over casserole. Microwave, **uncovered,** on HIGH for 5 to 7 minutes (LW 5 to 8 minutes) or until vegetables and sauce are hot and bubbly. (**Rotate** dish ½ turn after 3 minutes if not using turntable.)

Suggestions: Ritz cracker crumbs can be substituted for Saltine crumbs. Crush whole crackers in food processor or place in a plastic bag and roll with a rolling pin to crush.

Scalloped Tomato Bake

School lunches are notoriously awful, but at my high school there was a wonderful dish of scalloped tomatoes. Years later I kept thinking about that dish, and finally I managed to re-create it.

SERVES 4

EQUIPMENT:	medium mixing bowl, 1½-quart round casserole dish
COOKING TIME:	13 to 17 minutes (Low wattage ovens 15½ to 20 minutes)
STANDING TIME:	none required

4 slices whole wheat bread
1 28-ounce can whole tomatoes, undrained, *or* 6 to 8 large fresh tomatoes, skinned
½ cup tomato juice
2 tablespoons butter or margarine, sliced
½ cup chopped onion
½ cup chopped celery
½ cup chopped green bell pepper
1 tablespoon sugar
1 teaspoon dried oregano
1 teaspoon salt
¼ teaspoon pepper
¼ cup grated Parmesan cheese
grated Parmesan cheese and fresh parsley sprigs for garnish

Toast and butter bread slices and cut into ½-inch cubes. In a medium bowl, combine whole tomatoes along with their juice and the tomato juice. **Stir** in the toast cubes and set the dish aside.

Place butter, onion, celery, and green pepper in round casserole dish. **Cover** dish with plastic wrap, pulling back one corner to vent the steam. (If dish is flat-bottomed, **elevate** it on an inverted saucer.) Microwave on HIGH for 4 to 6 minutes (LW 5 to 7 minutes) or until vegetables are crisp-tender, **stirring** every 3 minutes. **Stir** in sugar, oregano, salt, pepper, and Parmesan cheese. Add tomato mixture and **stir** gently.

Cover dish with wax paper and place on turntable if available. Microwave on HIGH for 9 to 11 minutes (LW 10½ to 13 minutes) or until hot and bubbly, **stirring** once during cooking. (**Rotate** dish ½ turn when stirring if not using turntable.) Sprinkle Parmesan cheese over casserole and garnish with sprigs of parsley.

Suggestions: If you're using fresh tomatoes, remove skins by microwaving about 2 cups water in a casserole dish on HIGH for 4 to 5 minutes or until boiling. Make a small X in the bottom of each tomato with a paring knife, place in the boiling water, microwave on HIGH for 1 minute, and plunge into cold water. Skins should slip off easily.

Zucchini Boats

I credit this recipe to my son Bill. I defrosted a package of what I thought was hamburger one day only to find it was ground pork. I thought I would try something new, but the only vegetable I had was zucchini. "Stuff them, Mom!" were my instructions from Bill. Since that day this recipe has become a favorite of the entire family as well as with the crew at WSUB Radio, where I have a weekly radio program.

SERVES 4

EQUIPMENT: plastic dishwasher-safe colander and casserole dish, medium mixing bowl, grapefruit
spoon, 12 × 8- or 9 × 13-inch baking dish

COOKING TIME: 13 to 18 minutes (Low wattage ovens 15½
to 21½ minutes)

STANDING TIME: none required

4 small zucchini, as uniform in size as possible
salt
1 pound ground pork
1 garlic clove, minced
½ cup chopped onion
½ cup chopped fresh mushrooms
1 8-ounce can tomato sauce
¼ teaspoon dried oregano
¼ teaspoon dried basil
¼ teaspoon seasoned salt
dash of pepper
¼ cup shredded mozzarella cheese
4 teaspoons grated Parmesan cheese

Wash zucchini, cut off the ends, and cut each squash in half
lengthwise. Place the halves skin side down on 2 layers of paper
towel on microwave floor. Microwave on HIGH for 4 to 6 minutes
(LW 5 to 7 minutes) or until still slightly firm. Sprinkle salt lightly
over the shells to extract the excess moisture and turn them over
onto several layers of paper towel to drain.

Crumble ground pork into colander and place colander in a
casserole dish to catch the drippings. Microwave on HIGH, **uncovered,** for 3 minutes (LW 3½ minutes). Break up the meat chunks
with a fork and add garlic, onion, and mushrooms. Microwave on
HIGH for 3 to 4 minutes (LW 3½ to 5 minutes) or until vegetables
are crisp-tender and meat is no longer pink. Place **drained** meat
mixture in mixing bowl and add tomato sauce, oregano, basil,
salt, pepper, and mozzarella.

Scoop the pulp out of the zucchini using a grapefruit spoon,
leaving the shells intact to form a boat. Fill each boat with the
pork mixture, mounding if necessary, and place the filled shells in

baking dish. **Cover** with wax paper. (If dish is flat-bottomed, **elevate** it on an inverted saucer.) Microwave on HIGH for 3 to 5 minutes (LW 3½ to 6 minutes) or until shells are fork-tender and stuffing is steaming. Sprinkle each boat with Parmesan cheese before serving.

Troubleshooting: Be sure to leave a bit of pulp at each end of the shell to hold the filling in.

Do not overcook shells, or they will soften and lose their shape.

Suggestions: Ground beef or turkey may be substituted for the pork.

Vegetarian Pasta

Legend tells us that the many shapes of macaroni came to be when pasta was first made in Italy. Some cooks became bored with the "long, slender tubes," so each community developed its own distinctive way of making macaroni. The Romans prepared macaroni in strips, Sicilians rolled their dough on knitting needles to form spiral shapes, and in Bologna it was flat ribbons. Not all Italians have an endless love for pasta. The people of northern Italy prefer rice, particularly in the form of risotto.

SERVES 6

EQUIPMENT:	3-quart round casserole dish, small mixing bowl
COOKING TIME:	23 to 27 minutes (Low wattage ovens 26 to 31 minutes)
STANDING TIME:	none required

   3   cups uncooked ditalini macaroni
   1   10-ounce paper-covered box frozen chopped broccoli
   3   tablespoons butter or margarine, sliced
   ½   cup diced celery
   1   cup chopped onion
   ½   pound fresh mushrooms, sliced
   1   cup thinly sliced carrots
   2   tablespoons snipped fresh parsley
   1   large garlic clove, minced
   1   10¾-ounce can condensed cream of celery soup
   1   cup sour cream
   1   teaspoon salt
   ½   teaspoon black pepper
       grated Parmesan cheese and green bell pepper slices
       for garnish

Cook pasta conventionally, according to package directions; drain and set aside. Place paper-covered box of broccoli on 2 layers of paper towel on microwave floor. Microwave on HIGH for 3 minutes (LW 3½ minutes). Shake, turn box over, and microwave on HIGH for 3 minutes (LW 3½ minutes); set aside.

Place butter, celery, onion, mushrooms, carrots, parsley, and garlic in round casserole dish. **Cover** with lid or plastic wrap, pulling back one corner to vent the steam. (If dish is flat-bottomed, **elevate** it on an inverted saucer.) Place on turntable if available and microwave on HIGH for 9 to 11 minutes (LW 10 to 12 minutes) or until vegetables are crisp-tender, **stirring** once during cooking. (**Rotate** dish ½ turn when stirring if not using turntable.) Add broccoli and cooked pasta, **stirring** together gently.

In small bowl, **whisk** together soup, sour cream, salt, and pepper and fold into vegetable mixture. **Cover** again and microwave on HIGH for 8 to 10 minutes (LW 9 to 12 minutes) or until heated through, **stirring** once during cooking. (**Rotate** dish ½ turn when stirring if not using turntable.) Sprinkle with Parmesan cheese and garnish with green pepper slices.

Troubleshooting: If frozen vegetable box has a foil wrapper, remove it before microwaving as it will arc and could ignite paper towels.

It doesn't save time to microwave pasta. Cook a double batch on your conventional stove and freeze half for quick defrost and heat-up in the microwave when preparing this recipe again.

Suggestion: There are many choices of pasta that you may use in place of ditalini. My favorites are ruffles, frills, twists, or rotini.

FROZEN BOXED OR BAGGED VEGETABLES

Nearly all brands of frozen vegetables come with microwave cooking instructions on the package, telling you to remove the vegetables to a casserole dish, add water, cover, and microwave. It is much easier—and there's no dish to wash—if you microwave them right in the package you purchase them in. The most important thing to remember is that you can microwave only plastic bags and paper-covered boxes.

Very few manufacturers package their frozen boxed vegetables with a foil wrapper, but if the brand you choose does so, just remove the foil label before microwaving, as it will arc and may ignite the paper towels you place it on.

Only plastic bags need to be vented—make an X in the top of plastic bags—as they will melt if you do not allow the steam to escape. Paper-covered boxes will not melt and do not need to be vented.

Place the bag or box on 2 layers of paper towels, do not add water, and follow the microwaving times listed on the package. There will be no excess liquid to drain, which contains all the vitamins and nutrients, no dish to wash, and the vegetables will microwave beautifully.

RICE

Both rice and pasta are dry foods that need time to absorb moisture and take just as long to cook in the microwave as they do on your conventional stove. However, they both reheat very easily in the microwave when placed in a covered container and need no added water, only a vented covering of plastic wrap.

The type of dish used to microwave rice is very important. Square-cornered dishes will overcook whatever is in the corners, so be sure always to use a round dish and one that is deep, rather than flat; it must be at least 2 quarts in size for 1 cup of raw rice.

There are several methods you can use, but I find that this method works best for plain white rice: Place 2 cups hot water and 1 tablespoon margarine (optional) in a deep 2-quart round casserole dish. **Cover** with the lid or plastic wrap, pulling back one corner to vent the steam. (If dish is flat-bottomed, **elevate** on an inverted saucer.) Place on a turntable if available and microwave on HIGH for 5 to 7 minutes (LW 6 to 9 minutes) or until boiling.

Stir in 1 cup uncooked long-grain rice, **cover** again, and reduce the power to 50 percent or MEDIUM. Microwave for 12 to 17 minutes (LW 14 to 20 minutes) or until all the liquid is absorbed and the rice is tender. (**Rotate** dish ½ turn every 6 minutes if not using turntable.) Let **stand, covered,** for 5 minutes and fluff with a fork before serving.

Baked Vegetable Rice

SERVES 4

EQUIPMENT:	1-quart round casserole dish, deep 2-quart round casserole dish
COOKING TIME:	30 to 41 minutes (Low wattage ovens 43½ to 47¾ minutes)
STANDING TIME:	5 minutes

1   tablespoon butter or margarine, sliced
½   cup chopped onion
½   cup chopped celery
¼   cup grated carrot
½   cup sliced fresh mushrooms
1   10½-ounce can beef broth
¾   cup hot water
1   teaspoon butter or margarine
1   envelope Lipton Onion Cup-a-Soup
1   cup uncooked long-grain white rice

Place 1 tablespoon butter, onion, celery, carrot, and mushrooms in 1-quart casserole dish. **Cover** with lid or plastic wrap, pulling back one corner to vent the steam. (If dish is flat-bottomed, **elevate** it on an inverted saucer.) Microwave on HIGH for 5 to 7 minutes (LW 5 to 8 minutes) or until vegetables are crisp-tender, **stirring** once during cooking.

In deep casserole dish, combine broth, hot water, 1 teaspoon butter, and envelope of soup mix. **Stir** well and **cover** with plastic wrap, pulling back one corner to vent the steam. (If dish is flat-bottomed, **elevate** on an inverted saucer.) Place on turntable if available and microwave on HIGH for 6 to 8 minutes (LW 7 to 9 minutes) or until liquid begins to boil, **stirring** every 3 minutes. (**Rotate** dish ½ turn when stirring if not using turntable.)

Stir in vegetable mixture and rice. **Cover** again and microwave on HIGH for 2 to 4 minutes (LW 2½ to 4¾ minutes) or until boiling. Reduce power to 50 percent or MEDIUM and microwave for 17 to 22 minutes (LW 20 to 26 minutes) or until rice is tender and liquid has been absorbed. (**Rotate** dish ½ turn every 10 minutes if not using turntable.) Let **stand, covered,** for 5 minutes before fluffing with a fork and serving.

Troubleshooting: If you're using a square-cornered dish in place of a round casserole, you may find overcooking occurring in the corners.

Suggestions: Add diced cooked ham, chicken, or pork and this dish will remind you of the fried rice served in many Chinese restaurants.

Spanish Rice

SERVES 4 TO 6

EQUIPMENT: deep 2-quart round casserole dish
COOKING TIME: 20 to 25 minutes (Low wattage ovens 24 to 30 minutes)
STANDING TIME: 5 minutes

1 **cup hot water**
1 **beef bouillon cube**
1 **cup uncooked long-grain white rice**
1 **14½-ounce can stewed tomatoes, undrained and cut up or mashed**
⅛ **teaspoon pepper**
⅛ **teaspoon paprika**
3 **tablespoons thinly sliced pitted black olives**

Place hot water in deep casserole dish and add bouillon cube, crushing and stirring until dissolved. **Stir** in rice, stewed tomatoes with juice, pepper, and paprika. **Cover** dish with lid or plastic wrap, pulling back one corner to vent the steam. (If dish is flat-bottomed, **elevate** it on an inverted saucer.) Place on turntable if available and microwave on HIGH for 5 minutes (LW 6 minutes). (**Rotate** dish ½ turn if not using turntable.)

Reduce power to 50 percent or MEDIUM and microwave for 15 to 20 minutes (LW 18 to 24 minutes) or until liquid is absorbed and rice is tender. (**Rotate** dish ¼ turn every 5 minutes if not using turntable.) **Stir** in black olives, **cover,** and let **stand** for 5 minutes before serving.

Suggestions: Sprinkle with grated Parmesan cheese before serving.

Meats

Summer Italian Stuffed Chicken

The winning recipe at the 1989 National Chicken Cook-Off was submitted by Melissa Mathie of Michigan, a housewife who created her recipe just for the contest. I converted Melissa's winning recipe to the microwave making only one change—the topping in Melissa's recipe called for an egg and bread crumb mixture, which doesn't appear cooked when it's microwaved.

SERVES 4

EQUIPMENT:	meat mallet, flat baking dish, medium mixing bowl, serving platter, small mixing bowl, meat rack
COOKING TIME:	7¾ to 11¾ minutes (Low wattage ovens 8¾ to 13 minutes)
STANDING TIME:	3 minutes

4 **broiler-fryer chicken breast halves, boned and skinned**
½ **cup plus ⅓ cup bottled oil-vinegar dressing**
1 **small head radicchio, torn into bite-size pieces**
1 **small bunch watercress, cut into bite-size pieces**
¼ **cup fresh basil leaves**
2 **fresh plum tomatoes, thinly sliced**
3 **tablespoons butter or margarine, sliced**
½ **cup crushed cornflakes**
⅓ **cup grated Parmesan cheese**
1 **tablespoon chopped fresh parsley**
¼ **teaspoon dried basil**
¼ **teaspoon dried oregano**
¼ **teaspoon garlic powder**
  tomato rosettes for garnish

On hard surface, with flat side of meat mallet or similar flattening utensil, pound chicken to ¼-inch thickness and place in baking dish. Add ½ cup dressing and turn to coat. **Cover** and refrigerate for 30 minutes.

Place radicchio and watercress in medium bowl; add remaining ⅓ cup dressing and **toss** to mix. Arrange mixture on platter and refrigerate.

Remove chicken from dressing and drain. Cut each breast half in half crosswise. Divide fresh basil and tomatoes evenly on top of 4 pieces of chicken and top each with another chicken piece. Using the textured side of a meat mallet, pound the edges together to seal.

In a small bowl, microwave butter on HIGH for 40 to 50 seconds (LW 50 to 60 seconds) or until melted. On a sheet of wax paper, combine cornflake crumbs, Parmesan cheese, parsley, dried basil, oregano, and garlic powder. Dip only one side of each chicken bundle first into the melted butter and then into the cornflake mixture.

Place chicken pieces on meat rack like the spokes of a wheel, with the thickest portions to the outside of the dish and the thinner ends pointing toward the center. **Cover** loosely with wax paper and microwave on HIGH for 7 to 11 minutes (LW 8 to 12 minutes) or until chicken is no longer pink and is tender, **rotating** dish ½ turn every 3 minutes.

Once done, remove dish from microwave, remove wax paper and **tent** with aluminum foil. Let **stand** for 3 minutes before arranging on top of chilled radicchio and watercress. Garnish with tomato rosettes.

Troubleshooting: Turning chicken bundles over while cooking will cause the topping to come off.

If you'd like to enter the contest, here's what you need to know. An independent recipe-judging agency selects the best chicken recipe submitted from each of the 50 states and the District of Columbia. Each of the 51 finalists receives an expense-paid trip to participate in the national cook-off and a chance to compete for the $25,000 first prize, plus additional runner-up prizes.

Each contestant prepares his or her own recipe at the contest site and is judged by well-known food experts on taste, appearance, simplicity, and appeal. The contest is held every other year, and you can enter by sending your own favorite chicken recipe, complete with your name, address, and telephone number on the front of each recipe, to Chicken Contest, Box 28158, Central Station, Washington, DC 20005.

The National Chicken Cook-Off is held in odd-numbered years, while the Delmarva Poultry Group holds its chicken cook-off in the even numbered years. To enter the next Delmarva Cook-Off, write Delmarva Poultry Industry, Inc., RD 2, Box 47, Georgetown, DE 19947.

Chili Chicken Fiesta

John Messer submitted this recipe to the 1989 National Chicken Cook-Off and was the chosen contestant from Connecticut, my home state. Unfortunately John's recipe didn't take a top prize, but it is definitely a winner. When I presented my microwave version of John's recipe on television, the response was fantastic, and rightfully so: it's just delicious.

SERVES 6

EQUIPMENT:	deep 2- or 3-quart round casserole dish
COOKING TIME:	22 to 28 minutes (Low wattage ovens 26 to 34 minutes)
STANDING TIME:	5 minutes

1 **broiler-fryer chicken breast, boned, skinned, and cut into 1-inch pieces**
1 **tablespoon vegetable oil**
½ **cup chopped celery**
½ **cup chopped onion**
1 **14½-ounce can chicken broth**
2 **tablespoons chopped fresh parsley**
2 **teaspoons chili powder**
1 **teaspoon dried oregano**
1 **garlic clove, minced**
½ **cup chopped fresh tomato**
1 **15-ounce can red kidney beans, undrained**
1 **12-ounce can Mexican corn, drained**
1 **6-ounce box quick-cooking long-grain and wild rice**
lettuce leaves for serving

Place chicken, oil, celery, and onion in deep casserole dish. **Cover** dish with wax paper. (If dish is flat-bottomed, **elevate** it on an inverted saucer.) Place on turntable if available and microwave on HIGH for 3 minutes (LW 3½ minutes) **Stir, cover** again, and microwave on HIGH for 3 minutes (LW 3½ minutes) or until the pieces lose their pink color. (**Rotate** dish ½ turn when stirring if not using turntable.)

Add chicken broth, parsley, chili powder, oregano, garlic, tomato, kidney beans with liquid, and Mexican corn. **Stir** in quick-cooking long-grain and wild rice and **cover** again. Microwave on HIGH for 16 to 22 minutes (LW 19 to 27 minutes) or until rice is tender and liquid is nearly absorbed. (**Rotate** dish ¼ turn every 5 minutes if not using turntable.) Let **stand, covered,** for 5 minutes and serve mounded in lettuce leaves.

Troubleshooting: Be sure to cut chicken into uniformly sized pieces, because things of the same size cook in the same length of time.

Olympic Seoul Chicken

Another Delmarva contest winner comes from Muriel Brody of Cumberland, Rhode Island. I converted Muriel's recipe to the microwave with no ingredient changes.

SERVES 4

EQUIPMENT: small mixing bowl, 12 × 8-inch baking dish
COOKING TIME: 14 to 18 minutes (Low wattage ovens 16½ to 21 minutes)
STANDING TIME: 5 minutes

¼ **cup white vinegar**
3 **tablespoons soy sauce**
1 **teaspoon cornstarch**
2 **tablespoons honey**
¼ **teaspoon minced fresh ginger**
8 **broiler-fryer chicken thighs, skinned**
10 **garlic cloves, chopped**
1 **teaspoon crushed red pepper**

In small bowl, mix together vinegar, soy sauce, cornstarch, honey, and ginger; set aside.

Place chicken thighs in baking dish like the spokes of a wheel, with the broader parts to the outside of the dish and the smaller ends toward the center of the dish. Add garlic and red pepper. **Cover** with plastic wrap, pulling back one corner to vent the steam. (If dish is flat-bottomed, **elevate** it on an inverted saucer.) Microwave on HIGH for 3 minutes (LW 3½ minutes). Turn pieces over and **rearrange, cover** again, and microwave on HIGH for another 3 minutes (LW 3½ minutes).

Rearrange chicken pieces, bringing the less cooked areas to the outside of the dish, pour vinegar mixture over and around pieces, **cover** dish with wax paper, and microwave on HIGH for 8 to 12 minutes (LW 9½ to 14 minutes) or until chicken is fork-tender. Let **stand, covered,** for 5 minutes and serve with hot cooked rice.

REARRANGING MEAT PIECES

Since the microwaves cook from the outside to the center, always rearrange meat pieces by bringing the areas closest to the outside of the dish into the center and the areas pointing into the center to the outside edges. This rearranging will help the meat cook evenly.

Caribbean Chicken Creole

The Curaçao Caribbean Hotel on the island of Curaçao features this terrific creole dish on its buffet—it works beautifully in the microwave.

SERVES 4 TO 6

EQUIPMENT: 13 × 9-inch baking dish, 4-cup glass measure
COOKING TIME: 29 to 36 minutes (Low wattage ovens 34¾ to 43½ minutes)
STANDING TIME: 5 minutes

1   2- to 3-pound broiler-fryer chicken, cut up
2   tablespoons butter or margarine, sliced
1   medium onion, chopped
1   celery stalk, chopped
1   medium green bell pepper, chopped
½   cup white wine
½   cup chicken bouillon
1   medium fresh tomato, diced
1   6-ounce can tomato paste
4   dried prunes, sliced in half

Rinse chicken pieces and pat dry. Place pieces in baking dish, meatiest portions to the outside of the dish with skin side down; set aside.

Put butter, onion, celery, and green pepper in glass measure. Microwave on HIGH for 4 to 6 minutes (LW 4¾ to 7½ minutes), until vegetables are crisp-tender. Add wine, bouillon, diced tomato, tomato paste, and prunes, **stirring** to combine. Pour vegetable mixture over chicken pieces and **cover** with plastic wrap, pulling back one corner to vent the steam. (If dish is flat-bottomed, **elevate** it on an inverted saucer.) Microwave on HIGH for 15 minutes (LW 18 minutes), **rotating** dish ½ turn after 7 minutes.

Rearrange and turn chicken pieces over, being sure to baste well with sauce. **Cover** again, **rotate** dish ½ turn, and microwave on HIGH for 10 to 15 minutes (LW 12 to 18 minutes) or until chicken is fork-tender and no longer pink near the bone. Let **stand, covered,** for 5 minutes and serve over hot cooked rice.

Suggestions: Chicken may be skinned before cooking if you're watching your cholesterol.

Sweet and Sour Chicken

SERVES 4

EQUIPMENT:	2-quart round casserole dish, 4-cup glass measure
COOKING TIME:	16 to 22 minutes (Low wattage ovens 19 to 25 minutes)
STANDING TIME:	none required

1 **broiler-fryer chicken breast (about 1 pound), skinned, boned, and cut into bite-size pieces**
2 **tablespoons peanut oil**
1 **large garlic clove, minced**
1 **cup diagonally sliced (⅛-inch thick) carrots**
1 **cup sliced fresh mushrooms**
4 **scallions, cut into 1-inch pieces**
1 **cup green bell pepper strips, ¼ by 2 inches**
1 **8-ounce can sliced water chestnuts, drained**

SAUCE
- ½ **cup light brown sugar**
- 3 **tablespoons cornstarch**
- ½ **teaspoon ground ginger**
- 1 **cup pineapple juice**
- ⅓ **cup white vinegar**
- 2 **tablespoons soy sauce**
- 1 **tablespoon ketchup**

Combine chicken, oil, and garlic in casserole dish. **Cover** with lid or plastic wrap, pulling back one corner to vent the steam. (If dish is flat-bottomed, **elevate** it on an inverted saucer.) Place on turntable if available and microwave on HIGH for 4 to 6 minutes (LW 5 to 7 minutes) or until chicken is no longer pink, **stirring** every 2 minutes. (**Rotate** dish ½ turn when stirring if not using turntable.) Remove chicken from casserole with slotted spoon and set aside.

To remaining cooking liquid in dish, add carrots, mushrooms, scallions, pepper strips, and water chestnuts. **Stir** and **cover** again. Microwave on HIGH for 7 to 9 minutes (LW 8 to 10 minutes) or until vegetables are crisp-tender, **stirring** several times during cooking. (**Rotate** dish ½ turn when stirring if not using turntable.) **Drain** and discard any liquid; **stir** in chicken pieces. **Cover** to keep vegetables and chicken warm and set aside.

Blend sugar, cornstarch, and ginger in glass measure. **Whisk** in remaining sauce ingredients and microwave, **uncovered,** on HIGH for 5 to 7 minutes (LW 6 to 8 minutes) or until sauce is thickened, **whisking** every minute. Pour sauce over chicken mixture and **toss** to coat. Serve over hot cooked rice.

Troubleshooting: Be sure to cut chicken and vegetables into uniformly sized pieces, because things of the same size cook in the same length of time.

Chicken and Spanish Rice

SERVES 4

EQUIPMENT:	4-cup glass measure, 9 × 13-inch casserole dish
COOKING TIME:	32 to 36 minutes (Low wattage ovens 39 to 43 minutes)
STANDING TIME:	5 minutes

2 **tablespoons olive oil**
½ **cup diced green bell pepper**
½ **cup diced onion**
2 **garlic cloves, minced**
1 **4-ounce can sliced mushrooms, undrained or ½ cup sliced fresh mushrooms**
2 **cups uncooked quick-cooking rice**
1 **6-ounce can tomato paste**
1 **8-ounce can tomato sauce**
¼ **cup burgundy wine**
¼ **teaspoon dried oregano**
¼ **teaspoon dried basil**
⅛ **teaspoon pepper**
¼ **teaspoon salt**
1 **2- to 3-pound broiler-fryer chicken, cut up**

Place oil, green pepper, onion, and garlic in glass measure. Microwave, **uncovered,** on HIGH for 6 minutes (LW 7 minutes), **stirring** once; vegetables should be crisp-tender. Transfer vegetables to casserole dish and add all remaining ingredients except chicken; **stir** together well. Arrange chicken, skin side down, on top of rice mixture with the meatiest portions to the outside of the dish. **Cover** with plastic wrap, pulling back one corner to vent the steam. (If dish is flat-bottomed, **elevate** it on an inverted saucer.)

Microwave on HIGH for 15 minutes (LW 18 minutes). **Stir** rice mixture, turn chicken over, and **rearrange** pieces so that the less cooked areas are to the outside of the dish. **Rotate** dish ½ turn and microwave, **uncovered,** on HIGH for 12 to 15 minutes (LW 14 to 18 minutes) or until chicken is tender and the juices run clear when pierced with a fork. Also check the meat near the bone to be sure it is no longer pink. Once chicken is done, remove dish from microwave, **tent** with aluminum foil, and let **stand** for 5 minutes before serving.

Troubleshooting: If one area of the rice mixture appears to be overcooking, you may have a hot spot in the oven and should rotate dish more often.

Suggestions: Chicken may be skinned before cooking if you're watching your cholesterol level.

CORNISH GAME HENS

If you're tired of having to find ways to use up leftover chicken, tasty little cornish game hens may just be the answer. Because of their small size, one hen per person is the usual serving, eliminating leftovers. Tender as they are, their low fat and small size make for short cooking times and no chance for browning. To solve the browning problem, you just glaze them or paint with a browning agent for color.

If you're starting with frozen hens, defrost them individually on 30 percent power or LOW for 6 minutes (LW 6 minutes), **elevated** on an inverted saucer. Allow the hen to **stand** for 5 minutes, turn over, **rotate** ½ turn, and microwave again for 3 to 5 minutes (LW 3½ to 6 minutes) on 30 percent power or LOW. Again, let the hen **stand** for 10 minutes. Remove the giblets and allow to **stand** for 10 minutes more, until cool but not icy. Like regular chicken, Cornish hens cook on HIGH power for 6 to 8 minutes (LW 7 to 9 minutes) per pound, breast side up, elevated on a meat rack. If you don't have a meat rack, balance each hen on an inverted custard cup set into a casserole dish to catch the drippings.

Cranberry-Glazed Game Hens

SERVES 2

EQUIPMENT:	4-cup glass measure, custard cup, meat rack or 2 custard cups and casserole dish
COOKING TIME:	15¾ to 28 minutes (Low wattage ovens 19 to 32½ minutes)
STANDING TIME:	5 to 10 minutes

1   8-ounce can jellied cranberry sauce
¼   cup white wine
2   tablespoons dark brown sugar
1   tablespoon grated orange zest
2   1- to 1½-pound Cornish game hens
1   tablespoon butter or margarine
1   celery stalk, cut into quarters
1   medium onion, cut into quarters

Combine cranberry sauce, wine, brown sugar, and orange zest in glass measure. Microwave on HIGH for 1 to 2 minutes (LW 1¼ to 2¼ minutes), **uncovered,** until cranberry sauce melts and mixture is smooth, **whisking** every minute.

Remove giblets from hens, rinse well under cold water, and pat dry. Insert 2 celery and onion chunks into each hen cavity. Place butter in custard cup, **cover** with a sheet of paper towel, and microwave on HIGH for 40 to 50 seconds (LW 1 to 1¼ minutes) or until melted.

Place hens on meat rack or balance each on a custard cup set into a casserole dish to catch the drippings. Brush hens with melted butter and then with cranberry mixture, coating well. **Cover** hens loosely with a tent of wax paper and microwave on HIGH for 14 to 25 minutes (LW 16¾ to 29 minutes), **basting** and **rotating** dish ½ turn every 5 minutes.

Hens are done when legs move easily and juices from center cavity run clear, not pink. Let **stand, covered,** for 5 to 10 minutes and serve.

Suggestions: For added flavor, microwave orange on HIGH for 15 seconds before grating zest.

Orange-Glazed Stuffed Game Hens

SERVES 2

EQUIPMENT:	meat rack or 2 custard cups and casserole dish, 4-cup glass measure
COOKING TIME:	16 to 28 minutes (Low wattage ovens 19 to 32½ minutes)
STANDING TIME:	5 to 10 minutes

STUFFING

1 6-ounce box long-grain and wild rice
2 scallions, minced
6 fresh mushrooms, diced
2 1- to 1½-pound Cornish game hens

GLAZE

⅓ cup orange marmalade
¼ cup dark brown sugar
⅓ cup orange-flavored liqueur, such as Cointreau
orange slices for garnish

Prepare rice according to box directions, adding scallions and mushrooms at start of cooking. Set aside.

Remove giblets from hens, rinse under cold water, and pat dry. Fill cavities with rice mixture and secure with wooden picks or truss with string. Place stuffed hens on a meat rack or balance each on an inverted custard cup set into a casserole dish to catch the drippings.

Place glaze ingredients into glass measure and microwave **uncovered** on HIGH for 2 to 3 minutes (LW 2¼ to 3½ minutes), **stirring** every minute until smooth. Brush glaze onto hens and **cover** with a tent of wax paper. Microwave on HIGH for 14 to 25 minutes (LW 16¾ to 29 minutes) or until legs move freely and juices run clear when thigh is pierced with a fork. **Baste** and **rotate** dish ½ turn every 5 minutes. Let **stand, covered,** for 5 to 10 minutes. Garnish with orange slices.

DUCK

I don't think I'll ever forget my first disaster roasting a duck. As I stood holding the picture in the cookbook next to my creation, there was nothing left to do but let the tears fall.

That was many years ago, and since then I have learned two things. First, the pictures in most cookbooks aren't really cooked food, and usually it is impossible to duplicate them; the second thing I learned was how to cook a duck.

Most ducks today are purchased frozen and of course must be defrosted before being cooked. Remove any metal closures and the wrappings, place duck in a baking dish, and defrost on 30 percent power or LOW for 8 to 10 minutes (LW 9 to 12 minutes). Let the duck **stand** for 5 to 10 minutes and repeat the process. It may be necessary to repeat the process several times, but defrosting for short periods of time and allowing the duck to stand will defrost it evenly, with no cooking taking place on the outside edges.

Wash the inside cavity and pull out any excess fat. There is so much fat under the skin in a duck that you must pierce the skin with a small knife or the tines of a large fork to allow the fat to escape while cooking.

Roast Duck with Cherry Sauce

SERVES 4

EQUIPMENT: meat rack or 2 custard cups and casserole dish large enough to hold duck, 4-cup glass measure

COOKING TIME: Duck—8 to 10 minutes per pound (Low wattage ovens 10 to 12 minutes per pound) Sauce—2 to 3 minutes (Low wattage ovens 2¼ to 3½ minutes)

STANDING TIME: 5 minutes

    1   **4- to 5-pound duck, defrosted, giblets removed**
    1   **16-ounce can pitted dark cherries, undrained**
    1   **tablespoon sugar**
    1   **tablespoon cornstarch**
  ¼   **cup red wine**
    1   **tablespoon lemon juice**

Rinse duck, remove excess fat from cavity, twist the wing tips behind the back, and pull the neck skin over the tips. Secure neck skin with a wooden skewer and pierce the skin in several places all over the duck. Place duck breast side down on a meat rack or balanced on 2 custard cups set into casserole dish. **Cover** duck with a tent of wax paper.

First calculate cooking time; duck microwaves for 8 to 10 minutes per pound (LW 10 to 12 minutes per pound). Figure entire estimated cooking time and divide in ½.

Microwave on HIGH for the first 10 minutes (LW 12 minutes); drain excess fat. For the balance of the first half of cooking time, reduce the power to 50 percent or MEDIUM; **drain** excess fat.

Turn duck over, breast side up, and microwave for the remaining time on 50 percent power or MEDIUM. Duck is done when the leg moves easily and the juices run clear when the skin is pierced between the leg and thigh. Once the duck is done, **drain** and **tent** with aluminum foil. Let **stand, covered,** for 5 minutes before serving.

For sauce, drain cherries, reserving ¾ cup of the juice. **Whisk** together cherry juice, sugar, and cornstarch in glass measure. Add wine and lemon juice. Microwave, **uncovered,** on HIGH for 2 to 3 minutes (LW 2¼ to 3½ minutes) or until thickened, **whisking** well every minute. Serve sauce with duck.

Suggestions: For a really crisp skin, place duck in preheated 400° conventional oven for 10 to 15 minutes.

Turkey Meatball Stew

SERVES 4 TO 6

EQUIPMENT: 3-quart round casserole dish, large mixing bowl, deep 10-inch round baking dish or dinner plate, 6-cup glass measure, medium mixing bowl

COOKING TIME: 29 to 35 minutes (Low wattage ovens 35 to 41 minutes)

STANDING TIME: none required

½ cup chopped carrots
1 medium onion, chopped
½ cup chopped celery
2 medium potatoes, cut into ½-inch cubes
1 cup sliced fresh mushrooms
¼ cup tomato juice
1 14½-ounce can stewed tomatoes, drained, juice reserved

MEATBALLS
1¼ pounds ground turkey
1 egg, slightly beaten
⅓ cup cold water
¼ cup unseasoned fresh bread crumbs
2 tablespoons grated Parmesan cheese
½ cup finely chopped onion
1 tablespoon snipped fresh parsley
½ teaspoon garlic salt
¼ teaspoon pepper
½ teaspoon paprika

2½ cups water
2 1⅛-ounce packages gravy mix for turkey
1 cup frozen peas

Place carrots, onion, celery, potatoes, mushrooms, and tomato juice in casserole dish. **Cover** with lid or plastic wrap, pulling back one corner to vent the steam. (If dish is flat-bottomed, **elevate** it on an inverted saucer.) Place on turntable if available and microwave on HIGH for 10 to 12 minutes (LW 12 to 14 minutes) or until vegetables are crisp-tender, **stirring** every 5 minutes. Add stewed tomatoes, **stir,** and set aside. (**Rotate** dish ½ turn when stirring if not using turntable.)

Combine all meatball ingredients in bowl, mixing together thoroughly. Shape mixture into 16 uniformly sized balls. Place balls in deep baking dish or on dinner plate and **cover** with wax paper. (If dish is flat-bottomed, **elevate** it on an inverted saucer.) Place on turntable if available and microwave on HIGH for 6 minutes (LW 7 minutes). (**Rotate** dish ½ turn after 4 minutes if not using turntable.) **Drain** liquid and rearrange balls, bringing the less cooked ones from the center of the dish to the outside edges and the ones along the outside into the center. **Cover** again and microwave on HIGH for 4 to 6 minutes (LW 5 to 7 minutes) or until the centers are no longer pink. (**Rotate** dish ½ turn after 4 minutes if not using turntable.) **Drain** and set aside.

Pour water into glass measure and **whisk** in gravy mix. Microwave **uncovered** on HIGH for 9 to 11 minutes (LW 11 to 13 minutes), **whisking** every minute, until smooth and thickened. Add to stewed tomato mixture, **stirring** well. Carefully **stir** in cooked meatballs and frozen peas. **Cover** dish with plastic wrap, pulling back one corner to vent the steam, and microwave on HIGH for 12 to 15 minutes (LW 14 to 18 minutes) or until heated through, **stirring** every 4 minutes. (**Rotate** dish ½ turn when stirring if not using turntable.) Serve over hot cooked pasta.

Troubleshooting: Be sure to make uniformly sized balls, because things of the same size cook in the same length of time.

Failing to whisk gravy mix may cause it to be lumpy.

Stuffed Turkey Burgers

Moist and delicious, these burgers hold a surprise in the middle.

SERVES 4

EQUIPMENT: small mixing bowl, 4-cup glass measure, deep 10-inch round baking dish
COOKING TIME: 19 to 22 minutes (Low wattage ovens 22¾ to 27¾ minutes)
STANDING TIME: 5 to 10 minutes

BURGERS
- **5 tablespoons butter or margarine, sliced**
- **¼ cup chopped onion**
- **¼ cup chopped celery**
- **⅓ cup hot water**
- **1 cup herb-seasoned stuffing mix**
- **1 egg, slightly beaten**
- **½ teaspoon poultry seasoning**
- **1 pound fresh ground turkey**
- **⅓ cup evaporated milk**
- **2 tablespoons grated Parmesan cheese**
- **1 teaspoon salt**
- **¼ teaspoon pepper**

GRAVY
- **1 10¾-ounce can condensed cream of mushroom soup**
- **1 tablespoon ketchup**
- **2 teaspoons Worcestershire sauce**
- **1 cup sliced fresh mushrooms**
- **1 tablespoon snipped fresh parsley**

Place 2 tablespoons butter, onion, and celery in small bowl. **Cover** with plastic wrap, pulling back one corner to vent the steam, and microwave on HIGH for 3 to 4 minutes (LW 3½ to 4½ minutes) or until vegetables are crisp-tender, **stirring** once.

Place hot water in glass measure and microwave on HIGH for 1 minute (LW 1¼ minutes). Add 3 tablespoons butter and **stir** until melted. **Stir** in stuffing mix, egg, poultry seasoning, and onion-celery mixture. Set aside.

Mix together ground turkey, evaporated milk, Parmesan cheese, salt, and pepper. Shape mixture into 8 uniformly sized patties (about 4 inches in diameter) on a sheet of wax paper that has been lightly moistened with water. Place ¼ of the stuffing mixture in the center of each of 4 patties, spreading stuffing to within 1 inch of the edge. Top with remaining 4 patties and press edges together to seal. Place stuffed patties in deep baking dish like the spokes of a wheel, with a space in the center of the dish.

Combine soup, ketchup, Worcestershire sauce, mushrooms, and parsley. Pour over and around patties and **cover** dish with wax paper. (If dish is flat-bottomed, **elevate** it on an inverted saucer.) Place on turntable if available and microwave on HIGH for 15 to 17 minutes (LW 18 to 21 minutes) or until turkey loses its pink color and the patties are firm. (**Rotate** dish ½ turn every 5 minutes if not using turntable.) Let **stand, covered,** for 5 to 10 minutes before serving.

Troubleshooting: Form patties as uniformly in size as possible, because things of the same size cook in the same length of time.

THE RECIPE DETECTIVE

Have you ever eaten something outstanding in a restaurant and wished you knew how to duplicate it at home? Gloria Pitzer, better known as "The Recipe Detective," has spent the last 20 years researching the secrets of the food and restaurant industry. She has developed recipes with which to duplicate—or approximate—those products and special dishes that are regarded as "secret recipes" by their creators.

Gloria is always quick to emphasize that she doesn't know what the famous food companies and restaurants actually put into their products, and she isn't interested. She feels that almost any restaurant dish or grocery shelf product can be duplicated if you have a basic knowledge of food preparation and a good memory for taste. She writes and publishes her own series of cookbooks filled with wit, easy and delicious recipes, and lots of good, commonsense ideas.

Gloria will be happy to share 13 of her most requested recipes with you if you simply send a self-addressed, stamped envelope to Gloria Pitzer's Secret Recipes, Dept. M, Box 152, St. Clair, MI 48079, and tell her I sent you.

Beef Short Ribs in BBQ Sauce

This great short rib recipe appears in Gloria's *Mostly 4-Ingredient Cookbook*. This easy classic dish is even easier to make in the microwave. Use the sauce on anything you want to barbecue.

SERVES 4 TO 6

EQUIPMENT:	medium mixing bowl, 12 × 8 or 13 × 9-inch baking dish and meat rack if available
COOKING TIME:	55 to 60 minutes (Low wattage ovens 66 to 71 minutes)
STANDING TIME:	10 minutes

1   cup Catalina salad dressing
1   cup ketchup
1   cup apple butter
1   cup Coca-Cola
3   to 4 pounds beef short ribs

Combine everything except ribs thoroughly in mixing bowl.

Place ribs in baking dish on meat rack, if available. Spread ½ the sauce mixture evenly over ribs and **cover** with plastic wrap, pulling back one corner to vent the steam. (If dish is flat-bottomed, **elevate** it on an inverted saucer.) Microwave on HIGH for 5 minutes (LW 6 minutes). Reduce power to 50 percent or MEDIUM and microwave for 25 minutes (LW 30 minutes). Turn ribs over, **drain** any excess fat, and spread with remaining sauce.

Cover again and microwave for 25 to 30 minutes (LW 30 to 35 minutes) on 50 percent power or MEDIUM or until meat is fork-tender. Let **stand, covered,** for 10 minutes to finish tenderizing before serving.

Troubleshooting: Be sure to place the thicker, meatier portions of the ribs to the outside of the dish and the thinner portions to the center of the dish.

MEATBALLS

Meatballs cooked in the microwave brown beautifully and very quickly while also saving spatters and pan washing. You can prepare meatballs from your own recipe and place them in a circle in a glass pie plate or arrange them in a baking dish.

Microwave large meatballs, **uncovered,** on HIGH for 7 to 9 minutes (LW 8 to 10 minutes) and small ones for 8 to 10 minutes (LW 9 to 11 minutes). Be sure to turn them over and **rearrange** after ½ the cooking time. (If dish is flat-bottomed, **elevate** it on an inverted saucer to allow the microwaves to get underneath as well as in through the sides and top.) Because the microwave extracts about ⅓ more fat from meat than conventional frying, you'll be surprised to see just how much fat is released. Be sure to **drain** excess drippings when you're rearranging meatballs.

Ruby Meatballs

The great American hero, hoagy, grinder, sub—what you call it depends on where you're from—all boils down to the same thing, a step above but nonetheless a sandwich. These terms usually denote some type of filling nestled into a long roll, whether soft, hard, or crusty. Serve these in hot crusty rolls for a hero lunch!

SERVES 6

EQUIPMENT:	large mixing bowl, small bowl, 9 × 13-inch baking dish, 2- or 3-quart round casserole dish
COOKING TIME:	18 to 24 minutes (Low wattage ovens 22 to 28 minutes)
STANDING TIME:	none required

MEATBALLS
1½ pounds lean ground beef or beef and pork
½ cup seasoned dry bread crumbs
1 egg
1 small onion, minced
½ teaspoon dry mustard
¼ teaspoon garlic powder
⅛ teaspoon pepper
dash of seasoned salt

SAUCE
1 16-ounce can whole-berry cranberry sauce
1 8-ounce can tomato sauce

Combine all meatball ingredients in bowl, mixing well to blend. Shape meat into 20 to 30 uniformly sized meatballs and place in baking dish. (If dish is flat-bottomed, **elevate** it on an inverted saucer.) Microwave, **uncovered,** on HIGH for 4 to 5 minutes (LW 5 to 6 minutes). Carefully turn over and **rearrange** meatballs, bringing the ones in the corners of the dish to the center and the ones in the center to the outside edges. **Rotate** dish ½ turn and microwave on HIGH for 4 to 5 minutes (LW 5 to 6 minutes) more.

Drain meatballs well and place in round casserole dish. Combine cranberry sauce and tomato sauce and pour over meatballs. **Cover** with lid or plastic wrap, pulling back one corner to vent the steam. (If dish is flat-bottomed, **elevate** it on an inverted saucer.) Place on turntable if available and microwave on 60 percent power or MEDIUM for 10 to 14 minutes (LW 12 to 16 minutes), until the flavors have combined, **stirring** carefully every 5 minutes. (**Rotate** dish ½ turn when stirring if not using turntable.)

Troubleshooting: Be sure to form uniformly sized meatballs, because things of the same size cook in the same length of time.

Beef-Stuffed Pasta Shells

SERVES 6

EQUIPMENT: plastic dishwasher-safe colander and casserole dish, medium mixing bowl, 9 × 13-inch
baking dish

COOKING TIME: 24 to 28 minutes (Low wattage ovens 27¾
to 34¾ minutes)

STANDING TIME: 5 to 10 minutes

24   jumbo pasta shells, cooked and drained
1¼ pounds lean ground beef
1   medium onion, finely chopped
½   cup diced celery
1   egg, slightly beaten
½   cup Italian-flavored dry bread crumbs
1   5-ounce can evaporated milk
1   cup diced mozzarella cheese
1   tablespoon snipped fresh parsley
½   teaspoon salt
⅛   teaspoon pepper
4   to 5 cups spaghetti sauce
¼   cup grated Parmesan cheese

Cool cooked and drained pasta in a single layer on wax paper to
prevent sticking.

Crumble ground beef into colander and place in casserole
dish to catch the drippings. Microwave, **uncovered,** on HIGH for 3
minutes (LW 3½ minutes). Break up meat chunks with a fork and
add onion and celery. Microwave on HIGH for 4 to 6 minutes (LW
5 to 7 minutes) or until meat is no longer pink and vegetables are
tender.

Discard drippings and transfer meat mixture to mixing bowl.
Add egg, crumbs, milk, mozzarella, parsley, salt, and pepper. Mix
together and stuff each shell with about 2 tablespoons of meat
mixture.

Spread about 2 cups of sauce on the bottom of baking dish.
Arrange shells on sauce and pour remaining sauce over and

around filled shells. **Cover** dish with wax paper. (If dish is flat-bottomed, **elevate** it on an inverted saucer.) Microwave on HIGH for 16 to 18 minutes (LW 18 to 23 minutes) or until heated through, **rotating** dish ½ turn every 5 minutes.

Sprinkle top with Parmesan cheese and microwave, **uncovered,** on HIGH for 1 minute (LW 1¼ minutes). Let **stand** for 5 to 10 minutes before serving.

Suggestions: Ground pork or turkey can be substituted for beef.

Round Steak Roulades

SERVES 4

EQUIPMENT:	meat mallet, 6-cup glass measure, 9 × 13-inch glass baking dish, small mixing bowl
COOKING TIME:	58 to 64 minutes (Low wattage ovens 69½ to 76½ minutes)
STANDING TIME:	10 minutes

2 **pounds boneless top round steak, ½-inch thick**
1 **6-ounce package mushroom and onion flavor stuffing mix**
1½ **cups hot water**
¼ **cup butter or margarine, cut into 1-inch pieces**
3 **medium onions, quartered**
½ **small red bell pepper, cut into ¼-inch strips**
2 **tablespoons snipped fresh parsley**
1 **14¼-ounce can beef gravy**
½ **cup water**
1 **envelope (1¼-ounces) onion soup mix**
¼ **pound fresh mushrooms, sliced**

Cut steak into 4 serving pieces. Flatten meat to ¼-inch thickness by pounding with a meat mallet or the edge of an unbreakable saucer; set aside.

Remove vegetable seasoning packet from package of stuffing mix and combine with hot water and butter in glass measure. Add stuffing crumbs and **stir** to moisten. **Cover** with plastic wrap, pulling back one corner to vent the steam, and microwave on HIGH for 5 minutes (LW 6 minutes); fluff with a fork.

Spread equal amounts of prepared stuffing over each piece of steak, leaving a ½-inch border on all sides. Roll steak pieces, jelly-roll style, and secure with wooden picks. Arrange roulades in baking dish with seam sides up. Place onions and pepper strips around the rolls and sprinkle with parsley.

In small bowl, **whisk** together gravy, ½ cup water, and onion soup mix. **Cover** with plastic wrap, pulling back one corner to vent the steam, and microwave on HIGH for 3 to 4 minutes (LW 3½ to 4½ minutes) or until hot and bubbly.

Pour hot gravy over roulades and vegetables. **Cover** dish with plastic wrap, pulling back one corner to vent the steam. (If dish is flat-bottomed, **elevate** it on an inverted saucer.) Microwave on HIGH for 5 minutes (LW 6 minutes). **Rotate** the dish ½ turn, reduce the power to 50 percent or MEDIUM, and microwave for 25 minutes (LW 30 minutes), **rotating** dish ½ turn every 10 minutes. Turn rolls over, **baste** well, add mushrooms, **cover**, and microwave on 50 percent power or MEDIUM for 20 to 25 minutes (LW 24 to 30 minutes) or until meat is fork-tender, **rotating** dish ½ turn every 10 minutes. Let **stand, covered,** for 10 minutes before serving.

Troubleshooting: If one area of the dish appears to be overcooking, you may have a hot spot and need to rotate the dish more often.

Suggestions: Serve each roll covered with sauce and vegetables.

Peking Roast

Adapted for the microwave from the famous recipe Heloise published years ago in her newspaper column.

SERVES 6

EQUIPMENT:	large mixing bowl, roasting bag and large flat baking dish
COOKING TIME:	3 hours and 5 minutes (Low wattage ovens 3 hours and 42 minutes)
STANDING TIME:	Marinating—24 to 48 hours Microwaving—15 to 20 minutes

1 3-pound flat cut of beef, such as chuck or brisket
1 large garlic clove, thinly sliced
1 cup white vinegar
1 cup strong black coffee
1 cup water
**   salt and pepper to taste**

Cut deep slits all over meat and insert garlic slices. Place in a large bowl or plastic bag and add vinegar. **Cover** or close bag tightly and let marinate in the refrigerator for 24 to 48 hours, turning over several times.

Drain vinegar and place meat in lightly floured roasting bag set into flat baking dish. Add coffee and water and loosely close bag using a piece of string or dental floss, being sure to leave a space for the steam to escape.

Microwave on HIGH for 5 minutes (LW 6 minutes), reduce power to 30 percent or LOW, and microwave for 60 minutes (LW 72 minutes) per pound, turning bag over and **rotating** dish ½ turn every 30 minutes. For faster cooking you can use 50 percent power or MEDIUM for 40 minutes (LW 48 minutes) per pound, but the meat won't be as tender. Let **stand** in roasting bag for 15 to 20 minutes to finish tenderizing.

Troubleshooting: Bag will melt if closed tightly, so be sure to leave an opening to allow the steam to escape. Be sure to use string, dental floss, or a rubber band, not a metal twist tie, to close bag.

Suggestions: Serve with baked potatoes, peas, and cranberry sauce to round out the meal.

Texas Ribs

To make shopping for ribs easier, you can estimate you will need ¾ to 1 pound of spareribs per person if you're serving them as a main course. If you're serving them as an appetizer, you can estimate about 4 servings per pound.

SERVES 3 TO 4

EQUIPMENT:	small mixing bowl, meat rack, 12 × 8-inch baking dish
COOKING TIME:	41 to 44 minutes (Low wattage ovens 46 to 51 minutes)
STANDING TIME:	5 minutes

2½ to 3 pounds spareribs, cut into 2-rib sections

MARINADE
- **3 teaspoons salt**
- **¼ cup soy sauce**
- **⅓ cup sugar**
- **4 teaspoons La Choy Brown Gravy Sauce**
- **1 teaspoon ground cinnamon**
- **3 large garlic cloves, crushed**

Combine marinade ingredients in small bowl, and **mix** well. Place ribs in large plastic bag and pour marinade mixture over them. Tie bag securely and place in a large bowl. Refrigerate for at least 6 to 8 hours or overnight, turning bag often so that all ribs are covered with sauce.

Set meat rack into baking dish to catch the drippings and place ribs on rack, with the larger, meatier pieces to the outside of the dish and the smaller, bonier pieces toward the center. **Cover** with wax paper. (If dish is flat-bottomed, **elevate** it on an inverted saucer.) Microwave on HIGH for 5 minutes (LW 6 minutes).

Drain excess fat, **cover,** reduce power to 80 percent or MEDIUM-HIGH, and microwave for 35 to 38 minutes (LW 40 to 45 minutes) or until meat is no longer pink. **Rearrange** and turn ribs over every 10 minutes, bringing the less cooked areas to the outside of the dish and the ones along the edges into the center. Let **stand, covered,** for 5 minutes before serving.

Troubleshooting: Microwave until meat is no longer pink, but be careful: ribs will char if overcooked, and the bonier the pieces, the less the cooking time.

If you don't have a meat rack and casserole dish big enough to hold it, use a 12 × 8- or 9 × 13-inch baking dish, but be sure to turn and rearrange the ribs frequently and drain grease as it builds up.

WARM HAND TOWELS

Completely dampen matching washcloths with water, sprinkle with lemon, lime, or orange juice, and roll them up jelly-roll style. Place the rolled cloths in either a decorative dish or a small wicker basket. Add a slice or 2 of fruit to the top of the rolls and microwave, **uncovered,** on HIGH for 20 to 25 seconds per towel. To avoid burning hands and faces, please check the temperature of the cloths before serving; if microwaved too long, the ones on the outside edges will become very hot.

Ham Slice with Oranges

SERVES 4

EQUIPMENT: 4-cup glass measure, 8- or 9-inch round baking dish
COOKING TIME: 12 to 15 minutes (Low wattage ovens 14¼ to 17½ minutes)
STANDING TIME: 5 minutes

1 small orange
¼ cup orange juice
¼ cup molasses
2 tablespoons water
1 tablespoon honey
1 tablespoon dark brown sugar
⅛ teaspoon ground cinnamon
⅛ teaspoon dry mustard
⅛ teaspoon ground cloves
1 16-ounce center-cut fully cooked ham slice, ¾-to 1-inch thick

Peel orange and cut into very thin slices. Set aside.

In glass measure, combine orange juice, molasses, water, honey, brown sugar, cinnamon, mustard, and cloves. Microwave, **uncovered,** on HIGH for 2 to 3 minutes (LW 2¼ to 3½ minutes) or until hot and bubbly. **Stir** well and set aside.

Place ham slice in round baking dish. **Cover** with wax paper. (If dish is flat-bottomed, **elevate** it on an inverted saucer.) Place on turntable if available and microwave on 70 percent power or MEDIUM-HIGH for 5 minutes (LW for 6 minutes). Turn ham slice over and arrange orange slices over the top. Pour glaze over all and microwave, **uncovered,** on HIGH for 5 to 7 minutes (LW 6 to 8 minutes) or until ham is thoroughly heated. Let **stand** for 5 minutes, then cut ham into wedges and serve each wedge with an orange slice.

Troubleshooting: Check ham slice carefully to be sure it doesn't overcook.

Cranberry Ham Sauce

Ham steaks cooked on a grill can dry out and be awfully plain without a little something to zip them up, and this sauce will do just that.

MAKES 2 CUPS

EQUIPMENT: 6-cup glass measure
COOKING TIME: 4 to 6 minutes (Low wattage ovens 5 to 7 minutes)
STANDING TIME: none required

1 16-ounce can jellied cranberry sauce
¼ cup steak sauce
1 tablespoon prepared brown mustard
1 tablespoon vegetable oil
1 tablespoon light brown sauce
dash of ground cloves

Place all ingredients in glass measure and **whisk** together until well combined and smooth. **Cover** with wax paper and microwave on HIGH for 4 to 6 minutes (LW 5 to 7 minutes) or until mixture is hot and bubbly, **stirring** once during cooking time.

Suggestions: Use as a glaze for a whole ham or served hot as a sauce over ham slices. Garnish with pineapple slices and maraschino cherries.

Ham Stew

This is an excellent way to use up leftover holiday ham. With the addition of a salad and garlic bread, it is also a convenient casserole for Mom to prepare for her night out.

SERVES 4

EQUIPMENT: deep 3-quart round casserole dish
COOKING TIME: 18 to 22 minutes (Low wattage ovens 21½ to 27 minutes)
STANDING TIME: 3 minutes

2 **tablespoons butter or margarine, sliced**
½ **cup chopped onion**
½ **cup chopped celery**
½ **cup sliced fresh mushrooms**
¼ **cup chopped red bell pepper**
1 **garlic clove, minced**
2 **tablespoons snipped fresh parsley**
3 **10¾-ounce cans condensed cream of potato soup**
1 **cup milk**
2 **cups diced cooked smoked or boiled ham**
1 **10-ounce package frozen peas and carrots, defrosted**

Place butter, onion, celery, mushrooms, red pepper, garlic, and parsley in casserole dish. **Cover** with lid or plastic wrap, pulling back one corner to vent the steam. (If dish is flat-bottomed **elevate** it on an inverted saucer.) Place on turntable if available and microwave on HIGH for 4 to 6 minutes (LW 4¾ to 7½ minutes) or until vegetables are crisp-tender, **stirring** every 3 minutes. (**Rotate** dish ½ turn when stirring if not using turntable.)

Whisk soup and milk into vegetable mixture. Fold in ham and defrosted frozen vegetables. **Cover** again and microwave on HIGH for 14 to 16 minutes (LW 16¾ to 19½ minutes) or until heated through and vegetables are tender, **stirring** every 5 minutes. (**Rotate** dish ½ turn when stirring if not using turntable.) Let **stand, covered,** for 3 minutes and serve.

Troubleshooting: To thaw vegetables, place paper-covered box on 2 layers of paper towel on oven floor and microwave on HIGH for 3 to 4 minutes (LW 3¼ to 4½ minutes). If box is covered with foil wrapper, remove before microwaving or wrapper will arc and may cause the paper towels to ignite.

Suggestions: For added flavor, replace 1 or 2 cans of soup with cream of chicken soup.

Ham and Asparagus Rolls

SERVES 4

EQUIPMENT: 12 × 8-inch baking dish, small mixing bowl, 6-cup glass measure
COOKING TIME: 9 to 14 minutes (Low wattage ovens 10½ to 16 minutes)
STANDING TIME: 2 to 3 minutes

8 thick *or* 16 thin cooked asparagus spears
8 boiled ham slices
1 tablespoon butter or margarine
¼ cup chopped red bell pepper
1 cup sliced fresh mushrooms
1 10¾-ounce can condensed cream of chicken soup
1 10¾-ounce can condensed cream of celery soup
½ cup white wine
sliced scallions for garnish

Place 1 thick or 2 thin asparagus spears on each ham slice and roll up jelly-roll style. Arrange rolls seam side down in baking dish. Combine butter, red pepper, and mushrooms in small bowl and **cover** with plastic wrap, pulling back one corner to vent the steam. Microwave on HIGH for 3 to 5 minutes (LW 3½ to 6 minutes) or until vegetables are crisp-tender, **stirring** once.

In glass measure, **whisk** together both soups and wine. **Stir** in vegetable mixture and pour over and around ham rolls. **Cover** dish with wax paper. (If dish is flat-bottomed, **elevate** it on an inverted saucer.) Microwave on HIGH for 6 to 9 minutes (LW 7 to 10 minutes) or until heated through, **rotating** dish ½ turn every 4 minutes. Let **stand, covered,** for 2 to 3 minutes and garnish with sliced scallions.

Suggestions: Make this recipe the night before and heat just before serving.

Serve rolls and sauce over hot cooked rice. You can make the rice in advance, add a pat of butter, and heat on HIGH while the ham rolls stand.

Stuffed Ham Wraparounds

SERVES 4

EQUIPMENT:	2 small mixing bowls, 12 × 8-inch flat baking dish, 6-cup measure
COOKING TIME:	19 to 25 minutes (Low wattage ovens 22½ to 30 minutes)
STANDING TIME:	4 minutes

1 **10-ounce package frozen rice pilaf**
½ **cup shredded American cheese**
8 **slices boiled ham, ¼-inch thick**
8 **thin scallion strips cut from stems**
1 **9-ounce package frozen small onions with cream sauce**
⅔ **cup milk**
1 **tablespoon butter or margarine**
1 **1⅛-ounce envelope white sauce mix**
1 **cup water**
1 **cup frozen peas, defrosted**
1 **tablespoon chopped pimiento**

Remove plastic pouch from rice pilaf box and make a small slit in the center of the bag. Place pouch slit side up on 2 layers of paper towel on floor of microwave. Microwave on HIGH for 5 to 7 minutes (LW 6 to 8 minutes) or until heated through, **rotating** bag ¼ turn every 2 minutes.

Cut pouch open and empty contents into small mixing bowl. Add shredded cheese and stir well. Place ⅛ of mixture on each ham slice, roll up jelly-roll style, and tie each roll with a strip of scallion stem. Arrange rolls seam side down in baking dish and set aside.

Remove frozen onions from packaging and place in glass measure. Add milk and butter and **cover** with plastic wrap, pulling back one corner to vent the steam. Microwave on HIGH for 3 minutes (LW 3½ minutes). **Stir, cover** again, and microwave on HIGH for 3 minutes (LW 3½ minutes). **Stir** until sauce is smooth and let dish **stand** for 2 minutes.

Whisk white sauce mix with water in a small bowl. **Stir** in peas and pimientos. **Cover** with plastic wrap, pulling back one corner to vent the steam, and microwave on HIGH for 4 to 6 minutes (LW 4¾ to 7½ minutes), **stirring** every 3 minutes

Add white sauce mixture to onion sauce and **stir** well. Pour combined mixture over and around prepared ham rolls. **Cover** dish with plastic wrap, pulling back one corner to vent the steam. (If dish is flat-bottomed, **elevate** it on an inverted saucer.) Microwave on HIGH for 4 to 6 minutes (LW 4¾ to 7½ minutes) or until thoroughly heated, **rotating** dish ½ turn every 4 minutes. Let **stand, covered,** for 2 minutes before serving.

Troubleshooting: Failing to whisk sauce may cause it to be lumpy.

Suggestions: Roast beef slices may be substituted for ham.

Babci's Favorite Stew

When I was young, my grandmother had an old Polish friend we all affectionately called Babci. This recipe is adapted from the wonderful pot of stew I remember Babci bringing to Grandmother's house when she didn't want to spend an evening alone.

SERVES 4 TO 6

EQUIPMENT:	deep 3-quart round casserole dish, small mixing bowl
COOKING TIME:	43 to 56 minutes (Low wattage ovens 51¾ to 67 minutes)
STANDING TIME:	5 to 10 minutes

1　**pound fully cooked smoked sausage (kielbasa), cut into ½-inch slices**
2　**10½-ounce cans condensed French Onion Soup**
1　**16-ounce can peeled tomatoes, undrained and cut up**
½　**teaspoon Worcestershire sauce**
1　**cup thinly sliced carrots**
½　**pound fresh mushrooms, sliced**
1　**cup thinly sliced celery**
4　**medium potatoes, cut into eighths**
1　**large garlic clove, crushed**
1　**10-ounce package frozen peas with pearl onions**
¼　**cup flour**
⅓　**cup cold water**

In deep casserole dish, combine sausage slices, onion soup, tomatoes with juice, Worcestershire sauce, carrots, mushrooms, celery, potatoes, and garlic. **Stir** and **cover** with lid or plastic wrap, pulling back one corner to vent the steam. (If dish is flat-bottomed, **elevate** it on an inverted saucer.) Place on turntable if available and microwave on HIGH for 30 to 40 minutes (LW 36 to 48 minutes) or until vegetables are crisp-tender, **stirring** several times during cooking. (**Rotate** dish ½ turn when stirring if not using turntable.)

Stir in frozen peas and onions, **cover** again, and microwave on HIGH for 10 to 12 minutes (LW 12 to 14 minutes) or until all vegetables are tender, **stirring** once during cooking time. (**Rotate** dish ½ turn when stirring if not using turntable.)

In small bowl, **whisk** flour into water and **stir** into stew. Microwave, **uncovered,** on HIGH for 3 to 4 minutes (LW 3¾ to 5 minutes) or until bubbly and thickened, **stirring** once. Let **stand** for 5 to 10 minutes.

Troubleshooting: Cut vegetables uniformly in size, because things of the same size cook in the same length of time.

Suggestions: I suggest serving this stew as Babci did, with a green salad and hot crusty bread and butter.

Casseroles

Chicken and Broccoli Bake

SERVES 4

> EQUIPMENT: small mixing bowl, 4- and 6-cup glass measures, 9-inch round baking dish
> COOKING TIME: 13 to 18 minutes (Low wattage ovens 16 to 20½ minutes)
> STANDING TIME: 5 minutes

2	tablespoons butter or margarine, sliced
½	cup chopped onion
½	cup chopped celery
⅔	cup hot water
½	cup (¼ pound) butter or margarine, sliced
1	8-ounce package corn bread stuffing mix
1	10-ounce package frozen broccoli spears, defrosted
1	11-ounce can condensed Cheddar cheese soup
¼	cup milk
½	cup sour cream
1½	to 2 cups cut-up cooked chicken in bite-size pieces
1	4-ounce can mushroom pieces, drained
1	cup canned french-fried onions

Combine 2 tablespoons butter, onion, and celery in small bowl. **Cover** with plastic wrap, pulling back one corner to vent the steam, and microwave on HIGH for 3 to 5 minutes (LW 3½ to 6 minutes) or until vegetables are crisp-tender.

Place hot water and remaining butter in 4-cup glass measure and microwave on HIGH for 3 to 4 minutes (LW 3½ to 4½ minutes) or until butter is melted. Add stuffing mix and onion-celery mixture, **tossing** to blend. Spread stuffing mixture over bottom of round baking dish. Arrange drained broccoli spears over stuffing in a pattern resembling the spokes of a wheel, with the flowerets framing the outer edge of the dish. Set aside.

Combine soup and milk in 6-cup glass measure and **whisk** until well blended. **Whisk** in sour cream. Add chicken and mushrooms and **stir** together. Pour over stuffing base and broccoli spears. **Cover** with plastic wrap, pulling back one corner to vent the steam. (If dish is flat-bottomed, **elevate** it on an inverted saucer.) Place on turntable if available and microwave on HIGH for 7 to 9 minutes (LW 9 to 10 minutes) or until heated through. (**Rotate** dish ¼ turn every 3 minutes if not using turntable.)

Sprinkle top of casserole with french-fried onions and microwave, **uncovered,** on HIGH for 1 minute. Let **stand** for 5 minutes before serving.

Troubleshooting: Failing to whisk soup mixture may cause it to be lumpy.

Chicken and Ham Tetrazzini

SERVES 6

EQUIPMENT:	deep 2- and 3-quart round casserole dishes, 1- and 6-cup glass measures
COOKING TIME:	15 to 20 minutes (Low wattage ovens 18¼ to 23½ minutes)
STANDING TIME:	5 minutes

    2   tablespoons butter or margarine, sliced
    ½   cup chopped onion
    ½   cup diced red bell pepper
    ½   cup chopped celery
    ½   cup sliced fresh mushrooms *or* 1 4-ounce can sliced
        mushrooms, drained
    2   cups cut-up cooked chicken in bite-size pieces
    1   cup cut-up cooked ham in bite-size pieces
    ½   pound fine egg noodles, cooked and drained
    1   10¾-ounce can condensed cream of chicken soup
    ⅓   cup evaporated milk
    ⅓   cup mayonnaise
    1   cup shredded Cheddar cheese

CRUMB TOPPING
    2   tablespoons butter or margarine, sliced
    ½   cup plain dry bread crumbs
    ½   teaspoon garlic powder
    ½   teaspoon paprika

Place 2 tablespoons butter, onions, red pepper, celery, and mushrooms in 2-quart casserole dish. **Cover** with lid or plastic wrap,
pulling back one corner to vent the steam. (If dish is flat-bottomed,
elevate it on an inverted saucer.) Microwave on HIGH for 5 to 7
minutes (LW 6 to 8 minutes) or until vegetables are crisp-tender,
stirring every 3 minutes. Add chicken and ham, **stir,** and set
aside.

   Place cooked noodles in 6-cup glass measure and add soup,
milk, mayonnaise, and cheese. **Stir** gently and **cover** with plastic
wrap, pulling back one corner to vent the steam. Microwave on
HIGH for 2 to 3 minutes (LW 2½ to 3½ minutes) or until cheese
becomes very soft; set aside.

   In 1-cup glass measure, microwave 2 tablespoons butter on
HIGH for 1 minute (LW 1¼ minute), until melted. **Stir** in crumbs,
garlic powder, and paprika.

   In 3-quart casserole dish, alternate layers of noodle mixture
and chicken and ham mixture. Sprinkle top with crumb mixture.
Cover with lid or plastic wrap, pulling back one corner to vent
the steam. (If dish is flat-bottomed, **elevate** it on an inverted
saucer.) Place on turntable if available and microwave on HIGH

for 7 to 9 minutes (LW 8½ to 10¾ minutes) or until hot and bubbly. (**Rotate** dish ¼ turn every 3 minutes if not using turntable.) Let **stand, covered,** for 5 minutes before serving.

Suggestions: Leftover turkey may be substituted for chicken.

Chicken and Rice Bake

SERVES 4 TO 6

EQUIPMENT:	deep 3-quart round casserole dish, medium mixing bowl, custard cup
COOKING TIME:	12¾ to 16¾ minutes (Low wattage ovens 15 to 19 minutes)
STANDING TIME:	none required

2 tablespoons butter or margarine, sliced
½ cup chopped onion
½ cup chopped celery
1 cup sliced fresh mushrooms
1 10¾-ounce can condensed creamy chicken mushroom soup
1 10¾-ounce can condensed cream of celery soup
½ cup mayonnaise
½ cup chicken broth
1 tablespoon lemon juice
2 cups cut-up cooked chicken in 1-inch pieces
3 cups hot cooked rice

TOPPING
2 tablespoons butter or margarine, sliced
½ cup garden vegetable snack cracker crumbs
½ teaspoon garlic powder

Place 2 tablespoons butter, onion, celery, and mushrooms in deep casserole dish. **Cover** with lid or plastic wrap, pulling back one corner to vent the steam. (If dish is flat-bottomed, **elevate** it on an inverted saucer.) Microwave on HIGH for 5 to 7 minutes (LW 6 to 8 minutes) or until vegetables are crisp-tender.

In medium bowl, **whisk** together soups, mayonnaise, broth, and lemon juice and then combine them with vegetable mixture. Add chicken and rice, mixing well.

For topping, place 2 tablespoons butter in custard cup, **covered** with paper towel and microwave on HIGH for 40 to 50 seconds (LW 50 to 60 seconds) or until melted. **Stir** in cracker crumbs and garlic powder. Sprinkle over casserole and place on turntable if available. Microwave **uncovered** on HIGH for 7 to 9 minutes (LW 8 to 10 minutes) or until hot and bubbly. (**Rotate** dish ½ turn every 3 minutes if not using turntable.)

Troubleshooting: If you're not using a whisk to blend liquids, be sure to blend them completely with fork or spoon.

If melting butter is spattering oven, cover with a paper towel.

Suggestions: Cooked turkey may be substituted for chicken.

You can use any flavor snack crackers you have on hand for the topping. Crush in a food processor or blender or place in a plastic bag and crush with a rolling pin.

TURKEY LEFTOVERS

Roasting a whole turkey makes the house smell so nice and produces a wonderful meal, but what do you do with all the leftovers? To save room in the refrigerator, remove all the meat from the bones, slice some for sandwiches, cube some for use in recipes, freeze the rest, and use the bones for soup.

Turkey reheats best in the microwave when covered with gravy. To freeze for later use, line the dish you will use for reheating with plastic wrap or freezer paper. Place pieces of turkey in paper-lined dish, cover with gravy, wrap, and freeze right in the dish. Once frozen, remove the dish, mark the package with the date and the dish you used, place in a plastic bag to return to the freezer, and you are all ready for defrosting and reheating. Defrost the frozen package for 3 to 4 minutes on LOW (30 percent) and let stand for 5 minutes. Repeat the process until thawed.

Turkey and Wild Rice Mescolanza

My Italian friend, Antonio, the gentleman farmer, says that this recipe is a "mixed-up-dish," which is what *mescolanza* means. It may be mixed up, but it is also delicious and great for using up leftover turkey or chicken.

SERVES 4

EQUIPMENT:	2½-quart round casserole dish
COOKING TIME:	39 to 40 minutes (Low wattage ovens 46¾ to 48 minutes)
STANDING TIME:	5 minutes

> 3 **tablespoons butter or margarine, sliced**
> ½ **cup diced celery**
> 1 **cup sliced fresh mushrooms**
> 2 **tablespoons snipped fresh parsley**
> 2 **cups hot water**
> 1 **10¾-ounce can condensed cream of celery soup**
> 1 **6-ounce package long grain and wild rice**
> 3 **tablespoons white wine**
> ¼ **teaspoon pepper**
> 2 **cups cubed cooked turkey or chicken**
> 2 **cups leftover cooked peas and carrots or defrosted frozen peas**

Place butter, celery, mushrooms, and parsley in casserole dish. **Cover** with lid or plastic wrap, pulling back one corner to vent the steam. (If dish is flat-bottomed, **elevate** it on an inverted saucer.) Place on turntable if available and microwave on HIGH for 4 to 5 minutes (LW 4¾ to 6 minutes) until crisp-tender.

Add hot water, soup, rice with seasoning packet, wine, and pepper, **stirring** together well. **Cover** and microwave on HIGH for 30 minutes (LW 36 minutes), **stirring** every 10 minutes. (**Rotate** dish ½ turn when stirring if not using turntable.)

Stir in turkey, peas, and carrots. **Cover** again and microwave on HIGH for 5 minutes (LW 6 minutes) or until hot. Let **stand, covered,** for 5 minutes.

Suggestions: Garnish casserole top with crumbled bacon and chopped scallions.

Turkey Salad Bake

SERVES 4

EQUIPMENT:	2-quart round casserole dish, small mixing bowl
COOKING TIME:	14 to 19 minutes (Low wattage ovens 16½ to 22½ minutes)
STANDING TIME:	none required

2 tablespoons butter or margarine, sliced
1 cup chopped celery
½ cup chopped onion
½ cup chopped red bell pepper
¼ cup grated carrot
¼ pound fresh mushrooms, sliced
2 cups cut-up cooked turkey in ½-inch pieces
1 cup canned french-fried onions
1 cup mayonnaise
2 tablespoons lemon juice
1½ teaspoons onion salt
½ cup shredded Cheddar cheese
¼ cup diced scallions

Place butter, celery, onion, red pepper, carrot, and mushrooms in casserole dish. **Cover** with lid or plastic wrap, pulling back one corner to vent the steam. (If dish is flat-bottomed, **elevate** it on an inverted saucer.) Place on turntable if available and microwave on HIGH for 7 to 9 minutes (LW 8¼ to 10¾ minutes) or until vegetables are crisp-tender, **stirring** every 4 minutes. (**Rotate** dish ½ turn when stirring if not using turntable.) **Stir** in turkey and french-fried onions.

Whisk together mayonnaise, lemon juice, and onion salt and add to turkey mixture, **stirring** well. **Cover** dish again and microwave on HIGH for 5 to 7 minutes (LW 6 to 8¼ minutes) or until hot and bubbly. (**Rotate** dish ½ turn after 3 minutes if not using turntable.) Sprinkle top with cheese and scallions, **cover** again, reduce power to 50 percent or MEDIUM, and microwave for 2 to 3 minutes (LW 2¼ to 3½ minutes) or until cheese melts.

Suggestions: Cooked chicken may be substituted for turkey.

Deep-Dish Turkey Pie

SERVES 4

EQUIPMENT:	2½-quart round casserole dish
COOKING TIME:	11 to 13 minutes (Low wattage ovens 12¼ to 14¼ minutes)
STANDING TIME:	3 minutes

1   **10-ounce paper-covered box frozen peas and carrots**
3   **cups diced cooked turkey or chicken**
1   **4-ounce can mushroom stems and pieces, drained**
1   **12-ounce jar turkey or chicken gravy**
½   **teaspoon poultry seasoning**
2   **cups seasoned hot mashed potatoes**
    grated Parmesan cheese for garnish
    paprika for garnish

Place paper-covered box of vegetables on 2 layers of paper towel on oven floor and microwave on HIGH for 3 minutes (LW 3¼ minutes). Shake box, turn over, and microwave on HIGH for 3 to 4 minutes (LW 3¼ to 4½ minutes) or until vegetables are crisp-tender.

Place turkey, mushrooms, gravy, and poultry seasoning in round casserole dish. Add peas and carrots and **stir.** Spoon mashed potatoes in mounds over top of casserole and sprinkle with Parmesan cheese and paprika. Place on turntable if available and microwave, **uncovered,** on HIGH for 8 to 10 minutes (9 to 11 minutes) or until heated through. (**Rotate** dish ½ turn every 4 minutes if not using turntable.) Let **stand** for 3 minutes before serving.

Troubleshooting: Microwave only paper-covered box of vegetables. If box has a foil wrapper, remove before microwaving as foil wrapper will arc and might cause the paper towels to ignite.

Suggestions: If you're using leftover mashed potatoes, heat before adding to casserole by placing on a flat dinner plate, distributing evenly over plate. **Cover** with plastic wrap, pulling back one corner to vent the steam. (If dish is flat-bottomed, **elevate** it on an inverted saucer.) Microwave on HIGH for 3 to 5 minutes (LW 3½ to 6 minutes), bringing the less heated areas from the center of the dish to the edges and the potatoes along the edges into the center of the dish every 2 minutes.

Turkey and Eggplant Casserole

SERVES 4 TO 6

EQUIPMENT:	2- and 3-quart round casserole dishes, plastic dishwasher-safe colander and casserole dish, 2-quart round baking dish
COOKING TIME:	24 to 33 minutes (Low wattage ovens 29½ to 41½ minutes)
STANDING TIME:	3 minutes

1½   pounds eggplant, peeled and cut into ½-inch cubes
3   tablespoons water
1   pound ground turkey
½   cup grated carrot
1   cup diced celery
1   large onion, diced
1   large garlic clove, minced
1   tablespoon snipped fresh parsley
1¼   cups hot water
½   cup (¼ pound) butter or margarine, sliced
1   7-ounce package corn bread stuffing
1   egg, slightly beaten
1   teaspoon poultry seasoning
½   teaspoon salt
¼   teaspoon pepper
1   cup shredded sharp Cheddar cheese
     paprika for garnish

Place eggplant cubes and 3 tablespoons water in 2-quart casserole dish. **Cover** with lid or plastic wrap, pulling back one corner to vent the steam. (If dish is flat-bottomed, **elevate** it on an inverted saucer.) Place on turntable if available and microwave on HIGH for 6 to 9 minutes (LW 7 to 12 minutes) or until eggplant is crisp-tender, **stirring** twice. (**Rotate** dish ½ turn when stirring if not using turntable.)

Crumble ground turkey into colander set into casserole dish to catch the drippings. Microwave, **uncovered,** on HIGH for 4 to 6 minutes (LW 5 to 7 minutes) or until turkey is no longer pink, **stirring** and breaking up meat chunks with a fork every 2 minutes. Discard fat and drippings from dish under colander and transfer cooked turkey to casserole dish, breaking up any meat chunks with a fork. **Stir** in carrot, celery, onion, garlic, and parsley. Microwave, **uncovered,** on HIGH for 4 to 6 minutes (LW 5 to 7 minutes) or until vegetables are crisp-tender, **stirring** once.

Place hot water in 3-quart casserole dish and microwave, **uncovered,** on HIGH for 2 minutes (LW 3 minutes) or until water is very hot. Add sliced butter and **stir** until melted. Add stuffing mix and egg, **tossing** until moisture is absorbed. Add eggplant, turkey, and vegetable mixture, poultry seasoning, salt, and pepper, **stirring** together gently.

Spoon mixture into 2-quart baking dish and **cover** with wax paper. (If dish is flat-bottomed, **elevate** it on an inverted saucer.) Place on turntable if available and microwave on HIGH for 6 to 7 minutes (LW 7 to 9 minutes) or until hot. (**Rotate** dish ½ turn every 3 minutes if not using turntable.)

Top dish with Cheddar cheese and microwave, **uncovered,** on HIGH for 2 to 3 minutes (LW 2½ to 3½ minutes) or until cheese begins to melt. (**Rotate** dish ½ turn after 2 minutes if not using turntable.) Let **stand** for 3 minutes and sprinkle with paprika before serving.

Troubleshooting: If you're using a square-cornered dish to microwave eggplant, be sure to move pieces out of corners frequently.

When stirring eggplant, bring the less cooked pieces from the center of the dish to the outside edges and the ones along the edges into the center.

Beef and Eggplant Bake

SERVES 4

EQUIPMENT:	plastic dishwasher-safe colander and casserole dish, 2-quart round casserole dish, deep plate, flat 2-quart baking dish
COOKING TIME:	30½ to 39 minutes (Low wattage ovens 36½ to 45¾ minutes)
STANDING TIME:	none required

1 pound lean ground beef
1 medium onion, chopped
½ cup chopped celery
½ cup chopped green bell pepper
1½ tablespoons flour
1 8-ounce can tomato sauce
¾ cup water
1 cup sliced fresh mushrooms
1 large garlic clove, minced
1 tablespoon snipped fresh parsley
1 teaspoon dried oregano
½ teaspoon salt
¼ teaspoon pepper
1 egg
1 tablespoon water
½ cup plain dry bread crumbs
2 tablespoons grated Parmesan cheese
⅛ teaspoon paprika
1 small (about 1-pound) eggplant, pared or unpared and cut into 8½-inch slices
½ cup shredded mozzarella cheese
paprika for garnish

Crumble beef into colander and place in casserole dish to catch the drippings. Microwave, **uncovered,** on HIGH for 3 minutes (LW 3½ minutes). Break up meat chunks with a fork and add onion, celery, and green pepper. Microwave, **uncovered,** on HIGH for 4 to 6 minutes (LW 5 to 7 minutes) or until beef is no longer pink, **stirring** and breaking up meat chunks once.

Transfer cooked meat and vegetables to 2-quart casserole dish and sprinkle with flour, combining well. Add tomato sauce, ¾ cup water, mushrooms, garlic, parsley, oregano, salt, and pepper, **stirring** well. **Cover** with plastic wrap, pulling back one corner to vent the steam. (If dish is flat-bottomed, **elevate** it on an inverted saucer.) Place on turntable if available and microwave on HIGH for 5 to 7 minutes (LW 6 to 8 minutes) or until hot and bubbly, **stirring** once. (**Rotate** dish ½ turn when stirring, if not using turntable.)

Beat egg with 1 tablespoon water in deep plate and combine crumbs, Parmesan, and ⅛ teaspoon paprika on a paper plate. Dip eggplant slices into egg mixture, then coat with crumb mixture. Place slices in a single layer in flat baking dish, overlapping slices if necessary, and **cover** dish with wax paper. **Elevate** dish on an inverted saucer and microwave on HIGH for 12 to 15 minutes (LW 14 to 18 minutes) or until eggplant is fork-tender, **rearranging** slices and **rotating** dish ½ turn every 6 minutes.

Top beef mixture with eggplant slices and **cover** dish with wax paper. Microwave on HIGH for 5 to 6 minutes (LW 6 to 7 minutes) or until hot and bubbly. **Uncover** dish, top with mozzarella cheese, and microwave for 1½ to 2 minutes (LW 2 to 2¼ minutes) or until cheese melts. Sprinkle with paprika.

Troubleshooting: Microwave mozzarella cheese just until it starts to melt as it will toughen if microwaved too long.

GROUND BEEF

When you brown ground beef on a stove top, you fry it in its own fat. In the microwave you use a plastic dishwasher-safe colander. Crumble ground beef into the colander and set it into a casserole dish to catch the drippings. As the meat cooks, the fat drips down through the holes in the colander and collects away from the meat in the casserole dish. Should you not have a plastic dishwasher-safe colander, crumble ground beef into a flat casserole dish or glass pie plate lined with several layers of paper towel. When the meat is no longer pink, transfer meat to several fresh layers of paper towel to **drain.** The microwave extracts about one-third more fat from meat than conventional frying would, so be prepared to drain the drippings if necessary.

Roast Beef Noodle Casserole

SERVES 4

EQUIPMENT: 2½-quart round casserole dish, 2 small mixing bowls, 2-quart round casserole dish
COOKING TIME: 13¾ to 18¾ minutes (Low wattage ovens 16 to 22 minutes)
STANDING TIME: 5 minutes

½ **cup chopped onion**
½ **cup chopped green bell pepper**
½ **cup chopped celery**
¼ **cup grated carrot**
½ **cup sliced fresh mushrooms**
1 **large garlic clove, minced**
2 **tablespoons butter or margarine, sliced**
1 **10¾-ounce can condensed tomato soup**
½ **cup water**
¼ **cup ketchup**
¼ **teaspoon salt**
¼ **teaspoon pepper**
2 **cups diced cooked roast beef**
3 **cups cooked and drained medium noodles**
1 **cup shredded Velveeta cheese**

TOPPING
2 **tablespoons butter or margarine, sliced**
½ **cup onion bread crumbs**
½ **teaspoon paprika**

Place onion, green pepper, celery, carrot, mushrooms, garlic, and 2 tablespoons butter in 2½-quart casserole dish. **Cover** with lid or plastic wrap, pulling back one corner to vent the steam, and microwave on HIGH for 6 to 8 minutes (LW 7 to 9 minutes) or until vegetables are crisp-tender, **stirring** once.

Whisk together soup, water, ketchup, salt, and pepper in a small bowl and add to vegetables. **Stir** in beef, cooked noodles, and cheese. Spoon mixture into 2-quart casserole dish.

For topping, place 2 tablespoons butter in small bowl and microwave on HIGH for 40 to 50 seconds (LW 50 to 60 seconds) or until melted. **Stir** in crumbs and paprika and sprinkle topping over casserole. **Cover** with lid or plastic wrap, pulling back one corner to vent the steam. (If dish is flat-bottomed, **elevate** it on an inverted saucer.) Place on turntable if available and microwave on HIGH for 7 to 10 minutes (LW 8¼ to 12 minutes) or until hot and bubbly. (**Rotate** dish ¼ turn every 3 minutes if not using turntable.) Let **stand, covered,** for 5 minutes before serving.

Suggestions: Any type of cooked beef, including ground beef, may be used in place of roast beef.

Hot Diggity Dog Casserole

As a young girl I was a member of the Junior Midshipmen of America. One summer the Lions International invited our group to join the organization in the traditional march down Fifth Avenue in New York. It was a very exciting day, and we were all very proud. Upon returning home we were honored by our families and friends with a backyard barbecue. This hot dog dish was made by a former 4H leader, Jessica Barnes, and was an instant hit. With a green salad and some crusty bread, it can become a great meal for your family too.

SERVES 4 TO 6

EQUIPMENT:	small mixing bowl, 2½-quart round casserole dish
COOKING TIME:	18½ to 24 minutes (Low wattage ovens 21½ to 28½ minutes)
STANDING TIME:	3 to 5 minutes

    4 **bacon strips, cooked and diced**
    1 **tablespoon butter or margarine**
  ½ **cup chopped onion**
    2 **16-ounce cans pork and beans**
    1 **15½-ounce can dark red kidney beans**
  ½ **cup dark brown sugar**
    1 **teaspoon prepared mustard**
    1 **tablespoon soy sauce**
  ½ **cup ketchup**
    1 **tablespoon cider vinegar**
  ¼ **teaspoon ground ginger**
  ½ **pound hot dogs, cut into 1-inch slices**

Spread bacon in a single layer on top of 3 layers of paper towel on microwave floor. **Cover** bacon with 1 sheet of paper towel. Microwave on HIGH for 3½ to 4 minutes (LW 4 to 4½ minutes) or until bacon looks slightly underdone. Let **stand, covered,** for 3 to 5 minutes to brown and crisp; dice and set aside.

    Place butter and onion in small bowl. **Cover** with plastic wrap, pulling back one corner to vent the steam, and microwave on HIGH for 3 to 5 minutes (LW 3½ to 6 minutes) or until onion is crisp-tender, **stirring** once.

    In casserole dish, combine diced bacon, onion, and all remaining ingredients, **stirring** in hot dogs last. **Cover** with lid or plastic wrap, pulling back one corner to vent the steam. (If dish is flat-bottomed, **elevate** it on an inverted saucer.) Place on turntable if available and microwave on HIGH for 12 to 15 minutes (LW 14 to 18 minutes) or until mixture is hot and bubbly, **stirring** twice during cooking time. (**Rotate** dish ¼ turn when stirring if not using turntable.)

PAPER TOWELS IN THE MICROWAVE

It is always advisable to use white paper towels when placing food directly on them. The only time I have had the print in paper towels come off onto the food was when I cooked bacon. If you have white paper towels with a colored print on them, turn them over and use the back side; usually the colored print is only on one side. Do *not* use newspaper under the paper towel for absorbing grease when cooking bacon—chemicals in the ink can cause arcing and ignite the paper towels.

Macaroni with Cheese, Ham, and Mushrooms

Looking for that quick-to-put-together supper when everyone is hungry and you just walked in the door? Cook a large batch of elbow macaroni and freeze it in individual packages that will thaw quickly in the microwave. Stop on the way home from work and pick up the ham and you can get supper ready while the kids set the table and make a salad.

SERVES 4 TO 6

EQUIPMENT:	2-cup glass measure, 2-quart round casserole dish
COOKING TIME:	15 to 19¼ minutes (Low wattage ovens 17½ to 22¾ minutes)
STANDING TIME:	none required

2 cups milk
4 tablespoons butter or margarine, sliced
¼ cup flour
2 tablespoons instant minced onion
½ teaspoon salt
¼ teaspoon pepper
1 teaspoon dry mustard
2 tablespoons snipped fresh parsley
2 cups shredded Cheddar cheese
1 4-ounce can sliced mushrooms, drained
1 cup cubed cooked ham
2 cups elbow macaroni, cooked and drained

Place milk in glass measure and microwave on HIGH for 2 minutes (LW 2¼ minutes). Set aside. Place butter in round casserole dish and microwave on HIGH for 1 to 1¼ minutes (LW 1¼ to 1½ minutes) or until melted. **Whisk** in flour, minced onion, salt, pepper, dry mustard, and parsley. Briskly **whisk** in warm milk, **blending** well. (If dish is flat-bottomed, **elevate** it on an inverted saucer.) Place on turntable if available and microwave, **uncovered,** on HIGH for 7 to 9 minutes (LW 8 to 11 minutes) or until mixture is slightly thickened, **whisking** every minute.

Add cheese and **whisk** until melted. Add mushrooms, ham, and cooked macaroni, **stirring** well. Microwave, **uncovered,** on HIGH for 5 to 7 minutes (LW 6 to 8 minutes) or until heated through, **stirring** every 3 minutes. (**Rotate** dish ½ turn when stirring if not using turntable.)

Troubleshooting: Failing to whisk sauce may cause it to be lumpy.

Suggestions: Other varieties of cooked cubed meats may be substituted for ham to change the flavor of the casserole.

Ham and Potato Scallop

What good is buying that big ham that's on sale if you don't have a good recipe to use up the leftovers? When I buy a smoked ham, I glaze it for supper one night and make sandwiches the next day. I then cube the leftover ham and freeze it in individual packages. In one package I include the bone for later use in pea soup, and the other packages I use when I need a quick casserole.

SERVES 4

EQUIPMENT:	deep 2-quart round casserole dish, 6-cup glass measure
COOKING TIME:	20 to 26 minutes (Low wattage ovens 24¼ to 20½ minutes)
STANDING TIME:	none required

2 tablespoons butter or margarine, sliced
½ cup chopped onion
½ cup chopped green bell pepper
½ cup chopped celery
2 tablespoons chopped pimiento
2 tablespoons snipped fresh parsley
2 cups cubed cooked ham
2 cups cubed cooked potatoes

SAUCE
6 tablespoons butter or margarine, sliced
6 tablespoons flour
1 teaspoon salt
1 teaspoon onion powder
¼ teaspoon white pepper
½ teaspoon paprika
2 cups milk
½ cup shredded sharp Cheddar cheese
paprika and chopped scallions for garnish

Place 2 tablespoons butter, onion, green pepper, celery, pimiento, and parsley in deep casserole dish. **Cover** with lid or plastic wrap, pulling back one corner to vent the steam. Microwave on HIGH for 6 to 8 minutes (LW 7½ to 9½ minutes) or until vegetables are crisp-tender, **stirring** every 3 minutes. **Stir** in ham and potatoes and set aside.

Place 6 tablespoons butter in glass measure and microwave on HIGH for 1 minute (LW 1¼ minutes) or until melted. **Whisk** in flour, salt, onion powder, pepper, and paprika until blended. Gradually add milk, **whisking** mixture until very smooth. Microwave on HIGH for 8 to 10 minutes (LW 9½ to 12 minutes) or until sauce is thick enough to coat whisk, **whisking** every minute. Add cheese and **whisk** until cheese is completely melted and sauce is smooth.

Stir sauce into ham and potato mixture and **cover** dish with wax paper. (If dish is flat-bottomed, **elevate** it on an inverted saucer.) Place on turntable if available and microwave on HIGH for 5 to 7 minutes (LW 6 to 8¼ minutes) or until hot and bubbly, carefully **stirring** every 3 minutes. (**Rotate** dish ½ turn when stirring if not using turntable.) Garnish casserole top with paprika and chopped scallions before serving.

Troubleshooting: Failing to whisk sauce may cause it to be lumpy. If cheese doesn't melt while you're whisking it into sauce, microwave on HIGH for 1 to 2 minutes and whisk again.

Suggestions: Cubed leftover roast beef may be substituted for ham.

Prepare casserole the night before and heat just before serving.

Sweet Sausage and Vegetable Bake

SERVES 4 TO 6

EQUIPMENT:	deep 3-quart round casserole dish, 6-cup glass measure
COOKING TIME:	40 to 44 minutes (Low wattage ovens 48 to 53 minutes)
STANDING TIME:	5 minutes

1	**pound sweet Italian sausage, cut in ½-inch slices**
½	**pound fresh mushrooms, sliced**
1	**cup chopped onion**
1	**large garlic clove, crushed**
2½	**cups water**
⅔	**cup milk**
1	**5¼-ounce box dry scalloped potato mix**
1	**16-ounce package frozen broccoli and carrot mixture** *or* **1 10-ounce package broccoli cuts and 1 cup frozen carrot slices**
1	**tablespoon snipped fresh parsley**

Place sausage slices, mushrooms, onion, and garlic in deep casserole dish. **Cover** with lid or plastic wrap, pulling back one corner to vent the steam. (If dish is flat-bottomed, **elevate** it on an inverted saucer.) Place on turntable if available and microwave on

HIGH for 6 to 8 minutes (LW 7¼ to 9½ minutes) or until sausage loses its pink color, **stirring** carefully every 3 minutes. (**Rotate** dish ½ turn when stirring if not using turntable.) **Drain** any excess fat.

Place water, milk, and sauce packet from potato mix in glass measure, **whisking** together until well blended. Pour mixture over sausages and add potato slices from box along with frozen vegetables. **Stir** all ingredients together well.

Cover again and microwave on HIGH for 34 to 36 minutes (LW 40¾ to 43½ minutes) or until vegetables are tender and mixture is slightly thickened, **stirring** every 5 minutes. (**Rotate** dish ¼ turn when stirring if not using turntable.) Let **stand, covered,** for 5 minutes and sprinkle with parsley before serving.

SAUSAGE

There are two methods for cooking sausage in the microwave. Always pierce the casing of sausage links before cooking to vent the steam, or they will explode. Either place sausage in a plastic dishwasher-safe colander set into a casserole dish to catch the drippings or place in a flat casserole dish. Always place the thicker pieces to the outside of the dish and the thinner pieces toward the center in a single layer.

Microwave on HIGH for 5 minutes (LW 6 minutes). Turn sausage over and **rearrange,** bringing the less cooked areas to the outside of the dish and the ones along the edges into the center. Microwave on HIGH for 6 to 10 minutes (LW 7 to 12 minutes), depending on quantity, until sausages lose their pink color. If you're using a colander, the fat will drip into the casserole dish; if you're using a flat baking dish, drain the sausage and place on paper towels to absorb any excess drippings.

JW's Bouillabaisse

I devised this recipe after I tasted the wonderful bouillabaisse prepared by Chef Charles Fierro in JW's at the New York Marriott Marquis. Keep in mind that Chef Charles has never tried his creation in the microwave, and this is my conversion. I think the intriguing challenge of this recipe is in the two different stocks used. In JW's bouillabaisse both fish and clam stock are used to give flavor to the hearty base. If you have never made fish stock before, it's really quite easy. You can use this broth to poach a whole fish, such as trout, one night and freeze the leftover stock for use in other recipes.

SERVES 6

EQUIPMENT:	deep 3-quart round casserole dish, strainer
COOKING TIME:	42 to 51 minutes (Low wattage ovens 49¼ to 59¾ minutes)
STANDING TIME:	3 minutes

2   **dozen littleneck clams**
3   **tablespoons butter or margarine, sliced**
½   **cup white wine**
½   **teaspoon snipped fresh parsley**
     dash of seasoned salt
     dash of garlic powder

BASE
2   **tablespoons butter or margarine, sliced**
2   **garlic cloves, minced**
1   **celery stalk, minced**
1   **carrot, diced**
¼   **teaspoon powdered saffron**
¼   **cup white wine**
2   **cups fish stock (recipe follows)**

FISH

1 **cull (one-clawed) lobster**
½ **pound sea scallops, cut in half**
1 **pound red snapper, flounder, sole, or swordfish fillets, cut into 1½-inch chunks**
1 **pound medium shrimp, shells removed to the tails salt and pepper to taste**

Place clams, 3 tablespoons butter, ½ cup white wine, parsley, seasoned salt, and garlic powder in deep casserole dish. **Cover** with lid or plastic wrap, pulling back one corner to vent the steam. (If dish is flat-bottomed, **elevate** it on an inverted saucer.) Place on turntable if available and microwave on HIGH for 10 to 12 minutes (LW 12 to 14 minutes) or until all clams have begun to open. (**Rotate** dish ½ turn every 3 minutes if not using turntable.) Remove clams from broth, set aside, and keep warm; **strain** broth and set aside.

Place 2 tablespoons butter, garlic, celery, and carrot in deep casserole dish and microwave on HIGH for 6 to 8 minutes (LW 7 to 9 minutes), **stirring** every 4 minutes, until soft. **Whisk** in saffron and microwave on HIGH for another 2 to 3 minutes (LW 2¼ to 3½ minutes) or just until the saffron turns color. Immediately add the wine, then the fish stock and 1 cup of the reserved clam broth. Microwave, **uncovered,** on HIGH for 3 to 4 minutes (LW 3½ to 4¾ minutes), until boiling, then **whisk.** Microwave on HIGH for 2 minutes (LW 2¼ minutes) and **whisk** again.

Add lobster and scallops and **cover** with lid or plastic wrap, pulling back one corner to vent the steam. Microwave on 50 percent power or MEDIUM for 10 minutes (LW 12 minutes). **Stir** and add the fish cubes and shrimp; **cover** again and microwave on 80 percent power or MEDIUM-HIGH for 8 to 10 minutes (LW 9 to 12 minutes). (**Rotate** dish ½ turn every 4 minutes if not using turntable.)

Add salt and pepper to taste, add clams, **cover** again, and microwave on HIGH for 1 to 2 minutes (LW 1¼ to 2¼ minutes) or until clams are hot and fish flakes easily. Be careful not to overcook the fish. Let **stand, covered,** for 3 minutes and serve this lovely main dish in large deep bowls with a basket of garlic toast.

Suggestions: I keep a large container in the freezer, where I place any broth left over from steaming clams to use in clam chowder, clam sauce, or this recipe. You can substitute bottled clam juice, but don't tell anyone I recommended it.

There is no set rule for how many varieties of seafood must be in a pot surrounded by broth and spices to make a bouillabaisse, so watch the fish sales and be creative.

Fish Stock

SERVES 3 OR 4

EQUIPMENT:	round 2- or 3-quart casserole dish, strainer
COOKING TIME:	12 to 15 minutes (Low wattage ovens 14½ to 18 minutes)
STANDING TIME:	2 minutes

1　**cup white wine or water**
1　**medium onion, sliced**
1　**medium carrot, sliced**
1　**celery stalk, sliced**
1　**garlic clove, minced**
½　**lemon, sliced**
1　**bay leaf**
6　**peppercorns**
1　**1-pound whole fish** *or* **1 pound fillets**

In a casserole dish large enough to accommodate your fish, place all broth ingredients except fish and **cover** tightly with plastic wrap, pulling back one corner to vent the steam. (If dish is flat-bottomed, **elevate** it on an inverted saucer.) Microwave on HIGH for 5 minutes (LW 6 minutes).

Uncover and lay fish, backbone facing the side of the dish, or fillets with tips tucked underneath, on top of broth. **Cover** again and microwave on HIGH for 7 to 10 minutes (LW 8½ to 12 minutes) or until fish flakes easily at thickest portion, **rotating** dish ½ turn every 3 minutes. Let **stand, covered,** for 2 minutes. Drain fish broth or stock before serving fish, strain, and freeze for later use.

Fish Baked in a Puff

This fish has a lovely soufflélike topping.

SERVES 4

EQUIPMENT:	12 x 8-inch baking dish, 1-quart round baking dish, small mixing bowl
COOKING TIME:	14 to 18 minutes (Low wattage ovens 16 to 21 minutes)
STANDING TIME:	2 minutes

1¼ **pounds fish fillets, such as haddock, sole, or scrod**
3 **tablespoons butter or margarine, sliced**
1 **medium onion, thinly sliced**
½ **medium green bell pepper, thinly sliced**
1 **large garlic clove, minced**
1 **tablespoon snipped fresh parsley**
1 **tablespoon white wine**
1 **teaspoon lemon juice**
½ **teaspoon salt**
¼ **teaspoon pepper**
1 **small fresh tomato, thinly sliced**
2 **egg whites**
½ **cup mayonnaise**
½ **cup shredded Cheddar cheese**
paprika for garnish

Cut fish fillets into 4 serving pieces and arrange in baking dish with the thickest portions to the outside of the dish and the thinner ends pointing toward the center.

Place butter, onion, green pepper, garlic, and parsley in 1-quart baking dish. **Cover** with lid or plastic wrap, pulling back one corner to vent the steam. (If dish is flat-bottomed, **elevate** it on an inverted saucer.) Microwave on HIGH for 5 to 6 minutes (LW 6 to 7 minutes) or until vegetables are crisp-tender, **stirring** and **rotating** dish ½ turn every 3 minutes. **Stir** in white wine, lemon juice, salt, and pepper. Spoon mixture over fillets and top with tomato slices.

In small bowl, **whisk** egg whites until well combined. **Whisk** in mayonnaise and stir in cheese. Spread mixture over fish, covering fish completely. (If dish is flat-bottomed, **elevate** it on an inverted saucer.) Place on turntable if available and microwave, **uncovered,** on HIGH for 9 to 12 minutes (LW 10 to 14 minutes) or until fish flakes easily and topping is set. (**Rotate** dish ½ turn every 3 minutes if not using turntable.) Let **stand** for 2 minutes and sprinkle with paprika before serving.

Troubleshooting: Be sure to completely cover fish with mayonnaise mixture; entire piece should be covered with the puff.

Fillets with Shrimp Sauce

SERVES 4

EQUIPMENT:	deep 2-quart round casserole dish, small mixing bowl
COOKING TIME:	27 to 30 minutes (Low wattage ovens 32¼ to 36 minutes)
STANDING TIME:	6 to 7 minutes

2 cups hot water
1 cup uncooked long-grain white rice
1 teaspoon butter or margarine
3 scallions, finely minced
¼ pound fresh mushrooms, sliced
1 tablespoon butter or margarine

 1 **tablespoon chopped pimiento**
 1 **tablespoon snipped fresh parsley**
 ½ **teaspoon salt**
 ⅛ **teaspoon pepper**
 1 **10¾-ounce can condensed cream of shrimp soup**
 ¾ **cup sour cream**
1¼ **pounds sole or flounder fillets**
     paprika

Place hot water, rice, 1 teaspoon butter, and scallions in casserole dish and stir. (If dish is flat-bottomed, **elevate** it on an inverted saucer.) Place on turntable if available and microwave, **uncovered,** on HIGH for 5 minutes (LW 6 minutes). **Stir, cover** with wax paper, and microwave on 40 percent power or MEDIUM for 10 minutes (LW 12 minutes). (**Rotate** dish ½ turn every 5 minutes if not using turntable.) Let **stand, covered,** for 5 minutes.

Place mushrooms and 1 tablespoon butter in small dish and microwave on 60 percent power or MEDIUM for 3 to 4 minutes (LW 3½ to 4¾ minutes) or until tender. **Drain.** Add mushrooms, pimiento, parsley, salt, and pepper to rice and **stir** well.

Whisk soup and sour cream together in small bowl. Reserve ¾ cup for the topping and add the remainder to the rice mixture. Arrange fish fillets over rice, tucking the pointed tips under the fillets. Spread the reserved soup topping over the fish and sprinkle with paprika. **Cover** with lid or plastic wrap, pulling back one corner to vent the steam. Microwave on HIGH for 9 to 11 minutes (LW 10¾ to 13¼ minutes) or until fish flakes easily. (**Rotate** dish ½ turn every 5 minutes if not using turntable.) Let **stand, covered,** for 1 to 2 minutes.

Troubleshooting: If you use too shallow a dish for the rice, the liquid may boil over.

Failing to tuck pointed tips of fish under the fillets may cause them to overcook.

Suggestions: Any type of relatively thin fish fillets may be substituted.

Salmon Vegetable Pie

SERVES 4

EQUIPMENT: 2-quart round casserole dish, 2- and 6-cup glass measures

COOKING TIME: 27 to 34 minutes (Low wattage ovens 32½ to 42 minutes)

STANDING TIME: none required

1 **15½-ounce can salmon**
2 **cups frozen peas and carrots, cooked and drained**
2 **hard-cooked eggs, sliced**
2 **tablespoons chopped pimiento**
1 **tablespoon snipped fresh parsley**
1 **10¾-ounce can condensed cream of celery soup**
⅓ **cup milk**

POTATO TOPPING

1½ **cups hot water**
½ **cup milk**
2 **tablespoons butter or margarine, sliced**
¼ **teaspoon salt**
⅛ **teaspoon pepper**
1 **packet (3¼ ounces) instant Idaho mashed potatoes paprika**

Drain and flake salmon and, if desired, remove bones and skin. Place salmon in casserole dish. Add peas and carrots, sliced egg, pimiento, and parsley.

In 2-cup glass measure, **whisk** together soup and milk. Microwave, **uncovered,** on HIGH for 3 to 5 minutes (LW 3½ to 6 minutes) or until hot. **Stir** and add to salmon mixture, **stirring** gently. Set aside.

For topping, place hot water, milk, butter, salt, and pepper in 6-cup glass measure and microwave on HIGH for 9 to 11 minutes (LW 11 to 14 minutes) or until heated but not boiling. Whisk in contents of potato packet and whip briskly until potatoes are light and fluffy. (You may also use an electric mixer.) Drop mashed potatoes in mounds over casserole and sprinkle with paprika. Microwave, **uncovered,** on HIGH for 15 to 18 minutes (LW 18 to 22 minutes) or until hot and bubbly.

Suggestions: If creamier and lighter potatoes are desired, add a little more milk to mixture.

PIE SHELLS FOR QUICHE

The microwave produces a very flaky pie shell, but it won't brown; in fact, if yours does brown, you've overcooked it. To add some color to the crust you can substitute orange juice for the water in your recipe or add several drops of yellow food coloring to the dough. Another idea is to microwave the pie shell in an amber pie dish or just quickly brown it in a conventional oven once it has cooked in the microwave. If you purchase frozen pie shells, be sure to remove them from the metal pans and place them in glass or plastic pie dishes.

Microwave a single pie shell on 60 percent or MEDIUM power for 7 to 9 minutes (8¼ to 10¾ minutes), **elevating** the dish on an inverted saucer if flat-bottomed and **rotating** the dish ¼ turn every 2 minutes. If the crust bubbles up, gently push the bubbles down. Always prebake a pie shell before filling and baking in the microwave to ensure that the crust bakes completely.

Chicken and Mushroom Quiche

This chicken and mushroom quiche works beautifully without a pie shell, which makes preparation even easier.

SERVES 6

EQUIPMENT:	small mixing bowl, 9-inch glass pie dish, 6-cup glass measure
COOKING TIME:	24 to 35 minutes (Low wattage ovens 28½ to 41 minutes)
STANDING TIME:	10 minutes

1 cup sliced fresh mushrooms
1 9-inch baked pie shell (shell may be omitted)
1 cup diced cooked chicken
1 tablespoon imitation bacon bits
1 cup shredded Cheddar or Monterey Jack cheese
4 eggs
1¾ cups half-and-half
¼ cup chopped scallions
1 tablespoon snipped fresh parsley
½ teaspoon salt
¼ teaspoon pepper

Place mushrooms in small bowl and microwave, **uncovered,** on HIGH for 3 to 5 minutes (LW 3½ to 6 minutes) or until crisp-tender, **stirring** once. **Drain** and pat dry on paper towels. Spread mushrooms in baked pie shell or on the bottom of glass pie dish if you're omitting the crust. Top mushrooms with chicken, bacon bits, and cheese.

In glass measure, **whisk** eggs together with the remaining ingredients. Microwave on 50 percent power or MEDIUM for 6 to 9 minutes (LW 7 to 10 minutes) or until thoroughly heated, **stirring** every 2 minutes.

Stir and pour gently into shell. (If dish is flat-bottomed, **elevate** it on an inverted saucer.) Place on turntable if available and microwave on 50 percent power or MEDIUM for 15 to 21 minutes (LW 18 to 25 minutes) or until a knife inserted halfway between the center and the edge comes out clean and filling is set. (**Rotate** dish ¼ turn every 3 minutes if not using turntable.) Let **stand** on a hard heat-proof surface for 10 minutes before cutting into wedges.

Troubleshooting: If one area seems to be cooking more than the rest, you may have a hot spot and need to rotate the dish more often.

Midwestern Pie

SERVES 4

EQUIPMENT: 9-inch glass pie plate, 4-cup glass measure
COOKING TIME: 20 to 27 minutes (Low wattage ovens 23½ to 32 minutes)
STANDING TIME: 10 minutes

4 eggs
1 12-ounce can evaporated milk
⅔ cup diced cooked ham
½ cup chopped fresh mushrooms
¼ cup chopped scallions
¼ cup finely chopped red bell pepper
1 cup finely shredded Swiss cheese
½ teaspoon salt
¼ teaspoon pepper
snipped fresh parsley for garnish

Lightly grease pie plate with butter or margarine and set aside. In glass measure, **whisk** together eggs and evaporated milk. Add remaining ingredients except parsley, **whisking** well. Microwave on 50 percent power or MEDIUM for 7 to 10 minutes (LW 8 to 12 minutes) or until hot, **stirring** every 2 minutes.

Stir well and pour into prepared pie plate. (If pie plate is flat-bottomed, **elevate** it on an inverted saucer.) Place on turntable if available and microwave, **uncovered,** on 50 percent power or MEDIUM for 13 to 17 minutes (LW 15½ to 20 minutes) or until a knife inserted halfway between the center and edge comes out clean and pie appears set. (**Rotate** dish ¼ turn every 3 minutes if not using turntable.) Let **stand** on a heat-proof surface for 10 minutes before cutting into wedges and serving garnished with fresh parsley.

Troubleshooting: If you have a hot spot in your oven or if pie appears to be overcooking in one area, you need to rotate the dish more often.

Suggestion: Serve wedges topped with heated bottled picante salsa, an extra-chunky, zesty sauce that goes well with eggs or egg dishes.

No-Crust Vegetable Pie

This quiche-type pie forms its own crust as it bakes. It's lovely served for brunch or a quick supper.

SERVES 6 TO 8

EQUIPMENT:	10-inch round glass dish, medium mixing bowl
COOKING TIME:	19 to 23 minutes (Low wattage ovens 22¾ to 27¼ minutes)
STANDING TIME:	5 minutes

  2 tablespoons butter or margarine, sliced
½ cup chopped onion
½ cup chopped red bell pepper
½ cup chopped green bell pepper
  2 cups diced zucchini
  1 garlic clove, minced
  4 eggs, slightly beaten
½ cup vegetable oil
  1 cup Bisquick
½ cup shredded Swiss cheese
½ teaspoon dried oregano
½ teaspoon salt
¼ teaspoon pepper
  2 tablespoons snipped fresh parsley
  2 scallions, thinly sliced

Place butter, onion, red pepper, green pepper, zucchini, and garlic in round dish. **Cover** with plastic wrap, pulling back one corner to vent the steam. (If dish is flat-bottomed, **elevate** it on an inverted saucer.) Place on turntable if available and microwave on HIGH for 9 to 11 minutes (LW 10¾ to 13¼ minutes) or until vegetables are crisp-tender, **stirring** every 3 minutes. (**Rotate** dish ½ turn when stirring if not using turntable.)

Place eggs and oil in medium bowl and **stir** together. Add biscuit mix, cheese, oregano, salt, pepper, and parsley, **mixing** well. Pour batter over vegetables and **stir** together. Sprinkle scallions over the top. Microwave, **uncovered,** on HIGH for 10 to 12 minutes (LW 12 to 14 minutes) or until a knife inserted 1 inch from the edge comes out clean. (**Rotate** dish ¼ turn every 3 minutes if not using turntable.) Let **stand** on a hard heat-proof surface for 5 minutes. To serve, cut into wedges and serve hot or very warm.

Troubleshooting: If one area of the pie seems to be overcooking or if you have a hot spot in your oven, rotate the dish more often if not using a turntable.

Fish

Ocean Fantasy

SERVES 4

EQUIPMENT: 1-cup glass measure, deep 2-quart round casserole dish, small mixing bowl, custard cup

COOKING TIME: 14 to 20 minutes (Low wattage ovens 16¾ to 23¼ minutes)

STANDING TIME: 3 minutes

1 tablespoon butter or margarine, sliced
¼ cup finely minced red onion
¼ cup sliced fresh mushrooms
1 pound medium shrimp (defrosted if frozen)
1 pound bay scallops (defrosted if frozen)
1 10¾-ounce can condensed cream of celery soup
2 tablespoons evaporated milk
1 tablespoon lemon juice
¼ teaspoon garlic powder

TOPPING
  1 tablespoon butter or margarine, sliced
  1 garlic clove, minced
  ¼ cup plain dry bread crumbs

Place 1 tablespoon butter, onions, and mushrooms in glass measure and microwave on HIGH for 2 to 4 minutes (LW 2¼ to 4¾ minutes), **stirring** once, until soft; drain liquid. Arrange shrimp in bottom of casserole dish and top with drained onion and mushroom mixture. Top mushroom mixture with scallops.

Whisk together soup, milk, lemon juice, and garlic powder in small bowl and spoon over the scallops. **Cover** with lid or plastic wrap, pulling back one corner to vent the steam. (If dish is flat-bottomed, **elevate** it on an inverted saucer.) Place on turntable if available and microwave on 70 percent power or MEDIUM-HIGH for 10 to 13 minutes (LW 12 to 15 minutes) or until shrimp and scallops are opaque. (**Rotate** dish ½ turn every 5 minutes if not using turntable.)

Place 1 tablespoon butter and garlic in custard cup and **cover** with a paper towel. Microwave on HIGH for 1 minute (LW 1¼ minutes), until melted. **Stir** in bread crumbs and sprinkle over casserole. Microwave, **uncovered,** on HIGH for 1 to 2 minutes (LW 1¼ to 2¼ minutes) or until hot and bubbly.

Troubleshooting: If one area of the casserole seems to be overcooking, or if you have a hot spot in your oven, rotate the dish more often.

Shrimp and Crabmeat Wiggle

I adapted this recipe from a dish my mother-in-law made years ago. When I presented this on television as an old recipe updated, I received dozens of letters from folks telling me they fondly remembered something similar from years ago and really loved the microwave version.

SERVES 4

EQUIPMENT: deep 3-quart round casserole dish, small mixing bowl

COOKING TIME: 12 to 17 minutes (Low wattage ovens 14 to 20¼ minutes)

STANDING TIME: none required

1 tablespoon butter or margarine, sliced
1 cup sliced fresh mushrooms
2 tablespoons chopped pimiento
2 10¾-ounce cans condensed cream of shrimp soup
½ cup half-and-half or milk
½ cup mayonnaise
¼ cup white wine
1 cup frozen peas and pearl onions, defrosted
½ pound cooked peeled shrimp, cut into ½-inch pieces
½ pound crabmeat or imitation crabmeat, cut into bite-size pieces
4 cups hot cooked rice _or_ 8 toast points

Place butter, mushrooms, and pimiento in casserole dish. **Cover** with lid or plastic wrap, pulling back one corner to vent the steam. (If dish is flat-bottomed, **elevate** it on an inverted saucer.) Microwave on HIGH for 3 to 5 minutes (LW 3½ to 6 minutes) or until vegetables are crisp-tender.

In small bowl, **whisk** together soup, half-and-half, mayonnaise, and wine. Combine with mushroom mixture and add peas, **stirring** well. **Cover** again, place on turntable if available, and microwave on HIGH for 7 to 8 minutes (LW 8¼ to 9½ minutes) or until heated through and peas are cooked. (**Rotate** dish ½ turn every 4 minutes if not using turntable.)

Stir in shrimp and crabmeat, **cover,** and microwave on HIGH for 2 to 4 minutes (LW 2¼ to 4¾ minutes) or until hot and bubbly. Serve over hot cooked rice or toast points.

Suggestions: You can use just a full pound of either shrimp or crabmeat if you prefer, but I like to mix the two.

Calico Seafood Casserole

SERVES 4 TO 6

EQUIPMENT: 2-quart round casserole dish, custard cup
COOKING TIME: 16¾ to 21¾ minutes (Low wattage ovens 19½ to 25¾ minutes)
STANDING TIME: 3 to 5 minutes

½ **cup chopped celery**
½ **cup chopped red onion**
¼ **cup chopped green bell pepper**
¼ **cup chopped red or yellow bell pepper**
1 **clove garlic, minced**
4 **tablespoons butter or margarine, sliced**
2 **tablespoons white wine**
½ **pound small bay scallops**
1 **10¾-ounce can condensed cream of shrimp soup**
¼ **cup milk**
1 **pound crabmeat or imitation crabmeat, cut into bite-size pieces**
1 **4-ounce can sliced mushrooms, drained**
2 **teaspoons lemon juice**
1 **tablespoon snipped fresh parsley**
½ **cup seasoned dry bread crumbs**
  paprika

Combine celery, onion, peppers, garlic, 2 tablespoons sliced butter, white wine, and scallops in casserole dish. **Cover** with lid or plastic wrap, pulling back one corner to vent the steam. (If dish is flat-bottomed, **elevate** it on an inverted saucer.) Microwave on HIGH for 5 to 6 minutes (LW 6 to 7 minutes) or until vegetables are crisp-tender and scallops are opaque, **stirring** every 3 minutes.

Stir in soup and milk, **cover** again, and microwave on HIGH for 2 to 4 minutes (LW 2¼ to 4¾ minutes) or until soup is heated through, **stirring** every 2 minutes. Add crabmeat, mushrooms, lemon juice, and parsley. **Stir** well, **cover,** and microwave on HIGH for 7 to 9 minutes (LW 8 to 10¾ minutes) or until hot and bubbly, **stirring** every 3 minutes.

Place 2 tablespoons butter in custard cup and microwave on HIGH for 40 to 50 seconds (LW 50 to 60 seconds) or until melted. **Stir** in crumbs and sprinkle crumb mixture over casserole top. Sprinkle paprika over all. Microwave, **uncovered,** on HIGH for 2 minutes (LW 2¼ minutes) or just until hot. Let **stand** for 3 to 5 minutes.

Suggestions: You can substitute shrimp for crabmeat or use ½ pound shrimp and ½ pound crabmeat for variety.

SQUID

Charlie's Bar and Restaurant is a free-spirited establishment located on the island of Aruba. Charlie's wife, Rosalba, shared her secret for cooking the most tender squid in the world. "Just blanch it before preparing it in your recipe," she says. "The toughness is gone, and the results are perfect every time." To blanch squid in the microwave, place 2 cups water in a deep 2-quart casserole dish and microwave on HIGH for 5 to 6 minutes (LW 6 to 7 minutes) or until the water is boiling. Place the squid in the boiling water and microwave on HIGH for another 3 to 4 minutes (LW 3½ to 4½ minutes) or until the water comes to another full boil. Remove the squid from the water and go on with your recipe.

Squid and Mussels over Linguine

SERVES 4

EQUIPMENT:	deep 2- and 3-quart round casserole dishes, 4-cup glass measure
COOKING TIME:	29 to 39 minutes (Low wattage ovens 34¼ to 39¾ minutes)
STANDING TIME:	2 minutes

   4 **small to medium squid, cleaned**
   48 **small fresh mussels in their shells**
   2 **tablespoons olive oil**
   1 **tablespoon finely chopped garlic**
   1 **medium onion, finely chopped**
   1 **teaspoon dried basil**
   1 **tablespoon snipped fresh parsley**
   ½ **cup white wine**
   1 **28-ounce can crushed tomatoes**
   2 **tablespoons tomato paste**
      dash of cayenne pepper
      hot cooked linguine
      grated Parmesan and Romano cheese for garnish

If squid are frozen, defrost completely. Remove tentacles, discard head and ink sack, and use your fingers to pull the thin bone from the length of the squid. Leave tentacles whole, but slice body into ½- to ¾-inch slices.

Place 2 cups water in 2-quart casserole dish and microwave on HIGH for 5 to 6 minutes (LW 6 to 7 minutes) or until boiling. Add squid, stir, and microwave on HIGH for 3 to 4 minutes (LW ovens 3½ to 4¾ minutes) or until water comes to a boil, then remove immediately.

Scrub mussels well with a stiff brush, discard any broken or open ones, remove the beard or black tuft on the outside of the shells, and set aside.

Place oil, garlic, onions, basil, and parsley in glass measure. Microwave on HIGH for 4 to 6 minutes (LW 4½ to 7½ minutes) or until vegetables are crisp-tender, **stirring** every 2 minutes. Add wine and cook, **uncovered,** on HIGH for 2 to 3 minutes (LW 2¼ to 3½ minutes) or until rapidly boiling. Add tomatoes, tomato paste, and dash of cayenne pepper to casserole dish and **stir** in wine and vegetable mixture. **Cover** with wax paper. (If dish is flat-bottomed, **elevate** it on an inverted saucer.) Place on turntable if available and microwave on 70 percent power or MEDIUM-HIGH for 10 to 12 minutes (LW 12 to 14½ minutes), **stirring** every 5 minutes. (**Rotate** dish ½ turn when stirring if not using turntable.)

Add scrubbed mussels and blanched squid. **Cover** with lid or plastic wrap, pulling back one corner to vent steam, and cook on HIGH for 5 to 8 minutes (LW 6 to 9½ minutes) or until mussels are open, **stirring** once. If all mussels aren't open, microwave 1 minute more on HIGH. (**Rotate** dish ½ turn when stirring if not using turntable.) Let **stand, covered,** for 2 minutes and discard any mussels that aren't open before serving over hot linguine. Pass cheeses at the table.

Suggestions: For ease of serving, you may want to remove the cooked mussels from their shells and discard the shells. Place hot linguine in a large serving bowl and cover with the fish and sauce and serve topped with grated cheese.

Charlie's Sautéed Shrimp

Charlie's is also famous for its shrimp—here's Rosalba's recipe, converted for the microwave.

SERVES 2 TO 3

EQUIPMENT:	1-quart round casserole dish
COOKING TIME:	14 to 20 minutes (Low wattage ovens 16½ to 23¼ minutes)
STANDING TIME:	2 minutes

- ½ **cup (¼ pound) salted butter, sliced**
- 2 **tablespoons minced garlic**
- ¼ **teaspoon minced fresh ginger**
- 1 **celery stalk, diced**
- ½ **medium green bell pepper, diced**
- 2 **tablespoons snipped fresh parsley**
- 1 **pound unshelled jumbo shrimp**

Place butter, garlic, ginger, celery, green pepper, and parsley in casserole dish. **Cover** with lid or plastic wrap, pulling back one corner to vent the steam. (If dish is flat-bottomed, **elevate** it on an inverted saucer.) Place on turntable if available and microwave on HIGH for 6 to 8 minutes (LW 7 to 9 minutes), **stirring** every 3 minutes, until vegetables are tender. (**Rotate** dish ½ turn when stirring if not using turntable.)

Add the shrimp, arranging them in the dish so that the tail sections are pointing toward the center of the dish. Spoon sauce over and around the shrimp and **cover** again. Microwave on 70 percent power or MEDIUM-HIGH for 8 to 12 minutes (LW 9½ to 14¼ minutes) or until shrimp are opaque, turning over and **rearranging** shrimp every 4 minutes. (**Rotate** dish ½ turn every 4 minutes if not using turntable.) Let **stand, covered,** for 2 minutes and serve with a dish for the shells and lots of paper napkins.

Brisas del Mar Red Snapper

Red snapper is also popular on Aruba, and one of my favorite versions is served at the Brisas del Mar Restaurant under the personal supervision of owner Lucia Rasmijn. Lucia doesn't use a microwave in her kitchen, but my conversion is quite tasty and lacks only the island atmosphere.

SERVES 4

EQUIPMENT:	4-cup glass measure, 12 x 8-inch baking dish
COOKING TIME:	13 to 19 minutes (Low wattage ovens 15½ to 22½ minutes)
STANDING TIME:	3 minutes

1 **tablespoon butter**
2 **tablespoons white wine**
1 **celery stalk, thinly sliced**
1 **onion, chopped**
2 **fresh tomatoes, skinned and cut into eighths**
4 **red snapper fillets (about 1 pound)**
½ **cup sliced pitted black olives**

Place butter, wine, celery, onions, and tomatoes in glass measure. Microwave on HIGH for 5 to 7 minutes (LW 6 to 8¼ minutes) or until vegetables are tender.

Place snapper fillets in baking dish with the broader ends of the fillets to the outside of the dish and narrower ends pointing toward the center. Pour the vegetable sauce over the fish and sprinkle olives over all. **Cover** dish with wax paper. (If dish is flat-bottomed, **elevate** it on an inverted saucer.) Microwave on 70 percent power or MEDIUM-HIGH for 8 to 12 minutes (LW 9½ to 14¼ minutes) or until snapper flakes easily, **rearranging** fillets and **rotating** dish ½ turn every 4 minutes. Let **stand, covered,** for 3 minutes. When serving, mound vegetable mixture on top of each fillet.

Troubleshooting: If fillets have very thin tips, be sure to tuck them underneath the fillets to prevent overcooking them.

Tuna Vegetable Casserole

How many times have you looked at a can of tuna and wanted to turn it into a low-cost, quick-to-prepare, interesting dinner for the family? A great deal of salt is used in the preserving of canned tuna. If you're watching your sodium, purchase tuna packed in spring water rather than oil.

SERVES 4 TO 6

EQUIPMENT:	2-quart round casserole dish, 6-cup glass measure, custard cup
COOKING TIME:	13½ to 18¾ minutes (Low wattage ovens 16 to 22 minutes)
STANDING TIME:	none required

  2 tablespoons butter or margarine, sliced
  ½ cup chopped red onion
  ½ cup chopped celery
  ½ cup chopped green bell pepper
  1 cup sliced fresh mushrooms
  1 tablespoon chopped pimiento
  1 10¾-ounce can condensed cream of celery soup
  ¼ cup milk
  1 tablespoon lemon juice
  1 12½-ounce can tuna, drained and flaked
  1 10-ounce package frozen green peas, defrosted

TOPPING
  2 tablespoons butter or margarine, sliced
  ½ cup Wheat Thin snack cracker crumbs
  1 tablespoon snipped fresh parsley

Combine 2 tablespoons butter, onion, celery, green pepper, mushrooms, and pimiento in casserole dish. **Cover** with lid or plastic wrap, pulling back one corner to vent the steam. (If dish is flat-bottomed, **elevate** it on an inverted saucer.) Microwave on HIGH for 6 to 8 minutes (LW 7 to 9 minutes) or until vegetables are crisp-tender, **stirring** every 3 minutes.

In glass measure, **whisk** together soup, milk, and lemon juice. **Stir** in tuna and spoon into vegetable mixture. Add peas and **stir** well.

Place 2 tablespoons butter in custard cup and microwave on HIGH for 30 to 45 seconds (LW 45 to 60 seconds) or until melted. **Stir** in cracker crumbs and parsley. Sprinkle topping over top of casserole. **Cover** with wax paper and place on turntable if available. Microwave on HIGH for 7 to 10 minutes (LW 8¼ to 12 minutes) or until hot and bubbly. (**Rotate** dish ½ turn every 4 minutes if not using turntable.)

Troubleshooting: This casserole works best when prepared in a round rather than a square container.

Suggestions: For a different flavor, try substituting various-flavored cracker crumbs for topping. Crush crumbs in food processor or place in plastic bag and roll with rolling pin to crush.

Tuna on the Half Shell

There are times when you want to serve a special-looking low-cost entrée, and tuna on the half shell will fit that bill perfectly.

SERVES 4

EQUIPMENT: 6-cup glass measure, 4 large baking shells or ramekins, meat rack
COOKING TIME: 14 to 20 minutes (Low wattage ovens 16¼ to 23¾ minutes)
STANDING TIME: none required

2 **tablespoons butter or margarine, sliced**
¼ **cup chopped celery**
¼ **cup chopped onion**
⅓ **cup plain dry bread crumbs**
1 **5-ounce can evaporated milk**
1 **tablespoon white wine**
2 **eggs, well beaten**
1 **6½-ounce can tuna, drained and mashed**
2 **tablespoons chopped pimiento**
½ **cup chopped fresh mushrooms**
½ **teaspoon salt**
¼ **teaspoon pepper**
½ **cup shredded Cheddar cheese**
paprika
fresh parsley sprigs or thin lemon slices for garnish

Place butter, celery, and onion in glass measure. Microwave on HIGH for 2 to 4 minutes (LW 2¼ to 4¾ minutes) or until crisp-tender, **stirring** once. **Stir** in crumbs, evaporated milk, wine, eggs, tuna, pimiento, mushrooms, salt, and pepper. Microwave, **uncovered,** on 50 percent power or MEDIUM for 9 to 11 minutes (LW 10¾ to 13 minutes) or until heated through (mixture will be moist, with all excess liquid absorbed), **stirring** every 3 minutes.

Divide mixture among baking shells and place shells on large meat rack. Sprinkle tops with Cheddar cheese and microwave on 50 percent power or MEDIUM for 3 to 5 minutes (LW 3¼ to 6 minutes) or until cheese melts, **rearranging** shells after 2 minutes. Sprinkle with paprika and garnish with fresh parsley or lemon slices.

Suggestions: If you don't have individual baking shells or ramekins, you can use single-serving bowls and omit placing the bowls on a roasting rack. The presentation may not be as attractive, but the delicious taste remains.

SQUARE-CORNERED CONTAINERS

Microwaves have a habit of overcooking food that sits in the corners of square-cornered dishes. This problem is easily avoided by using round cooking containers or moving the food out of the corners frequently. Many manufacturers are addressing this problem by rounding the inside corners of their square dishes. When you're selecting new dishes for microwave use, run your finger inside the corners to be sure the ones you select have rounded inside corners.

Desserts and Baked Goods

Baking in the microwave? Many people feel it's just not possible. Well, surprise: here I am to tell you it not only works extremely well in half the time your conventional oven takes but there is no added heat in your kitchen. Does this mean that you can pick up any brand of cake mix, prepare it according to box directions, and bake in the microwave? Well, there you have me; Pillsbury is the only cake manufacturer, at this writing, whose box mix can be prepared according to box directions and microwaved. Even the Pillsbury mixes must be beaten at medium speed to incorporate less air and microwaved with no added ingredients. (I'm not talking about the microwave cakes, which are made specifically for microwaving; I'm talking about regular boxed cake mixes.)

To microwave other manufacturers' cakes you really must either call the toll-free telephone number on the box or write to the address on the box and request specific microwave instructions. I've found that several of the other cake manufacturers find it necessary to add ingredients to their boxed cake mixes to have them microwave satisfactorily, and some companies don't recommend microwaving all of their flavors. You will notice that whenever I use a box cake mix in a recipe it is always Pillsbury; if you decide to change the brand, please check with the manufacturer before proceeding with the recipe.

Can you also microwave your own homemade recipes? That's a tricky question. I sometimes have to make a scratch cake recipe several times before I find the exact baking times, and once in a while I have to change the leavening ingredients. If you have a problem with a recipe, please feel free to write to me in care of my publisher, and I will certainly see if I can help you. Please be assured that the recipes you find in this chapter have been tested and retested; I guarantee their success as long as you follow the cooking times and use the ingredients and baking pans listed.

BREAD PUDDINGS

When my mom was a girl, bread puddings were made with layers of fruit and bread and called charlottes. Fruit sauces were served over these delicious creations, and both were usually served hot. If by chance a serving or two was left over and found in the icebox the next day, it was topped with a scoop of homemade ice cream.

Applesauce Bread Pudding

SERVES 4 TO 6

EQUIPMENT:	toaster, 2½-quart round casserole dish, medium mixing bowl
COOKING TIME:	17 to 21 minutes (Low wattage ovens 20¼ to 25 minutes)
STANDING TIME:	15 to 20 minutes

   8   slices white bread
   4   tablespoons soft butter or margarine
   ⅓   cup dark brown sugar
   1   teaspoon ground cinnamon
   ½   cup applesauce
   ½   cup golden raisins
   2   cups milk
   4   eggs, well beaten
   ⅓   cup sugar
   ⅛   teaspoon ground nutmeg
   1   teaspoon vanilla extract
   ⅛   teaspoon salt
       whipped topping and red currant jelly for garnish
       (optional)

Toast bread slices. Spread one side with butter, sprinkle with brown sugar, then sprinkle with cinnamon. Divide bread into 4 groups of sandwiches, removing crusts if desired. Cut each sandwich into 4 squares. Place a single layer of 8 squares (2 sandwiches) in casserole dish and top with applesauce and ½ the raisins. Add remaining sandwich squares in a layer.

Place milk in glass measure and microwave on HIGH for 5 to 7 minutes (LW 6 to 8 minutes) or until milk is hot and scalded. *(Do not boil.)* **Whisk** eggs in medium bowl until light and fluffy. Add sugar, nutmeg, vanilla, and salt, **mixing** well. Gradually **whisk** hot milk into egg mixture. **Stir** in remaining raisins and gently pour over casserole. Allow to **stand** for 10 minutes. (With a fork, push the toast under the milk mixture to absorb part of the liquid and become fluffy.)

Cover dish with lid or plastic wrap, pulling back one corner to vent the steam. (If dish is flat-bottomed, **elevate** it on an inverted saucer.) Place on turntable if available and microwave on 50 percent power or MEDIUM for 14 to 16 minutes (LW 16¾ to 19 minutes) or until a knife inserted in the center comes out clean. (**Rotate** dish ¼ turn every 4 minutes if not using turntable.) Let **stand, covered,** on a hard heat-proof surface, for 5 to 10 minutes.

Serve warm or cold. If desired, garnish with whipped topping and drizzle with red currant jelly.

Apricot Bread Pudding

SERVES 4 TO 6

EQUIPMENT:	toaster, 2-quart round casserole dish, 4-cup glass measure, medium mixing bowl
COOKING TIME:	17 to 21 minutes (Low wattage ovens 20¼ to 25 minutes)
STANDING TIME:	15 to 20 minutes

10 slices cinnamon raisin bread
3 tablespoons soft butter or margarine
⅓ cup apricot preserves
2 cups milk
3 eggs
⅛ teaspoon salt
3 tablespoons sugar
1 teaspoon vanilla extract
ground cinnamon or nutmeg or whipped topping for garnish (optional)

Lightly toast bread and immediately spread one side with butter and then with preserves. Cut slices into 1-inch squares and layer in casserole dish.

Place milk in glass measure and microwave on HIGH for 5 to 7 minutes (LW 6 to 8¼ minutes) or until hot and scalded. *(Do not boil.)* In mixing bowl, **whisk** eggs together until light and fluffy. Add salt, sugar, and vanilla. Gradually **whisk** the warm milk into the egg mixture.

Pour the egg and milk mixture over the prepared toast squares, pushing the toast under the milk mixture with a fork. Let **stand** for 10 minutes while the toast absorbs the liquid and becomes puffy. After standing, **cover** dish with lid or plastic wrap, pulling back one corner to vent the steam. (If dish is flat-bottomed, **elevate** it on an inverted saucer.) Place on turntable if available and microwave on 50 percent power or MEDIUM for 12 to 14 minutes (LW 14¼ to 16¾ minutes) or until a knife inserted in the center comes out clean. (**Rotate** dish ¼ turn every

4 minutes if not using turntable.) Let **stand, covered,** on a hard heat-proof surface for 5 to 10 minutes. Serve warm or cold, sprinkled with cinnamon or nutmeg or topped with whipped topping.

Cherry Pineapple Charlotte

SERVES 4 TO 6

EQUIPMENT: small mixing bowl, 2½-quart round casserole dish, medium mixing bowl

COOKING TIME: 14 to 16½ minutes (Low wattage ovens 17 to 19¾ minutes)

STANDING TIME: 5 to 10 minutes

1 **cup (½ pound) butter or margarine, sliced**
8 **slices white bread, cut into 1-inch cubes**
1 **20-ounce can crushed pineapple, well drained**
¼ **cup chopped maraschino cherries**
3 **eggs, slightly beaten**
½ **cup evaporated milk**
1 **cup light brown sugar**
1 **teaspoon coconut flavoring**
whipped topping for garnish (optional)

Place sliced butter in small bowl, **cover** with a sheet of paper towel, and microwave on HIGH for 1 to 1½ minutes (LW 1½ to 1¾ minutes) or until melted. Combine bread cubes, pineapple, and cherries in casserole dish. In mixing bowl, combine all remaining ingredients, including melted margarine. Pour over bread mixture, **blending** well.

Cover dish with lid or plastic wrap, pulling back one corner to vent the steam. (If dish is flat-bottomed, **elevate** it on an inverted saucer.) Place on turntable if available and microwave on 50 percent power or MEDIUM for 13 to 15 minutes (LW 15½ to 18

minutes) or until a knife inserted in the center comes out clean. (**Rotate** dish ¼ turn every 4 minutes if not using turntable.) Let **stand, covered,** on a hard heat-proof surface for 5 to 10 minutes. Serve warm or cold with whipped topping if desired.

STANDING TIME IN BAKING

When you're baking in the microwave, the bottom of the pan is the last place to cook. When microwaving time has finished, remove pan from the oven and place on a hard heat-proof surface to trap the heat and allow the bottom to finish cooking. If you forget and place the pan on a cooling rack, you will find raw batter on the bottom. Should this happen, microwave for 1 to 2 minutes more and allow to stand again, this time on a hard heat-proof surface. Don't, by the way, allow the cake to stand in the oven; excess moisture is absorbed, making removal from the pan very difficult.

Butter Rum Raisin Cake

I have always loved butter rum raisin ice cream, and this is as close as I could get to a dessert with the same flavorings.

SERVES 8 TO 10

EQUIPMENT:	12-cup bundt pan, large mixing bowl, electric mixer
COOKING TIME:	17 to 20 minutes (Low wattage ovens 20 to 25 minutes)
STANDING TIME:	10 minutes

  2   teaspoons sugar mixed with 1 teaspoon ground
      cinnamon *or* 1 to 2 teaspoons finely chopped nuts
      for dusting pan
  1   box Pillsbury Plus yellow cake mix
  1   3½-ounce box instant vanilla pudding mix
  4   eggs
  1   cup orange juice
  ½   cup vegetable oil
  1   rounded tablespoon grated orange zest
  1   teaspoon ground cinnamon
  ½   teaspoon ground nutmeg
  2   teaspoons rum flavoring
  ½   cup raisins
      Butter Rum Glaze (recipe follows)
      chopped nuts for garnish

Grease bundt pan and dust with cinnamon and sugar or sprinkle
with 1 or 2 teaspoons finely chopped nuts. Set aside. Place cake
mix in mixing bowl, reserving 2 tablespoons. Add pudding mix,
eggs, orange juice, oil, orange zest, cinnamon, nutmeg, and rum
flavoring. Mix at low speed with mixer until moistened. Increase
speed to medium and beat for 5 minutes.

Plump raisins in a small amount of hot water for 1 minute
(see box on page 220), dry well on paper towels, and dust with
the reserved 2 tablespoons cake mix. Add raisins to cake batter
and stir gently. Pour batter into prepared pan and place on
turntable if available.

Microwave on 50 percent power or MEDIUM for 6 minutes
(LW 7 minutes). (**Rotate** dish ¼ turn every 3 minutes if not using
turntable.) Increase power to HIGH and microwave for 11 to 14
minutes (LW 13 to 18 minutes) or until top appears almost dry
and cake begins to pull away from the sides of the dish. (**Rotate**
dish ¼ turn every 3 minutes if not using turntable.) Let **stand** on
a hard heat-proof surface for 10 minutes before inverting onto a
cake dish to cool completely before topping with glaze and gar-
nishing with nuts.

Troubleshooting: Failing to rotate dish while baking may cause an
uneven top on the cake.

Butter Rum Glaze

EQUIPMENT: 4-cup glass measure
COOKING TIME: 1 to 1¼ minutes (Low wattage ovens 1¼ to 1½ minutes)

¼ cup butter or margarine, sliced
1½ cups confectioners' sugar
1 teaspoon rum flavoring
1 teaspoon grated orange zest
1 to 2 tablespoons hot water

Place butter in glass measure and microwave on HIGH for 1 to 1¼ minutes (LW 1¼ to 1½ minutes) or until melted. Blend in sugar, rum flavoring, and orange zest. Stir in hot water until desired spreading consistency is reached.

CHERRIES

When you're selecting fresh cherries, take just a minute to look them over before filling your bag. Choose only those that are firm and brightly colored and reach to the back of the mound for the less picked-over cherries. Avoid those that are soft and sticky and have any splits in the skin. When they are overripe, they will lose their shiny color, start to shrivel, and the stems will fall off easily.

To store cherries, place them on paper towels and pat dry any moisture, as this is what causes the fresh fruit to mold. Discard any bruised cherries and refrigerate, washing just before using. If you don't have a cherry pitter, and I don't know many people who do, wash the cherries and remove the stems. Split each cherry in half and, using a paper clip, pop out the pit—and don't eat half of them during the pitting process.

Deep-Dish Cherry Cobbler

SERVES 6

EQUIPMENT:	deep 3-quart round casserole dish, deep 10-inch round baking dish, large mixing bowl, sifter
COOKING TIME:	17 to 22 minutes (Low wattage ovens 19½ to 25¾ minutes)
STANDING TIME:	10 minutes

- 1¼ **cups sugar**
- 3 **tablespoons cornstarch**
- 4 **cups pitted fresh cherries**
- ¼ **teaspoon almond extract**
- ½ **cup miniature marshmallows**
- ¼ **cup butter-flavored Crisco**
- 1 **cup sugar**
- 1 **egg**
- 2 **cups flour**
- 2 **teaspoons baking powder**
- ¼ **teaspoon salt**
- ¾ **cup milk**
- ½ **teaspoon vanilla extract**

TOPPING
- 1 **tablespoon sugar**
- ½ **teaspoon ground cinnamon**

Combine 1¼ cups sugar and cornstarch in deep casserole dish. Add cherries, **mixing** to combine with dry ingredients. Sprinkle cherries with almond extract, **mixing** gently. (If dish is flat-bottomed, **elevate** it on an inverted saucer.) Place on turntable if available and microwave, **uncovered,** on HIGH for 4 to 7 minutes (LW 4½ to 8 minutes) or until mixture is boiling and has thickened, **stirring** every 2 minutes. (**Rotate** dish ½ turn when stirring if not using turntable.)

Place thickened cherry mixture in bottom of round baking dish and sprinkle marshmallows over cherries; set aside.

In large bowl, cream together Crisco and 1 cup sugar until light and fluffy. Add the egg and blend well. Sift flour, baking powder, and salt together and add alternately with the milk to creamed mixture. Add vanilla and mix well.

Spoon batter very carefully over cherry-marshmallow mixture. Combine topping ingredients and sprinkle over batter. (If dish is flat-bottomed, **elevate** it on an inverted saucer.) Place on turntable if available and microwave on 50 percent power or MEDIUM for 6 minutes (LW 7 minutes). (**Rotate** dish ¼ turn every 3 minutes if not using turntable.) Increase power to HIGH and microwave for 7 to 9 minutes (LW 8¼ to 10¾ minutes) or until top appears almost dry and cake begins to pull away from the sides of the dish. (**Rotate** dish ¼ turn every 3 minutes if not using turntable.) Let **stand** on a hard heat-proof surface for 10 minutes. Serve warm with ice cream or your favorite whipped topping.

Troubleshooting: Remove cake from oven for standing time.

Suggestions: A can of cherry pie filling can be substituted for fresh cherries. If so, place pie filling in deep round baking dish, sprinkle with almond extract, stir, sprinkle with marshmallows, and continue with recipe.

Country Morning Coffee Cake

Breakfast is the meal we seem to give the least attention to. For those of you who don't want eggs or pancakes, there are always delectable coffee cakes to accompany your morning brew.

SERVES 8

EQUIPMENT:	large mixing bowl, electric mixer, 2 small mixing bowls, 9 x 13-inch glass baking dish, cooling rack
COOKING TIME:	16 to 19 minutes (Low wattage ovens 19 to 22½ minutes)
STANDING TIME:	5 to 10 minutes

1 box Pillsbury Butter Recipe yellow cake mix
1 cup sour cream
¼ cup water
3 eggs
1 cup finely chopped nuts
½ cup firmly packed light brown sugar
½ teaspoon ground cinnamon
¼ teaspoon ground cloves
½ cup cherry preserve
¼ teaspoon almond extract

Reserve 2 tablespoons cake mix and set aside. In mixing bowl, blend the remaining cake mix, sour cream, water, and eggs at low speed until moistened; then beat at medium speed for 5 minutes. Combine nuts, brown sugar, cinnamon, cloves, and reserved cake mix in one small bowl. In another small bowl, mix the preserves and almond extract together.

Pour ½ the batter into glass baking dish. Spoon the preserves mixture over the batter and swirl slightly. Sprinkle with ½ the nut mixture. Cover with remaining batter and sprinkle remaining nut mixture evenly over the entire top. (If dish is flat-bottomed, **elevate** it on an inverted saucer.)

Microwave on 50 percent power or MEDIUM for 7 minutes (LW 8¼ minutes), **rotating** the dish ½ turn every 3 minutes. Increase power to HIGH and microwave for 9 to 12 minutes (LW 10¾ to 14¼ minutes) or until done. No unbaked batter should be visible in the center of the dish when you look through the bottom, and the cake should be beginning to pull away from the sides of the pan. Let **stand** on a hard heat-proof surface for 5 to 10 minutes. Then place dish on a cooling rack until completely cooled.

Troubleshooting: Remove cake from oven for standing time.

Apple Coffee Cake

SERVES 8

EQUIPMENT: 12-cup bundt pan, small mixing bowl, large mixing bowl, electric mixer

COOKING TIME: 23 to 26 minutes (Low wattage ovens 27½ to 31¾ minutes)

STANDING TIME: 10 to 15 minutes

2 teaspoons sugar mixed with 1 teaspoon ground cinnamon for dusting pan
½ cup chopped walnuts or pecans
½ cup sugar
2 teaspoons ground cinnamon
1 box Pillsbury Plus yellow cake mix
1 4-ounce box instant vanilla pudding mix
4 eggs
½ cup oil
1 cup sour cream
2 McIntosh, Courtland, or Macoun apples, pared and sliced

Grease bundt pan and dust with cinnamon sugar. Combine nuts, sugar, and cinnamon in small bowl and set aside. In mixing bowl, combine cake mix, pudding mix, eggs, oil, and sour cream. Blend on low speed, then beat for 5 minutes on medium speed.

Pour ½ the batter into the prepared pan and arrange ½ the apple slices on top. Sprinkle with ½ the nut mixture and cover with the remaining batter. Cover batter with balance of apple slices and nut mixture.

Place on turntable if available and microwave on 30 percent power or LOW for 11 minutes (LW 13½ minutes). (**Rotate** dish ¼ turn every 3 minutes if not using turntable.) Increase power to HIGH and microwave for 12 to 15 minutes (LW 14 to 18¼ minutes) or until top appears almost dry and cake begins to come away from the sides of the dish. (**Rotate** dish ¼ turn every 3 minutes if not using a turntable.) Let **stand** on a hard heat-proof surface for 10 to 15 minutes before inverting onto a serving dish.

Troubleshooting: Remove cake from oven for standing time.

Orange Sour Cream Coffee Cake

SERVES 8 TO 10

EQUIPMENT:	12-cup bundt pan or tube dish, large mixing bowl, electric mixer, small mixing bowl, pastry blender or 2 table knives, medium mixing bowl
COOKING TIME:	13 to 16 minutes (Low wattage ovens 15½ to 19 minutes)
STANDING TIME:	10 minutes

2 teaspoons sugar mixed with 1 teaspoon ground cinnamon for dusting pan

BATTER
3 cups flour
1½ cups sugar
2 teaspoons baking powder
1 teaspoon baking soda
1 teaspoon salt
1 cup sour cream
¾ cup butter-flavored Crisco
2 tablespoons orange juice
1 tablespoon grated orange zest
3 eggs

FILLING

½ **cup light brown sugar**
⅓ **cup flour**
2 **teaspoons ground cinnamon**
¼ **cup finely chopped nuts**
¼ **cup butter-flavored Crisco**

GLAZE

1½ **cups confectioners' sugar**
2 **tablespoons butter or margarine, softened**
1 **teaspoon grated orange zest**
2 **to 3 tablespoons orange juice**

Grease bundt pan or tube dish and dust with cinnamon sugar. Set aside. Place cake batter ingredients in large mixing bowl. Blend on low speed until moistened, then mix at medium speed for 5 minutes. Pour ⅓ of batter into prepared dish.

Combine all filling ingredients except Crisco in small bowl. With a pastry blender or 2 table knives, cut Crisco into filling mixture until it resembles cornmeal. Sprinkle ½ the filling over the cake batter. Top with another ⅓ of the batter and the balance of the filling mixture, ending with the remaining batter.

Place on turntable if available and microwave on 50 percent power or MEDIUM for 6 minutes (LW 7 minutes). (**Rotate** dish ¼ turn every 3 minutes if not using turntable.) Increase power to HIGH and microwave for 7 to 10 minutes (LW 8½ to 12 minutes) or until top appears almost dry and cake begins to come away from the sides of the dish. (**Rotate** dish ¼ turn every 3 minutes if not using turntable.) Let **stand** on a hard heat-proof surface for 10 minutes. Invert onto a serving plate and allow to cool completely.

Blend glaze ingredients together in medium bowl, using enough orange juice to make a glaze consistency, and spoon over cake, allowing some of the glaze to drizzle over the sides of cooled cake.

Troubleshooting: Remove cake from oven for standing time.

Suggestion: Garnish with fresh orange slices and walnut halves.

PREPARING CAKE PANS

PREPARING CAKE PANS

The general rule when microwaving any baked good is to grease
and sugar the pan if you're going to remove the cake for frosting or glazing. If you're going to serve right from the glass or plastic baking dish, no greasing is necessary. If you're using a flat
baking dish, you may omit the greasing if you line the bottom of
the pan with a piece of wax paper, cut to fit the pan exactly.
Wax paper will not work with a bundt pan or tube dish; grease
and dust them with sugar or finely chopped nuts, graham cracker
crumbs, brown sugar, cinnamon sugar, or cocoa for chocolate cakes.
Whatever you dust the pan with will remain on the outside of
the cake, so please remember not to use flour, as you would when
conventionally baking a cake.

Raspberry Apple Coffee Cake

SERVES 10

EQUIPMENT: 12-cup bundt pan, small mixing bowl
COOKING TIME: 11 to 13 minutes (Low wattage ovens 13 to
15½ minutes)
STANDING TIME: 5 minutes

**2 10½-ounce packages Aunt Jemima Easy Mix Coffee
Cake**
⅓ cup red raspberry jam
½ cup finely diced peeled apple (½ apple)
½ teaspoon ground cinnamon
¼ cup chopped nuts
2 eggs
1 cup milk

Generously grease bundt pan and sprinkle the bottom and sides
with only 1 packet of crumb topping from the coffee cake box.
(Second packet of topping may be used at another time, with any
other coffee cake recipe.)

Combine jam, apple, cinnamon, and nuts in small bowl and set aside. Mix each package of coffee cake mix in its own plastic bag with 1 egg and ½ cup of milk per package. (Follow directions on box for mixing.)

Squeeze batter from one bag into the prepared pan and top with jam mixture. Squeeze the batter from the second packet over the top of the jam. Place on turntable if available and microwave on HIGH for 11 to 13 minutes (LW 13 to 15½ minutes) or until top springs back when touched lightly and cake starts to pull away from sides of pan. (**Rotate** dish ¼ turn every 3 minutes if not using turntable.) Let **stand** on a hard heat-proof surface for 5 minutes before inverting onto a serving dish. Once cool, sprinkle with confectioners' sugar and serve warm or cold.

Troubleshooting: Remove cake from oven for standing time.

BUTTERMILK

Buttermilk is an ingredient you may need in small amounts—instead of buying an entire quart, make your own. To a 1-cup glass measure, add 1 tablespoon vinegar or lemon juice plus enough milk to fill the measure, mix, and you have a substitute for buttermilk called *sour milk*. An alternative is to mix equal amounts of sour cream and milk together, which produces a truer buttermilk replacement.

Cranberry Date Nut Cake

SERVES 6 TO 8

EQUIPMENT:	2-quart ring mold or 9-inch tube pan, medium and large mixing bowls, cooling rack
COOKING TIME:	15 to 18 minutes (Low wattage ovens 17¾ to 21½ minutes)
STANDING TIME:	5 to 10 minutes

2¼ cups flour
  1 cup sugar
  1 teaspoon baking soda
  ¼ teaspoon salt
1½ cups cranberries coarsely chopped
  1 cup chopped pitted dates
  ½ cup chopped walnuts
  2 eggs, beaten
  1 cup buttermilk
  ¾ cup vegetable oil
  1 tablespoon finely grated orange zest
     Orange Glaze (recipe follows)

Grease ring mold or tube pan and dust with sugar; set aside. In large bowl, **stir** together flour, sugar, baking soda, and salt. Add cranberries, dates, and nuts, **mixing** together well. Combine eggs, buttermilk, oil, and orange zest; add to the flour mixture and **mix** well.

Spread batter in prepared dish. (If dish is flat-bottomed, **elevate** on an inverted saucer.) Place on turntable if available and microwave on 50 percent power or MEDIUM for 9 minutes (LW 10¾ minutes). (**Rotate** dish ¼ turn every 3 minutes if not using a turntable.) Increase power to HIGH and microwave for 6 to 9 minutes (LW 7 to 10¾ minutes) or until cake begins to come away from the sides of the dish and no raw batter appears on top of the cake. (**Rotate** dish ¼ turn every 3 minutes if not using turntable.) Let **stand** on a hard heat-proof surface for 5 to 10 minutes, then remove cake to cooling rack. While warm, spoon glaze over cake.

Suggestions: Excellent served for breakfast when heated in the microwave for 10 to 15 seconds per slice, wrapped in a paper towel. If desired, spread with butter or cream cheese.

Orange Glaze

EQUIPMENT: small mixing bowl
COOKING TIME: 3 to 4 minutes (Low wattage ovens 3½ to
4¾ minutes)

½ **cup orange juice**
1 **tablespoon grated orange zest**
¾ **cup sugar**

Combine orange juice, orange zest, and sugar in small bowl. Microwave on HIGH for 3 to 4 minutes (LW 3½ to 4¾ minutes), **stirring** every 2 minutes, until hot and the sugar has dissolved.

Cream of Tomato Soup Cake

SERVES 6 TO 8

EQUIPMENT: 12-cup bundt pan or tube dish, large mixing bowl, electric mixer, sifter, small mixing bowl
COOKING TIME: 15 to 18 minutes (Low wattage ovens 17¾
to 21 minutes)
STANDING TIME: 10 minutes

2 **teaspoons sugar mixed with 1 teaspoon ground cinnamon for dusting pan**
¾ **cup butter-flavored Crisco**
1 **cup sugar**
2 **eggs**
3 **cups flour**
1 **teaspoon baking soda**
1 **tablespoon baking powder**
1 **teaspoon ground cinnamon**
1 **teaspoon ground nutmeg**
1 **teaspoon ground cloves**
1 **11-ounce can Campbell's condensed Homestyle Cream of Tomato Soup**

½ **cup hot water**
½ **cup raisins, softened**
½ **cup chopped nuts (optional)**
   confectioners' sugar for dusting cake (optional)

Grease bundt pan or tube dish and dust with cinnamon sugar; set aside. In mixing bowl, cream together Crisco and sugar. Add eggs, beating well. Sift together flour, soda, baking powder, cinnamon, nutmeg, and cloves. Combine soup and hot water in small bowl and add to the Crisco mixture alternately with the sifted dry ingredients. **Stir** well after each addition, adding the raisins and nuts last.

Spoon batter into prepared pan, place on turntable if available, and microwave on 50 percent power or MEDIUM for 6 minutes (LW 7 minutes). Increase power to HIGH and microwave for 9 to 12 minutes (LW 10¾ to 14 minutes) or until cake begins to pull away from the sides of the dish and the top appears almost dry. (**Rotate** dish ¼ turn every 3 minutes if not using turntable.) Let **stand** on a hard heat-proof surface for 10 minutes, then invert onto a cake plate. If desired, dust with confectioners' sugar.

Troubleshooting: Remove cake from oven for standing time.

Suggestions: Perfect for afternoon tea.

Saucy Fruit Medley

When I was a child, my mother did a lot of entertaining. I remember my mom's buffet table, especially at family and holiday dinners, when the dessert attraction was fruit medley surrounded by her homemade butter cookies. When I was old enough to take a ceramics course, one of the first things that caught my eye was a watermelon half. I painted it so carefully that when it was finished it looked just like the real thing—it has held Mom's lovely fruit desserts since the day I gave it to her.

SERVES 10 TO 12

EQUIPMENT: deep 3-quart round casserole dish, 2-cup glass measure

COOKING TIME: 13 to 16 minutes (Low wattage ovens 15½ to 18½ minutes)

STANDING TIME: 3 minutes

1 **16-ounce can apricot halves, drained and cut into bite-size pieces**
1 **29-ounce can sliced peaches, drained and cut into bite-size pieces**
1 **16-ounce can pear halves, drained and cut into bite-size pieces**
1 **20-ounce can pineapple chunks, drained**
1 **11-ounce can mandarin orange segments, drained**
2 **10-ounce jars maraschino cherries, drained**
½ **cup golden raisins**
½ **cup dark raisins**
2 **bananas, sliced (optional)**
¼ **cup brown sugar**
½ **cup orange liqueur, such as Triple Sec**
¼ **cup orange juice**
1 **thin lemon slice, cut into quarters**

Combine all fruits in deep casserole dish and set aside. In glass measure, combine brown sugar, liqueur, orange juice, and lemon slices. **Cover** with wax paper and microwave on HIGH for 3 to 4 minutes (LW 3½ to 4½ minutes), **stirring** to dissolve the sugar. Add liquid to fruit mixture and **toss** together. **Cover** dish with lid or plastic wrap, pulling back one corner to vent the steam. (If dish is flat-bottomed, **elevate** it on an inverted saucer.) Place on turntable if available and microwave on HIGH for 10 to 12 minutes (LW 12 to 14 minutes) or until mixture is heated through, **stirring** gently twice during cooking time. (**Rotate** dish ½ turn when stirring if not using turntable.) Let **stand, covered,** for 3 minutes before serving. Serve warm or cold.

Suggestions: This is an excellent year-round first course or dessert delight. Serve warm or cold with sour cream sprinkled with cinnamon or a dollop of whipped cream topped with a cherry. It may also accompany your favorite meat dish, or you can serve it over sponge cake with whipped topping.

Apple Raisin Gingerbread

SERVES 6

EQUIPMENT: 6-cup glass measure, 2-quart round casserole dish, medium mixing bowl, cooling rack
COOKING TIME: 16 to 20 minutes (Low wattage ovens 19 to 23 minutes)
STANDING TIME: 7 minutes

1 **20-ounce can sliced apples, drained**
½ **cup sugar**
¼ **cup hot water**
½ **teaspoon ground cinnamon**
½ **cup raisins**
1 **14¼-ounce box gingerbread mix**
1¼ **cups lukewarm water**
1 **egg**

Place apple slices in glass measure. Dissolve sugar in hot water and pour over apples. Add cinnamon and **stir** gently. **Cover** with plastic wrap, pulling back one corner to vent the steam, and microwave on HIGH for 5 to 7 minutes (LW 6 to 8 minutes) or until hot. *(Do not boil.)*

Add raisins, **stir** gently, **cover,** and let **stand** on a hard heat-proof surface for 2 minutes to let the raisins plump. **Drain** the liquid and spoon the apple mixture into the bottom of round casserole dish.

Place the gingerbread mix, lukewarm water, and egg in mixing bowl and **stir** vigorously with a fork for about 2 minutes, until batter is of uniform color and consistency. Pour batter over the apple mixture and place on turntable if available. (If dish is flat-bottomed, **elevate** it on an inverted saucer.) Microwave on 80 percent power or MEDIUM-HIGH for 11 to 13 minutes (LW 13 to 15 minutes) or until a toothpick inserted in the center comes out clean. (**Rotate** dish ¼ turn every 3 minutes if not using turntable.) Let **stand** on a hard heat-proof surface for 5 minutes, then invert onto cooling rack. Serve warm.

Suggestions: Top with Blushing Cherry Topping (page 196), vanilla ice cream, or whipped topping.

Lemon Jell-O Cake

This cake was very popular in the 1960s. It's very moist and cool-tasting and has become a favorite at our house. Keep it tightly covered and it will keep well, right to the very last crumb.

SERVES 8 TO 10

EQUIPMENT:	12-cup bundt or tube pan, large mixing bowl, electric mixer, small mixing bowl
COOKING:	19 to 21 minutes (Low wattage ovens 22½ to 25 minutes)
STANDING TIME:	10 minutes

- **1 box Pillsbury Plus lemon cake mix**
- **4 eggs, well beaten**
- **¾ cup water**
- **½ cup vegetable oil**
- **1 3-ounce package lemon Jell-O gelatin**

GLAZE
- **1 cup confectioners' sugar**
- **1 tablespoon butter or margarine, softened**
- **¼ teaspoon lemon extract**
- **1 teaspoon grated lemon zest**
- **1 to 2 tablespoons milk**

Grease bundt or tube pan and dust with sugar; set aside. Place cake mix, eggs, water, oil, and gelatin in large bowl. Blend at low speed, then beat at medium speed for 5 minutes and pour into prepared pan. (If dish is flat-bottomed, **elevate** it on an inverted saucer.) Place on turntable if available and microwave on 30 percent power or LOW for 11 minutes (LW 13 minutes). (**Rotate** dish ¼ turn every 3 minutes if not using turntable.)

Increase power to HIGH and microwave for 8 to 10 minutes (LW 9½ to 12 minutes) or until cake comes away from the sides of the dish and no wet spots appear on top. (**Rotate** dish ¼ turn every 3 minutes if not using turntable.) Let **stand** on a hard heat-proof surface for 10 minutes, then invert onto a cake plate and let cool completely.

For glaze, combine confectioners' sugar, butter, lemon extract, and lemon zest in small bowl. Add milk until the mixture has the consistency of a glaze; drizzle over cake.

Troubleshooting: Be sure to use a 12-cup baking pan as the batter may rise over the sides of a smaller one.

Suggestions: You can vary the flavor by substituting orange Jell-O, orange extract, and zest for the lemon and using an orange or yellow cake mix.

Lemon Yogurt Bread

SERVES 6

EQUIPMENT: 9-inch ring mold, large mixing bowl, cooling rack
COOKING TIME: 9 to 11 minutes (Low wattage ovens 10¾ to 13 minutes)
STANDING TIME: 5 minutes

1 **egg, lightly beaten**
1 **8-ounce container plain yogurt**
1 **box Pillsbury Plus yellow cake mix**

2   teaspoons grated lemon zest
¼   cup chopped nuts

Grease ring mold and set aside. Combine egg and yogurt in large bowl. Add cake mix and lemon zest, **stirring** to combine. **Stir** in chopped nuts.

Spread batter in prepared mold. (If dish is flat-bottomed, **elevate** it on an inverted saucer.) Place on turntable if available and microwave on 70 percent power or MEDIUM-HIGH for 9 to 11 minutes (LW 10¾ to 13 minutes) or until a toothpick inserted in the center comes out clean. (**Rotate** dish ¼ turn every 3 minutes if not using turntable.) Let **stand** on a hard heat-proof surface for 5 minutes. Cool completely on a cooling rack.

Troubleshooting: Remove bread from microwave for standing time.

Suggestions: Wrap individual portions in a paper towel and heat on HIGH for 15 to 25 seconds. Spread with butter and serve for breakfast.

Mincemeat Bread with Orange Spread

SERVES 6

EQUIPMENT:	2-quart ring mold, large mixing bowl, cooling rack
COOKING TIME:	15 to 17 minutes (Low wattage ovens 17¾ to 20¼ minutes)
STANDING TIME:	5 to 10 minutes

1   package Nut Quick bread mix
½   cup plain yogurt
¾   cup water
1   egg
1   cup rum-flavored mincemeat
     Orange Spread (recipe follows)

Line bottom only of ring mold with wax paper cut to fit; set aside. Combine bread mix, yogurt, water, and egg in large bowl. **Stir** 50 to 75 strokes by hand, until dry particles are moistened. **Stir** in mincemeat, mixing well. Pour into prepared dish. (If dish is flat-bottomed, **elevate** it on an inverted saucer.) Place on turntable if available and microwave on 30 percent power or LOW for 8 minutes (LW 9½ minutes). (**Rotate** dish ¼ turn every 3 minutes if not using turntable.) Increase power to HIGH and microwave for 7 to 9 minutes (LW 8¼ to 10¾ minutes) or until a toothpick inserted comes out clean. (**Rotate** dish ¼ turn every 3 minutes if not using turntable.) Let **stand** on a hard heat-proof surface for 5 to 10 minutes. Turn out onto a cooling rack. Serve with orange spread.

ORANGE SPREAD

EQUIPMENT: small mixing bowl, electric mixer

1   8-ounce package cream cheese
⅓   cup orange marmalade

Remove cream cheese from foil wrapper and place in bowl. Microwave on 50 percent power or MEDIUM for 1 minute (LW 1¼ minutes). Add marmalade and beat until smooth and spreadable.

Orange Marmalade Pound Cake

Orange-flavored cakes have always been my personal favorites, and I'm always looking for new ways to incorporate the taste I love into something a little different.

SERVES 12 TO 14

EQUIPMENT: 12-cup bundt pan or tube dish, large mixing bowl, electric mixer
COOKING TIME: 16 to 18 minutes (Low wattage ovens 18 to 21 minutes)
STANDING TIME: 10 minutes

1 box Pillsbury Plus yellow cake mix
½ cup sour cream
⅓ cup butter-flavored Crisco
½ cup orange juice
1 tablespoon grated orange zest
3 eggs
½ cup orange marmalade
½ cup chopped nuts
Orange Glaze (recipe follows)

Grease bundt pan or tube dish and dust with sugar; set aside. In mixing bowl, blend first 6 ingredients on low speed until moistened. Beat on medium speed for 5 minutes. Fold in marmalade and nuts. Pour into prepared dish. Place on turntable if available and microwave on 30 percent power or LOW for 9 minutes (LW 10 minutes). (**Rotate** dish ½ turn once during cooking if not using turntable.)

Increase power to HIGH and microwave for 7 to 9 minutes (LW 8 to 11 minutes) or until cake begins to come away from the sides of the dish and there are no moist spots on top of the cake. (**Rotate** dish ½ turn every 3 minutes if not using turntable.) Let **stand** on a hard heat-proof surface for 10 minutes before inverting onto a serving plate. When cool, drizzle with glaze.

Troubleshooting: Remove cake from microwave for standing time.

Suggestions: Try using the Pineapple Icing that I use with the Mandarin Orange Cake on page 182 instead of the glaze, but I warn you it will be a hard choice, as they are both delicious.

ORANGE GLAZE

> EQUIPMENT: small mixing bowl

1   cup confectioners' sugar
1   to 2 tablespoons orange juice
½   teaspoon grated orange zest

In small bowl, blend all glaze ingredients together until smooth, using enough orange juice to make a glaze consistency.

Mandarin Orange Cake

SERVES 8 TO 10

> EQUIPMENT: 12-cup bundt pan or tube dish, large mixing bowl, electric mixer
> COOKING TIME: 20 to 22 minutes (Low wattage ovens 24 to 26 minutes)
> STANDING TIME: 10 minutes

1   package Pillsbury Plus yellow cake mix
4   eggs
¾   cup vegetable oil
1   11-ounce can mandarin orange segments in light syrup, undrained
1   tablespoon grated orange zest
**   Pineapple Icing (recipe follows)**

Grease bundt pan and dust with sugar; set aside. Place cake mix, eggs, oil, orange segments with syrup, and orange zest in mixing bowl. Blend at low speed until moistened, then increase speed to medium and beat for 5 minutes. Pour batter into prepared dish and place on turntable if available.

Microwave on 30 percent power or LOW for 11 minutes (LW 13 minutes). (**Rotate** dish ¼ turn every 3 minutes if not using turntable.) Increase power to HIGH and microwave for 9 to 11 minutes (LW 11 to 13 minutes) or until cake pulls away from the sides of the dish and no wet spots appear on the top of the cake. (**Rotate** dish ¼ turn every 3 minutes if not using turntable.) Let **stand** on a hard heat-proof surface for 10 minutes before removing to a cake plate to cool completely before frosting with pineapple icing.

Troubleshooting: Remove cake from microwave for standing time.

Suggestions: For a change of pace, glaze cake with Orange Glaze (page 181).
   Decorate iced cake with orange slices, coconut, or walnut halves.

PINEAPPLE ICING

EQUIPMENT: small mixing bowl

1   cup confectioners' sugar
¼   cup pineapple ice cream topping
2   to 3 teaspoons light cream

Combine all ingredients in small bowl, using enough cream to make a frosting consistency and blending well.

Peach Sponge Soufflé

SERVES 6 TO 8

EQUIPMENT:	2½-quart round casserole dish, 4-cup glass measure, medium mixing bowl
COOKING TIME:	28 to 33 minutes (Low wattage ovens 33 to 39 minutes)
STANDING TIME:	10 to 15 minutes

1   **store-bought prebaked sponge cake (2-layer cake size)**
½   **cup peach preserves**
1   **16-ounce can sliced peaches, drained**
3   **cups milk**
4   **eggs, beaten**
¼   **cup sugar**
⅛   **teaspoon salt**
1½ **teaspoons vanilla extract**

Cut sponge cake layers into 24 slices. Spread preserves between slices, making 12 sandwiches. Cut each sandwich into 3 cubes. Layer ½ the cubes in the bottom of casserole dish. Top with the entire can of drained peaches, arranging the remaining cubes over the peaches.

Place milk in glass measure and microwave on HIGH for 6 to 8 minutes (LW 7 to 9 minutes) or until hot. *(Do not scald or boil.)* In medium bowl, **whisk** the eggs and then add the sugar, salt, and vanilla. Gradually **whisk** the hot milk into the egg mixture. Pour the whisked mixture over the cake cubes and firmly press the cubes down into the milk so that the milk-egg mixture will be absorbed. Let **stand** for 5 minutes.

Cover dish with lid or plastic wrap, pulling back one corner to vent the steam. (If dish is flat-bottomed, **elevate** it on an inverted saucer.) Place on turntable if available and microwave on 50 percent power or MEDIUM for 22 to 25 minutes (LW 26 to 30 minutes) or until knife inserted in the center comes out clean. (**Rotate** dish ¼ turn every 4 minutes if not using turntable.) Let **stand, covered,** on a hard heat-proof surface for 5 to 10 minutes. Cool completely before serving.

Suggestions: Garnish with whipped topping and drizzle with additional peach preserves.

Peachy Delight

SERVES 4

EQUIPMENT:	1-quart round baking dish, 2 small mixing bowls
COOKING TIME:	11½ to 12 minutes (Low wattage ovens 13¾ to 14¼ minutes)
STANDING TIME:	none required

1   16-ounce can cling peach halves, drained, reserving syrup
¼   cup peach preserves
¼   cup brown sugar
½   teaspoon ground cinnamon
¼   teaspoon ground nutmeg
3   tablespoons butter or margarine, sliced
½   cup Lorna Doone or any vanilla cookie crumbs
2   tablespoons finely chopped nuts

Arrange peach halves, cut side up, in round baking dish. In small bowl, combine ¼ cup reserved peach syrup, preserves, brown sugar, cinnamon, and nutmeg, **stirring** well. Microwave on HIGH for 1½ to 2 minutes (LW 1¾ to 2¼ minutes) or until heated, **stirring** once.

Pour mixture over peach halves. (If dish is flat-bottomed, **elevate** it on an inverted saucer.) Place on turntable if available and microwave on 60 percent power or MEDIUM for 5 minutes (LW 6 minutes), **basting** with sauce several times.

Place butter in another small bowl and microwave on HIGH for about 1 minute (LW 1¼ minutes) or until melted. **Stir** in crumbs and nuts. Mound the topping into the peach cavities. Microwave on 60 percent power or MEDIUM for 4 minutes (LW 4¾ minutes) to heat peaches and topping. (**Rotate** dish ½ turn every 2 minutes if not using turntable.)

Suggestions: Serve each peach half with sauce remaining in the dish, top with whipped topping, and sprinkle with cinnamon.

PINEAPPLES

Pineapples must be picked when they are ripe. Next time you're in the market with a few minutes to spare, stand back and watch all the various techniques people employ to test ripeness. In my experience shaking, thumping, and pulling individual leaves from the crown won't help. However, I'm always interested in new testing methods, and if you have one that works, please let me know.

Pineapples are at the peak of their season from April through June. When selecting your fresh pineapples, try to get a large one that is as heavy as possible. A large, heavy pineapple usually means a good deal of edible fruit is inside. Try not to pick one that has brown leaves or bruises. Don't leave your pineapple on the counter; refrigerate it and use as soon as possible.

In case you're having trouble tackling your fresh pineapple, here's how: Cut off the top, just below the leaves, and slice off the stem end. Stand the pineapple up, stem end down, and slice rind off in thin strips. Remove the eyes by making diagonal cuts on both sides of each row of eyes. Quarter the fruit and remove the core, then slice, chunk, or wedge the fruit for salads, desserts, or main dishes.

Orange-Pineapple Float

SERVES 8 TO 10

EQUIPMENT:	2 8- or 9-inch round glass baking dishes, electric mixer, 6-cup glass measure
COOKING TIME:	10½ to 13 minutes (Low wattage ovens 12¼ to 15¾ minutes)
STANDING TIME:	10 minutes

    1 box Pillsbury Plus yellow cake mix
2½ cups crushed pineapple, undrained
    1 box (3½ ounces) vanilla pudding mix (not instant)
  ½ cup shredded coconut
    1 12-ounce container whipped topping *or* 1 pint whipping cream, whipped
  ½ cup chopped pecans

Prepare cake mix according to box directions, but add 1 teaspoon orange extract and beat at medium speed for 4 minutes. Grease baking dishes and dust with sugar or cover bottom of each dish with wax paper cut to fit the dish. Divide batter evenly between dishes. (If dish is flat-bottomed, **elevate** it on an inverted saucer.) Place on turntable if available and microwave, one layer at a time, on 30 percent power or LOW for 5 minutes (LW 6 minutes).

Increase power to HIGH and microwave for 2½ to 3 minutes (LW 2¾ to 3¾ minutes) or until no moist spots appear on top and cake begins to come away from sides of pan. (**Rotate** dish ½ turn every 2 minutes if not using turntable.) Let **stand** on a hard heat-proof surface for 10 minutes before inverting onto serving dish. Set aside and follow baking instructions for second layer.

Place crushed pineapple with juice, vanilla pudding mix, and coconut in glass measure. **Whisk** mixture together well and microwave on HIGH for 3 to 5 minutes (LW 3½ to 6 minutes) or until mixture is thick, **whisking** every minute. Let mixture cool. Once pineapple mixture has cooled, fold in whipped topping and pecans.

Cut each cake layer in half lengthwise, forming 4 layers. Spread pineapple mixture evenly between layers and over the top. Chill and serve cold.

Stella Novack's
Hawaiian Pineapple Cake

Stella Novack and her family have lived next door to my parents ever since I can remember. Stella is a marvelous cook, and her Polish recipes have always been among my favorites. This particular cake really sparked my interest because it is so cool and refreshing.

SERVES 10 TO 12

EQUIPMENT: 9 x 13-inch baking dish, large mixing bowl, electric mixer, cooling rack, 6-cup glass measure

COOKING TIME: 16 to 18½ minutes (Low wattage ovens 18¾ to 21¾ minutes)

STANDING TIME: 10 minutes

1   **box Pillsbury Plus yellow cake mix**
1   **cup water**
⅓   **cup vegetable oil**
3   **eggs**
1   **8-ounce package cream cheese**
1   **3½-ounce package instant vanilla pudding mix**
1   **cup cold milk**
1   **20-ounce can crushed pineapple, well drained**
1   **12-ounce container whipped topping, defrosted if frozen**
1   **cup sweetened flaked coconut**
⅔   **cup chopped drained maraschino cherries**

Line bottom of baking dish with wax paper cut to fit. Combine cake mix, water, oil, and eggs in large bowl and beat at low speed until moistened. Beat for 5 minutes at medium speed. Pour batter evenly into prepared dish. (If dish is flat-bottomed, **elevate** it on an inverted saucer.) Microwave on 50 percent power or MEDIUM for 7 minutes (LW 8 minutes).

Increase power to HIGH and microwave for 8 to 10 minutes (LW 9½ to 12 minutes), **rotating** dish ¼ turn every 3 minutes, until cake begins to come away from the sides and there are no moist spots on top. Let **stand** on a hard heat-proof surface for 10 minutes. Remove cake to cooling rack and cool completely. Place cooled cake on cake plate and prepare filling.

Remove cream cheese from wrapper and place in glass measure. Microwave on 50 percent power or MEDIUM for 1 to 1½ minutes (LW 1¼ to 1¾ minutes), just to soften. Add instant pudding and milk. Combine at low speed on mixer until blended. Spread mixture over cake. Spread well-drained pineapple over pudding filling. Frost entire cake with whipped topping, press coconut into the sides of the cake, and sprinkle chopped cherries over the top.

Troubleshooting: Watch cream cheese carefully as you want it to just soften, not melt.

Suggestions: An excellent addition to the buffet table for parties and showers.

Sweet Potato Dump Cake

The name "dump cake" has always fascinated me. I have read many recipes where you actually dump the ingredients into the baking dish, give them a whirl, and bake. This recipe works best in a round baking dish with an open center, so you'll have to "dump" the ingredients into a bowl first, but I guarantee the results will be worth the extra step.

SERVES 6

EQUIPMENT: 2-quart ring mold, small and medium mixing bowls

COOKING TIME: 9¾ to 12 minutes (Low wattage ovens 12 to 14¼ minutes)

STANDING TIME: 10 minutes

3-4 tablespoons finely chopped nuts for dusting ring mold
4 tablespoons unsalted butter, sliced
1¼ cups flour
1 cup sugar
2 teaspoons ground cinnamon
1 teaspoon baking soda
½ teaspoon salt
1 egg
1 4½-ounce jar Gerber strained sweet potatoes
1 8-ounce can crushed pineapple, undrained
1 teaspoon vanilla extract
confectioners' sugar for dusting cake

Grease ring mold, sprinkle with finely chopped nuts, and set aside. In small bowl, microwave butter on HIGH for 45 to 55 seconds (LW 1 to 1¼ minutes) or until melted. Place melted butter in medium bowl and add all remaining ingredients except confectioners' sugar. Mix with a fork until smooth and well blended. Pour batter into prepared dish. (If dish is flat-bottomed, **elevate** it on an inverted saucer.) Place on turntable if available and microwave on 30 percent power or LOW for 4 minutes (LW 5 minutes). (**Rotate** dish ¼ turn every 2 minutes if not using turntable.)

Increase power to HIGH and microwave for 5 to 7 minutes (LW 6 to 8 minutes) or until top appears almost dry. (**Rotate** dish ¼ turn every 3 minutes if not using turntable.) Let **stand** on a hard heat-proof surface for 10 minutes, then turn out onto serving plate. When completely cool, dust with confectioners' sugar.

Suggestions: If a ring mold isn't available, substitute a bundt pan.

Ricotta Cheese Cake Squares

SERVES 8 TO 10

EQUIPMENT:	2 large mixing bowls, electric mixer, 9 x 13-inch baking dish
COOKING TIME:	35 to 37 minutes (Low wattage ovens 41 to 44 minutes)
STANDING TIME:	10 minutes

1 **box Pillsbury Plus yellow cake mix**
1 **cup water**
⅓ **cup vegetable oil**
3 **eggs**
2 **pounds whole-milk ricotta cheese**
¾ **cup sugar**
4 **eggs, well beaten**
½ **teaspoon vanilla extract**
1 **teaspoon lemon extract**
1 **teaspoon lemon juice**
1 **tablespoon grated lemon zest**
1 **21-ounce can cherry, strawberry, or blueberry pie filling**

Mix cake mix, water, oil, and 3 eggs in large bowl at low speed until moistened. Beat for 5 minutes at medium speed and pour into baking dish.

In another large bowl, combine ricotta cheese, sugar, 4 eggs, vanilla, lemon extract, lemon juice, and lemon zest. Carefully pour over cake batter and spread evenly. (Be sure not to mix the cheese mixture with the cake batter; just layer it.) (If dish is flat-bottomed, **elevate** it on an inverted saucer.) Microwave on 30 percent power or LOW for 11 minutes (LW 13 minutes), **rotating** dish ¼ turn every 3 minutes.

Increase power to HIGH and microwave for 24 to 26 minutes (LW 28 to 31 minutes) or until a toothpick inserted in the center comes out clean and there is no raw batter on top of the cake, **rotating** dish ¼ turn every 3 minutes. Let **stand** on a hard heat-proof surface for 10 minutes. Cool completely and cut into squares. Serve with cherry, strawberry, or blueberry pie filling spooned over the top. Refrigerate any leftovers.

Troubleshooting: If your oven has only HIGH power, divide the cake batter and topping evenly between 2 8 x 12-inch baking dishes and microwave on HIGH for 8 to 12 minutes (LW 9 to 14 minutes). If recipe is prepared in a 9 x 13-inch dish on HIGH power, it will rise so fast that it will spill over the top of the dish.

Suggestions: Sliced fresh strawberries or peaches can be placed attractively over each serving in place of pie filling.

Strawberry Banana Cake

SERVES 8 TO 10

EQUIPMENT:	12-cup bundt pan, large mixing bowl, electric mixer, sifter, medium mixing bowl
COOKING TIME:	13 to 15 minutes (Low wattage ovens 15 to 17¾ minutes)
STANDING TIME:	10 minutes

½ **cup butter-flavored Crisco**
1¼ **cups sugar**
2 **eggs**
2 **cups flour**
1 **teaspoon baking powder**
¼ **teaspoon baking soda**
½ **teaspoon salt**
1 **cup sour cream or plain yogurt**
1 **teaspoon vanilla extract**
1 **cup (about 2 medium) mashed bananas**
¾ **cup strawberry preserves**

Grease bundt pan, dust with sugar or chopped nuts, and set aside. In large bowl, cream shortening and sugar together. Add eggs, one at a time, beating well after each addition. Sift together flour, baking powder, baking soda, and salt.

In medium bowl, **whisk** together sour cream, vanilla, and mashed bananas. Add alternately with flour mixture to creamed mixture, mixing until well blended. Spoon batter into prepared pan, place on turntable if available, and microwave on 50 percent power or MEDIUM for 6 minutes (LW 7 minutes). (**Rotate** dish ¼ turn every 3 minutes if not using turntable.)

Increase power to HIGH and microwave for 7 to 9 minutes (LW 8 to 10¾ minutes) or until cake begins to pull away from the sides of the dish and the top appears almost dry. (**Rotate** dish ¼ turn every 3 minutes if not using turntable.) Let **stand** on a hard heat-proof surface for 10 minutes, then turn out onto a serving plate. When completely cooled, split cake and spread with strawberry preserves.

Troubleshooting: Remove cake from oven for standing time.

Suggestions: For a different flavor, substitute peach, apricot, blueberry, cherry, or raspberry preserves.

Zucchini Nut Quick Bread

SERVES 6 TO 8

EQUIPMENT: 2-quart ring mold, large mixing bowl
COOKING TIME: 15 to 17 minutes (Low wattage ovens 16 to
18½ minutes)
STANDING TIME: 5 to 10 minutes

1   package Nut Quick bread mix
1   cup shredded (unpeeled) zucchini
1   teaspoon ground cinnamon
1   teaspoon vanilla extract
⅔   cup milk
2   tablespoons vegetable oil
1   egg
½   cup raisins

Line bottom only of ring mold with wax paper cut to fit and set aside. In large bowl, combine bread mix, zucchini, cinnamon, vanilla, milk, oil, and egg. **Stir** by hand for 50 to 75 strokes or until dry particles are moistened. **Stir** in raisins and pour into prepared dish. (If dish is flat-bottomed, **elevate** it on an inverted saucer.) Place on turntable if available and microwave on 30 percent power or LOW for 8 minutes (LW 9½ minutes). (**Rotate** dish ¼ turn every 3 minutes if not using turntable.)

Increase power to HIGH and microwave for 7 to 9 minutes (LW 8 to 10½ minutes) or until toothpick inserted in the center comes out clean. (**Rotate** dish ¼ turn every 3 minutes if not using turntable.) Let **stand** on a hard heat-proof surface for 5 to 10 minutes before removing to serving dish.

Troubleshooting: Be sure to remove cake from oven for standing.

Suggestions: For breakfast, wrap slice of bread in a paper towel and heat on HIGH for 15 to 25 seconds, or until just warm. Spread with butter or cream cheese.

Chocolate Zucchini Cake

SERVES 8 TO 10

EQUIPMENT:	large mixing bowl, electric mixer, 9 x 13-inch baking dish, small mixing bowl
COOKING TIME:	24 to 28 minutes (Low wattage ovens 28¼ to 32¾ minutes)
STANDING TIME:	10 minutes

1½ **cups sugar**
½ **cup margarine**
¼ **cup vegetable oil**
1 **teaspoon vanilla extract**
2 **eggs**
2½ **cups flour**
¼ **cup unsweetened cocoa powder**
1 **teaspoon baking soda**
½ **cup buttermilk**
2 **cups grated (unpeeled) zucchini**
¾ **cup Nestlé Mini-Morsels**
½ **cup chopped nuts**
⅓ **cup miniature semisweet chocolate chips**
1 **7-ounce jar marshmallow creme**

Combine sugar, margarine, oil, vanilla, and eggs in large bowl. Beat well. Add flour, cocoa, baking soda, and buttermilk, mixing well until blended thoroughly. Fold in zucchini, Nestlé Mini-Morsels, and nuts. Spread batter in baking dish. (If dish is flat-bottomed, **elevate** it on an inverted saucer.) Microwave on 50 percent power or MEDIUM for 7 minutes (LW 8 minutes).

Increase power to HIGH and microwave for 15 to 18 minutes (LW 18 to 21½ minutes) or until top is dry and cake begins to come away from the sides of the dish, **rotating** dish ½ turn every 4 minutes. Let **stand** on a hard heat-proof surface for 10 minutes.

To frost, place chocolate chips in small bowl and microwave on 50 percent power or MEDIUM for 2 to 3 minutes (LW 2¼ to 3¼ minutes), until soft and shiny, **stirring** every minute. Spoon tablespoons of marshmallow creme over warm cake and carefully spread with a knife dipped in hot water. Swirl melted chocolate through marshmallow creme to marble. Cool completely.

Troubleshooting: Be sure to remove cake from oven for standing.

Suggestions: If buttermilk isn't available, combine 1½ teaspoons of vinegar or lemon juice with enough milk to make ½ cup or combine equal parts sour cream and milk.

Apricot Dessert Sauce

How many times have you had a plain piece of cake or ice cream that needed just a quick garnish, but whipped topping just wouldn't do? Here are several ideas to help, each of them so good it's going to be a difficult choice.

MAKES 1 CUP

EQUIPMENT:	small mixing bowl
COOKING TIME:	2 to 3 minutes (Low wattage ovens 2¼ to 3½ minutes)
STANDING TIME:	none required

> **1   12-ounce jar apricot preserves**
> **¼   cup apricot-flavored brandy**

Combine preserves and brandy in small bowl. Microwave on HIGH for 2 to 3 minutes (LW 2¼ to 3½ minutes) or until heated, **stirring** once. Cool slightly before spooning over ice cream or pound cake.

Fresh Blueberry Sauce

My mother attended a "recipe exchange dinner," where each woman brought a favorite dish and provided the others attending with a copy of the recipe. This fresh blueberry sauce was served over cheesecake and became the "ladies' choice" of the evening.

MAKES 3 CUPS

EQUIPMENT:	6-cup glass measure
COOKING TIME:	9 to 11 minutes (Low wattage ovens 10½ to 12 minutes)
STANDING TIME:	25 minutes

3 cups fresh blueberries, sorted and rinsed
¼ cup minute tapioca
⅔ cup sugar
1¼ cups water
2 teaspoons lemon juice

Sort and rinse blueberries and set aside. Combine tapioca, sugar, and water in glass measure and allow to **stand** for 5 minutes. Add blueberries and **stir.** Microwave on HIGH for 9 to 11 minutes (LW 10½ to 13 minutes) or until mixture comes to a full boil, **stirring** every 2 minutes. Add lemon juice, **stir** well, and let **stand** on a hard heat-proof surface for 20 minutes. The sauce will thicken as it cools. **Stir** and serve warm over pound cake, ice cream, and especially cheesecake.

Suggestions: I pick blueberries in season and freeze them, unwashed, in plastic bags to use all winter. Sort and rinse the frozen berries and then go on with the recipe.

Blushing Cherry Topping

This sauce has a bit of a zip to it and can make a piece of plain cake look very inviting.

MAKES 3 CUPS

EQUIPMENT: 4-cup glass measure
COOKING TIME: 5½ to 6½ minutes (Low wattage ovens 6½ to 7¾ minutes)
STANDING TIME: none required

1 20-ounce can cherry pie filling
½ cup burgundy
½ cup red currant jelly
⅛ teaspoon ground cinnamon

Combine all ingredients in glass measure. Microwave on 80 percent power or MEDIUM-HIGH for 5½ to 6½ minutes (LW 6½ to 7¾ minutes) or until heated but not boiling, **stirring** every 2 minutes. Serve hot or cool slightly.

Suggestions: Great over gingerbread, waffles, pancakes, and, of course, ice cream.

RHUBARB

Rhubarb's nickname is "pieplant"—many years ago it grew in almost every garden and made the most delicious and inexpensive pies. Choose firm, crisp, brightly colored stalks. Avoid very thin or overly large and tough stalks; as the young ones will be the most tender. Be sure to remove and throw away the leaves, which contain poisonous oxalic acid. Dark red stalks with many leaves indicate a very tart flavor, while bright pink stalks with a few small leaves are less acidic and will have a milder flavor. Rhubarb, which contains a large supply of potassium, will wilt rapidly at room temperature but will keep in the refrigerator for up to 4 weeks if you remove and discard the leaves, wash and pat dry stalks, and wrap them loosely in plastic wrap. One pound of fresh rhubarb makes 2 cups of cooked fruit.

Rosy Rhubarb Sauce

MAKES 4 CUPS

EQUIPMENT: 2-quart round casserole dish
COOKING TIME: 14 to 16 minutes (Low wattage ovens 15 to 18½ minutes)
STANDING TIME: 4 minutes

2 pounds rhubarb, cut into 1-inch pieces
⅓ cup water
¾ cup sugar
1 or 2 drops red food coloring
⅛ teaspoon lemon juice

Place rhubarb pieces and water in casserole dish. **Cover** with lid or plastic wrap, pulling back one corner to vent the steam. (If dish is flat-bottomed, **elevate** it on an inverted saucer.) Place on turntable if available and microwave on HIGH for 13 to 16 minutes (LW 14 to 17½ minutes) or until rhubarb is tender, **stirring** several times during cooking time. (**Rotate** dish ¼ turn when stirring if not using turntable.)

Stir in sugar, **cover,** and microwave on HIGH for 1 minute (LW 1¼ minutes). Let **stand, covered,** on a hard heat-proof surface, for 4 minutes. Add 1 to 2 drops of red food coloring, as desired, and **stir** in lemon juice. **Stir** mixture well and serve warm or cold.

Troubleshooting: Be sure to cut rhubarb into uniformly sized pieces to ensure that all pieces cook evenly.

Suggestions: For a variation, try my favorite: add 1 cup sliced fresh strawberries when you add the sugar and microwave for 2 minutes (LW 2¼ minutes) instead of 1 minute.

Delicious when served with any type of meat or chicken or over ice cream, cheesecake, or a slice of pound cake.

Strawberry Rhubarb Chill

SERVES 6 TO 8

EQUIPMENT:	2-quart round casserole dish, electric mixer, small mixing bowl, dessert dishes
COOKING TIME:	6 to 9 minutes (Low wattage ovens 7½ to 10½ minutes)
STANDING TIME:	4 minutes

> **3** cups (1½ pounds) rhubarb, cut into ½-inch chunks
> **1** cup orange juice
> **1** 3-ounce box strawberry Jell-O gelatin
> **½** cup whipping cream
> **3** tablespoons confectioners' sugar
> **6** cleaned fresh strawberries

Place rhubarb and orange juice in casserole dish. **Cover** with lid or plastic wrap, pulling back one corner to vent the steam. (If dish is flat-bottomed, **elevate** it on an inverted saucer.) Place on turntable if available and microwave on HIGH for 6 to 9 minutes (LW 7½ to 10½ minutes) or until rhubarb is crisp-tender. Let **stand, covered,** for 4 minutes. After standing, thoroughly **stir** in powdered gelatin until dissolved. Set dish aside to cool.

Beat whipping cream until foamy. Gradually add confectioners' sugar and continue beating until soft peaks form. Fold whipped cream into gelatin mixture and spoon into dessert dishes. Chill until firm. Garnish each dish with a fresh strawberry before serving.

Suggestions: Desserts always look even more inviting when served in footed champagne or dessert glasses. To stretch to serve 8, divide mixture into 8 dessert dishes and top each serving with whipped cream before adding a large fresh strawberry.

Holidays

NEW YEAR'S DAY

New Year's Good Luck Cake

Rather than just hope for a healthy and prosperous New Year, give it a helping hand. My grandmother's Good Luck Cake may be just the ticket. Grandma recalled that serving this cake was an old European custom at family get-togethers, brought to this country by our ancestors. This cake is easy to bake, delicious to eat, and its hidden secret remains a mystery to the very last slice.

SERVES 8 TO 10

EQUIPMENT:	12-cup bundt pan, large mixing bowl, electric mixer, sieve, pastry brush
COOKING TIME:	16 to 18 minutes (Low wattage ovens 19¾ to 21½ minutes)
STANDING TIME:	10 minutes

½ **cup finely chopped almonds**
1 **box Pillsbury Plus yellow cake mix**
3 **eggs**
⅓ **cup vegetable oil**
1 **cup water**
2 **tablespoons grated orange zest**
1 **whole almond, shelled**

GLAZE
½ **cup apricot, pineapple, or peach preserves**
2 **teaspoons pineapple or orange juice**

Grease bundt pan and sprinkle with finely chopped almonds. Set aside. Combine cake mix, eggs, oil, and water in large bowl at low speed on electric mixer until moistened, then beat for 5 minutes at medium speed. **Stir** in orange zest.

Pour batter into prepared pan and press the whole almond about ½ inch below the surface of the batter. Place pan on turntable if available and microwave on 30 percent power or LOW for 11 minutes (LW 13¼ minutes). (**Rotate** dish ¼ turn every 3 minutes if not using a turntable.)

Increase power to HIGH and microwave for 5 to 7 minutes (LW 6 to 8¼ minutes) or until there are no moist spots on the top of the cake and it begins to pull away from the sides of the pan. (**Rotate** dish ½ turn after 3 minutes if not using a turntable.) Allow dish to **stand** on a hard heat-proof surface for 10 minutes.

Invert cake onto serving plate and cool completely before glazing. For glaze, press preserves through a sieve and combine with the juice. Using a pastry brush, cover the top and sides of the cake with glaze.

Troubleshooting: If cake top looks uneven during cooking, rotate dish more often.

Suggestions: Grandma always used a yellow cake, but feel free to substitute any flavor of your choice.

A colored Jordan almond might be a pretty alternative to a plain almond, especially if children are looking to see whose slice contains the surprise.

CHINESE NEW YEAR

If I had wondered whether there was a magic lamp that could grant me a cooking wish, I found it during Chinese New Year when I visited the Silver Palace Restaurant in East Haven, Connecticut. Owner Billy Gee asked, "Would you like to watch our chefs in the kitchen?" Believe me, he didn't have to ask twice. Armed with pen and paper, I entered a kitchen completely different from any I had ever seen. One entire wall housed a specially made stainless-steel unit that held a row of various-sized woks. Underneath each wok were gas jets that sent adjustable amounts of very high heat flaming up to the wok.

In the center of this long row of woks was an enormous pot even bigger than an old-fashioned washtub. Simmering inside was chicken broth, made fresh and continually all day; in some way it's included in most dishes.

Head Chef Yu worked with a very long-handled spoonlike tool that had obviously seen a lot of action. It's his special utensil, and it always goes with him, just as other chefs might carry and use their own knives from kitchen to kitchen.

The cooking process in the super-hot woks is even faster than microwaving. But try this New Year special dish in your microwave.

Silver Palace Supreme

SERVES 6

EQUIPMENT:	2 small mixing bowls, 10-inch covered browning dish
COOKING TIME:	15 to 18 minutes (Low wattage ovens 16¾ to 21¾ minutes)
STANDING TIME:	Marinating—15 to 20 minutes
	Finished dish—3 minutes

¼　pound boneless, skinless chicken breast, thinly sliced
¼　pound flank steak or tender beef, thinly sliced
2　tablespoons minced garlic
¼　teaspoon minced fresh ginger
1　tablespoon rice wine
2　tablespoons peanut oil
1　10-ounce paper-covered box frozen broccoli spears
4　jumbo shrimp, peeled
¼　pound fresh sea scallops
¼　pound fresh lobster meat
¼　pound roast pork, thinly sliced
1　can (1 cup) whole baby corn, drained (available at Chinese grocery stores)
½　can (1 cup) water chestnuts, drained
½　can (1 cup) bamboo shoots
1　10-ounce box frozen snow peas, defrosted
⅔　cup thinly sliced celery
1　cup chopped bok choy

SAUCE
2　tablespoons soy sauce
1　tablespoon oyster sauce
1　teaspoon rice wine
2　tablespoons chicken broth
½　teaspoon sugar
½　teaspoon salt
¼　teaspoon pepper
¼　teaspoon dark sesame oil
1　tablespoon cornstarch

Combine chicken and beef in small bowl. Mix in 1 tablespoon of the minced garlic, ginger, rice wine, and 1 tablespoon of the peanut oil. Let **stand** for 15 to 20 minutes.

Place paper-covered box of broccoli spears on 2 layers of paper towel on oven floor and microwave on HIGH for 5 minutes (LW 6 minutes); **drain** and set aside.

Preheat 10-inch browning dish for 5 to 7 minutes (LW 6 to 8 minutes), or according to manufacturer's instructions. While dish is preheating, **whisk** together all sauce ingredients in another small bowl and set aside.

Using pot holders, remove hot browning dish from microwave to a hard heat-proof surface. Coat dish with remaining tablespoon peanut oil and add remaining tablespoon minced garlic. To sizzling garlic, add chicken and beef, **stirring** with wooden spoon to prevent sticking.

Cover and microwave on HIGH for 1 to 2 minutes (LW 1¼ to 2¼ minutes). Add shrimp, scallops, lobster, and pork. **Cover** and microwave on HIGH for 2 minutes (LW 2½ minutes). **Stir** and add all remaining vegetables, including broccoli spears. **Cover** and microwave on HIGH for 4 to 5 minutes (LW 4¾ to 6 minutes) or until vegetables are crisp-tender.

Mix sauce ingredients into dish and microwave, **uncovered,** on HIGH for 3 to 4 minutes (LW 3½ to 4¾ minutes). **Cover** and let **stand** for 3 minutes. Serve with hot cooked rice.

Troubleshooting: If frozen vegetable box is covered with a foil wrapper, remove it before microwaving as it will arc and may ignite the paper towels.

Do not try to cover browning dish with plastic wrap or wax paper. Dish is very hot and should be covered with its own heat-proof lid only.

Fish finishes cooking while the dish stands, so do not overcook.

Silver Palace Scallop Beef

SERVES 4

EQUIPMENT:	10-inch covered browning dish, small mixing bowl
COOKING TIME:	7 to 10 minutes (Low wattage ovens 8¼ to 12 minutes)
STANDING TIME:	3 minutes

2 tablespoons soybean or peanut oil
2 garlic cloves, minced
6 thin slices fresh ginger, 4 grated and 2 minced
½ pound flank steak, thinly sliced
1 cup shredded bok choy
1 8-ounce box frozen snow peas, defrosted
½ red bell pepper, cut into ½-inch slices
½ cup drained whole baby corn (available at Chinese grocery stores)
¼ cup sliced bamboo shoots
¼ cup sliced water chestnuts
1 cup broccoli flowerets
6 scallions, white parts only, cut into ½-inch slices
½ pound bay scallops

SAUCE
⅛ teaspoon salt
½ teaspoon sugar
1 tablespoon hoisin sauce
1 tablespoon oyster sauce
1 tablespoon rice wine or sweet white wine

Preheat a 10-inch covered browning dish according to manufacturer's instructions, usually 5 to 7 minutes (LW 6 to 8 minutes). Using pot holder, remove dish from microwave to hard heat-proof surface. Add oil, garlic, and minced ginger, swirling in dish to keep from sticking. Add beef and **stir** with a wooden spoon to prevent sticking. Microwave, **uncovered,** on HIGH for 2 minutes (LW 2½ minutes). **Whisk** sauce ingredients together in small bowl.

Add all the vegetables, **stirring** to combine. **Cover** and microwave on HIGH for 3 to 4 minutes (LW 3½ to 4¾ minutes) or until vegetables are crisp-tender.

Add scallops and sauce, **stirring** to coat meat and vegetables. **Cover** again and microwave on HIGH for 2 to 4 minutes (LW 2¼ to 4¾ minutes) or until scallops are opaque and tender. Let **stand, covered,** for 3 minutes and serve with hot cooked rice.

Troubleshooting: Do not try to cover browning dish with plastic wrap or wax paper. Dish is very hot and needs to be covered with its own heat-proof lid.

Scallops will continue to cook while standing, so cook only until tender; do not overcook.

BROWNING DISHES

Browning dishes are specially constructed dishes that gather microwave energy and thus get hot. The surface of the dish becomes the closest thing to a frying pan there is, right now, for use in the microwave. Because the surface gets hot, you must use pot holders to avoid burning yourself or dropping the dish. When stir-frying, a deep microwave browning dish with a cover is necessary. There are flat browning skillets on the market for steaks, patties, and sandwiches, but they do not have sides or a cover. Don't try to cover a browning dish that does not come with a cover with plastic wrap or wax paper as the heat of the dish may burn or melt the coverings; use only the cover that comes with it.

VALENTINE'S DAY

Sweetheart Cake

A heart-shaped cake is appropriate for those of any age on Valentine's Day.

SERVES 10 TO 15

EQUIPMENT: 8-inch round and square baking dishes, large mixing bowl, electric mixer, cooling rack

COOKING TIME: 14 to 16 minutes per layer (Low wattage ovens 16¾ to 19¼ minutes per layer)

STANDING TIME: 10 minutes

1 box Pillsbury Plus yellow cake mix
1 cup water
⅓ cup oil
3 eggs
1 12-ounce container whipped topping, defrosted if frozen
2 20-ounce cans cherry pie filling

Line bottom only of round and square baking dishes with wax paper cut to fit and set aside. Place cake mix, water, oil, and eggs in large bowl and blend on low speed with mixer until moistened. Increase speed to medium and beat for 5 minutes. Pour ½ the batter into each of the prepared baking dishes. (If dishes are flat-bottomed, **elevate** them on an inverted saucer.) Place on turntable if available and microwave one layer at a time on 30 percent power or LOW for 11 minutes (LW 13¼ minutes). (**Rotate** dish ¼ turn every 3 minutes if not using turntable.)

Increase power to HIGH and microwave for 3 to 5 minutes (LW 3½ to 6 minutes) or until cake pulls away from the sides of the dish and top appears almost dry. (**Rotate** dish ½ turn once during cooking time if not using a turntable.)

Let each dish **stand** on a hard heat-proof surface for 10 minutes, remove cake from dish, and cool completely on a cooling rack.

Decorating: Cover a 16-inch-diameter circle of heavy cardboard (I got mine from a pizza restaurant) with foil to form a cake plate. Place the square cake on the foil-covered base in a diamond position. Cut the round cake in half and place the cut sides of each half next to the 2 top sides of the diamond, forming a heart.

Place a small amount of whipped topping on the cut sides of the round cake to keep them in place. Frost the entire heart with the balance of whipped topping, building a rim around the outer top edge to keep the pie filling from running over the edges.

Fill the entire top of the heart with pie filling and refrigerate.

Suggestions: This cake is excellent for showers, buffets, or family parties. You can change the fruit filling flavor to correspond to taste and the occasion.

SAINT PATRICK'S DAY

Malachi McCormick's book, *Irish Country Cooking*, is a personal collection of recipes, lore, proverbs, and quotations selected to "stimulate a nostalgic appetite." McCormick sprinkles Irish folklore and customs among his special recipes.

He "dismisses as spurious the claim that corned beef and cabbage is Ireland's national dish—without in any way disparaging its delectability." Ironically, he says, "corned beef was largely unknown to many Irish people until they set foot in the famine boats that bore them away to the New World."

If corned beef and cabbage isn't, according to McCormick, the national dish, then what is? He feels the honor should go to colcannon, made from boiled new potatoes, boiled white cabbage, and boiled leeks or onions, to which are added butter, milk, mace, and wild garlic.

Colcannon

(Adapted from Malachi McCormick's *Irish Country Cooking*, published by Clarkson N. Potter, Inc.)

SERVES 6

EQUIPMENT:	12 x 8-inch baking dish, deep 2-quart round casserole dish, 4-cup glass measure, potato masher
COOKING TIME:	23 to 33 minutes (Low wattage ovens 27¼ to 39½ minutes)
STANDING TIME:	2 to 3 minutes

    1 pound green cabbage, core removed
    ¼ cup water
    2 pounds unpeeled potatoes in 1-inch cubes
    ¼ cup water
    ½ teaspoon salt
    2 medium leeks, thoroughly washed and sliced
    1 cup milk
    ½ teaspoon ground mace
    2 garlic cloves, minced
    salt and pepper to taste
    ½ cup (¼ pound) unsalted butter

Cut cored cabbage into 4 wedges. Place wedges in baking dish with the broader ends to the outside of the dish and add ¼ cup water. **Cover** with plastic wrap, pulling back one corner to vent the steam. (If dish is flat-bottomed, **elevate** it on an inverted saucer.) Microwave on HIGH for 12 to 15 minutes (LW 14¼ to 18 minutes) or until tender. Let **stand, covered,** for 2 to 3 minutes. After standing, **drain,** chop, and set aside.

    Place potato cubes in casserole dish. Mix salt into ¼ cup water and add to potatoes. **Cover** with lid or plastic wrap, pulling back one corner to vent the steam. (If dish is flat-bottomed, **elevate** it on an inverted saucer.) Microwave on HIGH for 7 to 10 minutes (LW 8¼ to 12 minutes) or until fork-tender; **drain** and set aside.

    Place milk and leeks in glass measure. Microwave on 50 percent power or MEDIUM for 4 to 8 minutes (LW 4¾ to 9½ minutes) or until tender, **stirring** every 2 minutes.

    To drained potatoes, add mace, garlic, salt, and pepper. Mash with potato masher and add leeks and milk, **mixing** to combine. Mash in cabbage and then butter.

    Transfer the mixture to an oven-proof dish, make a furrowed pattern by drawing a fork along the surface, and place under a conventional broiler to brown.

Troubleshooting: The texture you want to achieve is smooth and buttery potato with interesting pieces of leek and cabbage well distributed throughout.

PASSOVER

During the Passover holiday everything used for food preparation must be koshered, and that includes the microwave. To kosher the microwave, begin by filling a completely clean micro-safe container, one that has not been used for 24 hours, with water. Place the filled container in the microwave, microwave on HIGH for 10 to 12 minutes, and let it steam heavily. Once the interior is heavily misted, completely wipe out the top, sides, and bottom of the oven with a soft cloth.

When you're ready to cook, use a flat piece of Styrofoam (or any other thick object that is not metal and doesn't get hot) to separate the bottom of the oven from the cooking dish. I experimented with both wooden and acrylic cutting boards and discovered that they both got hot. I also tested a piece of Styrofoam for 2 minutes with a glass of water on it, and it stayed cool. Since the piece of Styrofoam I used had a depression in it, I filled the cavity with water and microwaved for 2 minutes on HIGH power to find the Styrofoam didn't get hot or melt, so Styrofoam is my recommendation. Or you might try using a meat rack or saucer.

Whenever possible, keep the food you are microwaving for Passover covered from all sides. If you're covering your dishes with plastic wrap, be sure to pull back one corner to allow the steam an avenue of escape, or it will melt the plastic.

TESTING THE SAFETY OF
UTENSILS FOR MICROWAVE USE

Place a glass filled with water inside or right next to—touching—the utensil whose safety you question. Microwave on HIGH power for 1 to 2 minutes. If the test piece remains cool, it is safe for microwave use. Test any questionable pieces of glass, plastic, crockery, or ceramic dishes you plan to use first: some of them are made of material that attracts microwaves, and they may get hot. When a utensil gets hot, it is absorbing some of the microwave energy that is supposed to be cooking the food. Hot utensils can burn you, crack, or break with repeated use, and your food will take longer to cook because it's not getting all of the available energy.

Mom's Chicken Soup

SERVES 6

EQUIPMENT:	deep 3-quart round casserole dish, strainer
COOKING TIME:	20 to 25 minutes (Low wattage ovens 24 to 30 minutes)
STANDING TIME:	none required

1   **2½- to 3½-pound broiler-fryer chicken, cut up and skinned**
2   **large celery stalks, cut into 4 pieces**
3   **carrots, cut into 2-inch pieces**
1   **medium onion, peeled**
½   **teaspoon salt**
⅛   **teaspoon pepper**
1½   **quarts water**
     Matzo Balls (recipe follows)

Arrange chicken pieces in casserole dish with the thickest parts to the outside of the dish. Add all remaining ingredients except matzo balls. **Cover** dish with lid or plastic wrap, pulling back one corner to vent the steam. (If dish is flat-bottomed, **elevate** it on an inverted saucer.) Place on turntable if available and microwave on HIGH for 20 to 25 minutes (LW 24 to 30 minutes), turning chicken over after 10 minutes. (**Rotate** dish ½ turn every 10 minutes if not using turntable.) Microwave until chicken is no longer pink near the bone or until it falls easily away from the bone. Skim away any fat and remove the chicken. (Cool chicken and refrigerate for use in another recipe.)

Remove carrots to a large serving bowl and strain the soup into the same bowl. Adjust salt and pepper to taste. **Cover** tightly to keep warm while you prepare matzo balls. When matzo balls are done, carefully remove them from water and transfer to the warm clear soup. Serve pieces of carrots with the matzo balls and soup.

Suggestions: Use a micro-safe bowl to keep soup warm so you can reheat before serving, should it cool.

MATZO BALLS

Have you ever been seated at a seder table eating your matzo ball soup, trying to come up with a polite adjective to describe the "baseball-like" matzo balls you were eating? Hard matzo balls can be a problem but not with this recipe. These little morsels should be light and fluffy—and of course they're delicious.

MAKES 12 DUMPLINGS

EQUIPMENT:	small mixing bowl, deep 3-quart round casserole dish
COOKING TIME:	18 to 21 minutes (Low wattage ovens 21½ to 25 minutes)
STANDING TIME:	none required

2 **eggs**
2 **tablespoons vegetable oil**
1 **packet (2½ ounces) Matzo Ball Mix**
1½ **quarts hot water**

Blend eggs and oil in small bowl and add packet of dry matzo ball mix. Using a fork, **stir** until evenly mixed. **Cover** bowl and place in refrigerator for 15 minutes.

Place hot water in casserole dish. (If dish is flat-bottomed, **elevate** it on an inverted saucer.) Microwave on HIGH for 5 minutes (LW 6 minutes) or until a rolling boil begins.

With wet hands, form 12 1-inch-diameter balls and drop them into the boiling water. **Cover** with lid or plastic wrap, pulling back one corner to vent the steam. Place on turntable if available and microwave on HIGH for 3 to 4 minutes (LW 3½ to 4¾ minutes) or until water comes to a boil again.

Reduce power to 50 percent or MEDIUM and microwave for 10 to 12 minutes (LW 12 to 14¼ minutes). (**Rotate** dish ½ turn every 5 minutes if not using turntable.)

Troubleshooting: Be sure to wet your hands well before forming mixture into balls to keep them from sticking to dry hands.

Suggestions: The completed soup with matzo balls freezes beautifully. Any extra matzo balls may be added to stews, pot roasts, or roast brisket during the last 15 minutes of cooking. Be sure to baste with gravy for added flavor.

Borscht with Meatballs

Borscht is another Passover favorite, and this recipe adds a little excitement to plain beet soup.

SERVES 4

EQUIPMENT: medium mixing bowl, deep 10-inch round baking dish, deep 3-quart round casserole dish

COOKING TIME: 18 to 21 minutes (Low wattage ovens 21½ to 25 minutes)

STANDING TIME: none required

MEATBALLS
- ½ **pound lean ground beef**
- 1 **egg, slightly beaten**
- ¼ **cup cold water**
- 3 **tablespoons matzo meal**
- 1 **tablespoon snipped fresh parsley**
- ½ **teaspoon salt**
- ¼ **teaspoon pepper**

SOUP
- 1 **1-quart jar borscht with beets**
- 1 **10½-ounce can chicken broth**

Combine all meatball ingredients in medium bowl. Shape mixture into 28 uniformly sized meatballs and arrange in baking dish. **Cover** with wax paper. (If dish is flat-bottomed, **elevate** it on an inverted saucer.) Microwave on HIGH for 3 minutes (LW 3½ minutes), **rotating** dish ½ turn once during cooking time. Drain any liquid and rearrange meatballs, bring those in the center to the outside edges and the ones along the edges into the center.

Cover again and microwave on HIGH for 1 to 2 minutes (LW 1¼ to 2½ minutes) or until the center is no longer pink. **Drain, cover** with foil to keep warm, and set aside.

Place borscht and chicken soup in deep casserole dish and **stir** well. **Cover** with lid or plastic wrap, pulling back one corner to vent the steam. (If dish is flat-bottomed, **elevate** it on an inverted saucer.) Place on turntable if available and microwave on HIGH for 10 minutes (LW 12 minutes), **stirring** every 5 minutes. (**Rotate** dish ½ turn when stirring if not using turntable.)

Add meatballs, stir, and **cover** again. Microwave on HIGH for 4 to 6 minutes (LW 4¾ to 7 minutes) or until soup and meatballs are heated. (**Rotate** dish ½ turn when stirring if not using turntable.)

Troubleshooting: The microwave extracts ⅓ more fat from meat than conventional frying does. Be sure to drain fat from meatballs as they cook or they will be very greasy.

Suggestions: Follow an old European custom and add broken matzos to the soup before serving.

Mama's Gefilte Fish Patties

Gefilte fish is usually served as an appetizer on lettuce leaves but this recipe turns it into a really different main dish, wonderful on nights when only dairy is being served.

SERVES 4

EQUIPMENT:	small and medium mixing bowls, dinner plate
COOKING TIME:	9 to 13 minutes (Low wattage ovens 10½ to 15¼ minutes)
STANDING TIME:	none required

1 24-ounce jar gefilte fish, drained
1 egg, slightly beaten
3 tablespoons margarine, sliced
¼ cup grated carrot
¼ cup chopped onion
¼ cup chopped celery
1 tablespoon snipped fresh parsley
1 teaspoon sugar
2 tablespoons matzo meal
Cucumber Sauce (recipe follows)

In medium bowl, mash drained fish and add beaten egg; set aside. Place margarine, carrot, onion, celery, and parsley in small bowl. **Cover** with plastic wrap, pulling back one corner to vent the steam, and microwave on HIGH for 3 to 5 minutes (LW 3½ to 6 minutes) or until crisp-tender. **Stir** into fish mixture and add sugar and matzo meal.

Shape mixture into 4 uniformly sized patties and arrange in a circle on dinner plate. **Cover** with wax paper. (If plate is flat-bottomed, **elevate** it on an inverted saucer.) Place on turntable if available and microwave on HIGH for 6 to 8 minutes (LW 7 to 9¼ minutes) or until heated through. (**Rotate** dish ½ turn every 4 minutes if not using turntable.) Serve warm or cold with cucumber sauce.

CUCUMBER SAUCE

MAKES ABOUT 1½ CUPS

EQUIPMENT: small mixing bowl

½ cup sour cream
½ cup mayonnaise
½ cup chopped peeled and seeded cucumber
2 tablespoons chopped scallions
1 large garlic clove, minced
1 teaspoon prepared horseradish
½ teaspoon salt

Combine all ingredients in small bowl and refrigerate for several hours to blend flavors.

Suggestions: This sauce makes an excellent dip served with carrot sticks, green bell pepper strips, fresh cauliflower and broccoli flowerets, and cherry tomatoes. You can also serve this sauce as a dressing over lettuce wedges.

EASTER

Easter Basket Cake

This lovely cake makes a pretty centerpiece for your Easter dessert table.

SERVES 8 TO 10

EQUIPMENT:	11 x 7-inch baking dish, strip of white cardboard ¼ inch wide and 17 inches long, frosting bag and decorating tube no. 30
COOKING TIME:	15 to 17 minutes (Low wattage ovens 18 to 20¾ minutes)
STANDING TIME:	10 minutes

1 box Pillsbury Plus yellow cake mix
½ pint ripe fresh strawberries
1 12-ounce container whipped topping, defrosted if frozen

Prepare cake mix according to box directions, beating for 5 minutes at medium speed.

For each layer, line only the bottom of baking dish with wax paper cut to fit. Pour ½ the prepared batter into dish. (If dish is flat-bottomed, **elevate** it on an inverted saucer.) Place on turntable if available and microwave on 30 percent power or LOW for 11 minutes (LW 13¼ minutes). (**Rotate** dish ¼ turn every 3 minutes if not using turntable.)

Increase power to HIGH and microwave for 4 to 6 minutes (LW 4¾ to 7½ minutes) or until cake pulls away from the sides of the dish and there are no moist spots on the top of the cake. (**Rotate** dish ½ turn halfway through baking if not using turntable.) Let **stand** on hard heat-proof surface for 10 minutes, then invert onto a cooling rack. Repeat directions for second layer.

Decorating: Clean, dry, and slice strawberries in half. Place one completely cooled layer on a doily-covered serving dish and cover with a small amount of whipped topping. Place the second layer on top and, reserving ¾ cup whipped topping, use the balance to frost sides and top of entire cake.

Using ½ cup of the reserved topping and decorating tube no. 30, decorate around the top edge of the cake to resemble the outer edge of a basket. Fill the entire top of the cake with the halved strawberries.

Insert the ends of the strip of cardboard into the top sides of the cake to form a handle. Decorate the handle with tube no. 30 and remaining ¼ cup reserved topping.

Suggestions: Any fresh or canned fruit may be used in place of the fresh strawberries.

You may also substitute a can of prepared frosting for the whipped topping and use candy Easter eggs in place of strawberries.

HARD-COOKING EGGS FOR EASTER

Please don't even think of putting a whole raw egg in its shell into your microwave oven. The steam that builds up inside the egg will cause it to explode. In fact, there have been cases where the explosion has caused severe damage to the microwave.

You can't even reheat conventionally hard-cooked and peeled eggs without first slicing or quartering them. They've been known to explode in the face of the person they are served to.

Boil your eggs on your conventional stove and if you plan on eating leftover dyed Easter eggs, be sure to color them with non-toxic vegetable dyes and store them in the refrigerator. Hard-cooked eggs will keep for up to one week in the refrigerator.

To shell your egg, tap it gently all over to crack the shell. Roll the egg between your hands to loosen the shell, then peel, starting at the large end. Hold the egg under cold running water or dip in a bowl of water to help ease off the shell.

Deviled Egg Casserole

SERVES 4

EQUIPMENT:	2 small mixing bowls, 1½-quart round baking dish, 4-cup glass measure
COOKING TIME:	9 to 14½ minutes (Low wattage ovens 11½ to 17 minutes)
STANDING TIME:	none required

6 hard-cooked eggs, shelled
¼ cup mayonnaise
½ teaspoon prepared brown mustard
¼ cup finely minced ham
1 tablespoon finely chopped onion (optional)
dash of salt
dash of pepper
dash of paprika

CHEESE SAUCE
3 tablespoons butter or margarine, sliced
2 tablespoons flour
¼ teaspoon salt
dash of pepper
1 cup milk
½ cup shredded Cheddar or American cheese

TOPPING
2 tablespoons butter or margarine, sliced
½ cup Ritz or other cracker crumbs
1 tablespoon snipped fresh parsley
½ teaspoon paprika

Halve the shelled hard-cooked eggs lengthwise. Remove the yolks and place in a small bowl; set aside the whites. Mash the yolks with a fork or press through a sieve.

Add the mayonnaise, mustard, ham, onion, salt, pepper, and paprika and mix until well blended. Fill egg white halves, using 1 tablespoon of yolk mixture per egg half. Place stuffed egg halves in round baking dish and set aside.

For the sauce, place 3 tablespoons butter in glass measure and microwave on HIGH for 30 to 45 seconds (LW 40 to 60 seconds) or until melted. **Whisk** in flour, salt, and pepper until well blended and a smooth paste forms.

Gradually **whisk** in milk until well blended and smooth. Microwave, **uncovered,** on HIGH for 4 to 6 minutes (LW 5 to 7 minutes), until sauce thickens and coats the whisk, **whisking** every minute. Add cheese, **whisking** until melted and sauce is smooth. Pour sauce over and around stuffed eggs and set aside.

Place 2 tablespoons butter in small bowl and microwave on HIGH for 30 to 45 seconds (LW 40 to 55 seconds) or until melted. **Stir** in crumbs, parsley, and paprika. Sprinkle topping over casserole and **cover** with wax paper. (If dish is flat-bottomed, **elevate** it on an inverted saucer.) Place on turntable if available and microwave on HIGH for 4 to 7 minutes (LW 5 to 8 minutes) or until hot and bubbly. (**Rotate** dish ½ turn every 2 minutes if not using a turntable.)

Troubleshooting: Forgetting to whisk sauce may cause it to be lumpy.

Suggestions: This is a lovely dish any time of the year on a buffet table or as an addition to Sunday brunch.

MOTHER'S DAY

Ever since I can remember, my mom has practiced her philosophy that it's always better to give than to receive. I have carried this over with my own children, along with the idea that sometimes the most treasured gifts are those that someone has taken the time to create personally.

Keeping this in mind, I want to share a "Happy Mother's Day," "Happy Birthday," "Welcome to the Neighborhood," "Hope You're Feeling Better," or just a little "Hello, Hope This Brings a Smile" gift that my mom taught me. Each gift can be personalized individually to anyone's taste and pocketbook.

Begin by baking individual muffins in paper drinking cups. Place a pretty cloth napkin inside a new clay flowerpot. Add small houseplant gardening tools, a gift certificate to a local clothing store, a bag of herbs to make mulled apple cider, gourmet coffee or tea for a hot drink to accompany the muffin. A magazine subscription tucked in would be nice, or try plane tickets to visit a special friend or relative.

You'll probably find there is still enough room to add a small gift box that can hold earrings, a bracelet, a pretty hair comb, or a locket with a loved one's picture. Tickets to dinner and a play are certainly a treat that anyone would love to discover. A bow tied to the outside of the gift pot completes the gift.

Pumpkin Raisin Muffins

MAKES 14 TO 16 MUFFINS; 8 TO 10 IN 9-OUNCE PAPER CUPS

EQUIPMENT:	medium mixing bowl, muffin pan or 6 custard cups or 6 9-ounce paper drinking cups, cooling rack, custard cup
COOKING TIME:	3 to 4 minutes (Low wattage ovens 3½ to 4¾ minutes)
STANDING TIME:	none required

¾ **cup canned pumpkin**
½ **cup orange juice**
1 **egg**
1 **teaspoon ground cinnamon**
½ **teaspoon ground nutmeg**
1 **package Nut Quick bread mix**
1 **cup raisins, plumped (see box; page 220)**
 apple jelly, maraschino cherries, and sliced almonds for garnish

Blend pumpkin, orange juice, egg, cinnamon, and nutmeg in medium bowl. Add bread mix and **stir** until dry particles are moistened—50 to 75 strokes. **Stir** in raisins.

Line a muffin pan or 6 custard cups with 2 paper cupcake liners (see box on page 241). (If you're using 9-ounce paper drinking cups, do not use paper liners.) Fill cups ⅔ full. If you're using custard or drinking cups, place them in a circle in the oven. Cook 6 muffins at a time on HIGH for 3 to 4 minutes (LW 3½ to 4¾ minutes), until the tops are no longer doughy.

Rearrange cups or **rotate** muffin pan ½ turn after 2 minutes. Remove muffins from their containers and immediately discard the outer wet paper. (If you're using drinking cups, place entire cup on rack to cool.) Place muffins on wire rack to cool.

To garnish muffins, melt 1 tablespoon apple jelly in custard cup on HIGH for 40 to 50 seconds (LW 1 minute) and spread over the top of the cooled muffin. Add a cherry and several sliced almonds to form a flower.

Troubleshooting: When you're using the paper drinking cups, fill only ½ full of batter. They bake so fast that the batter will go over the sides if you use too much.

Suggestions: To place in flowerpots, do not remove muffins from drinking cups but place entire muffin-filled paper cup in flowerpot. To remove muffin from paper cup, loosen muffin all around the cup with blade of a knife, gently shake, and the muffin will pop out.

PLUMPING RAISINS

Raisins will be distributed throughout the cake if they are plumped up before being added to the batter. Place 1 cup raisins and 2 teaspoons water in a 2-cup glass measure. **Cover** with plastic wrap, pulling back one corner to vent the steam, and microwave on HIGH for 15 to 20 seconds (LW 18 to 24 seconds). **Stir** and let **stand** for 1 minute.

FATHER'S DAY

Father's Day Red Devil Pound Cake

Why not change your routine for Dad's special day and create a delectable home-baked gift in less time than it takes to select a tie from the store? A luscious, chocolaty indulgence will show your favorite guy just how much you care.

SERVES 8 TO 10

EQUIPMENT: 2-quart ring mold or bundt pan, small dish, large mixing bowl, electric mixer
COOKING TIME: 14 to 16½ minutes (Low wattage ovens 17½ to 19½ minutes)
STANDING TIME: 10 minutes

1 **8-ounce package cream cheese**
¾ **cup butter-flavored Crisco**
1¼ **cups sugar**
4 **eggs**
1 **teaspoon vanilla extract**
4 **envelopes unsweetened Nestlé Choco Bake**
½ **teaspoon red food coloring**
1¾ **cups flour**
1¼ **teaspoons baking powder**
¼ **teaspoon salt**
Sweet Buttercream Frosting (recipe follows)

Grease ring mold or bundt pan and dust with sugar; set aside. Remove cream cheese from foil wrapper and place in a shallow dish. Microwave on 50 percent power or MEDIUM for 60 to 90 seconds (LW 1¼ to 1¾ minutes) or until softened. Place softened cream cheese, Crisco, and sugar in large bowl. Beat with an electric mixer at medium speed until light and fluffy. Beat in eggs one at a time, then blend in vanilla, Choco Bake, and red food coloring. Add flour, baking powder, and salt, **mixing** well.

Spoon batter into prepared dish. Place on turntable if available and microwave on 30 percent power or LOW for 7 minutes (LW 8¼ minutes). (**Rotate** dish ½ turn after 3 minutes if not using turntable.) Increase power to HIGH and microwave for 6 to 8 minutes (LW 7½ to 9½ minutes) or until top is dry and cake begins to come away from the sides of the dish. (**Rotate** dish ½ turn every 3 minutes if not using turntable.) Let **stand** on a hard heat-proof surface for 10 minutes, then invert onto cake plate and cool completely before frosting with Sweet Buttercream Frosting.

To Assemble Cake:

Slice cake into 3 layers. Place bottom layer on a cake dish covered with a paper doily and frost. Add second layer and frost. Add third layer and spread frosting over the top and sides of cake. Sprinkle completely cooled almonds over entire frosted cake and chill until ready to serve. Allow cake to **stand** at room temperature for 30 minutes before serving.

SWEET BUTTERCREAM FROSTING

MAKES 2 CUPS

EQUIPMENT:	glass pie plate, deep 2-quart bowl, electric mixer
COOKING TIME:	4¾ to 5¾ minutes (Low wattage ovens 5½ to 7 minutes)
STANDING TIME:	5 minutes

1 tablespoon butter or margarine, sliced
½ cup slivered almonds
1 8-ounce container unsalted whipped butter *or* 1 cup (½ pound) unsalted butter
1 to 1½ cups sugar
1 box (3½ ounces) vanilla pudding mix, prepared according to package directions and cooled

Place 1 tablespoon butter or margarine in pie plate; **elevate** on an inverted saucer if plate is flat-bottomed, and microwave on HIGH for 40 to 50 seconds (LW 50 to 60 seconds) or until melted. Add slivered almonds, **tossing** to coat. Place on turntable if available and microwave on HIGH for 3 to 4 minutes (LW 3½ to 4¾ minutes), **stirring** every 2 minutes or until almonds are light golden brown. Let **stand** on a hard heat-proof surface for 5 minutes as the almonds will continue to brown, then allow to cool.

Place 1 cup butter in deep bowl and microwave on 50 percent power or MEDIUM for 1 minute (LW 1¼ minutes) or until softened but not melted.

Using an electric mixer, begin beating until smooth. Gradually add 1 cup sugar, beating until all the sugar has dissolved and you can no longer feel or taste the granules. The amount of sugar you use depends on your own personal taste for sweetness; taste and adjust as you beat. (You must beat for 10 to 20 minutes to be sure all granules are dissolved.)

Once smooth, gradually add about 1 cup of the prepared pudding into the butter mixture, beating until smooth and creamy.

Suggestions: Any leftover frosting can be frozen and defrosted on 30 percent power or LOW for 1½ to 2 minutes and whipped up with a fork.

You can also add a tablespoon or 2 of cocoa powder to about ½ cup of the frosting. Use the chocolate frosting to frost the center layer of the cake, which looks lovely when sliced.

CRISCO AND CHOCO BAKE

Butter-flavored Crisco is a convenient shortening that has a delicate butter flavor and taste. It can be kept on your pantry shelf year-round, doesn't need to be softened as butter does, has no sodium or cholesterol, and, best of all, makes cakes high, light, moist, and long-keeping. Nestlé Choco Bake is a premelted, unsweetened chocolate-flavor substitute. One packet is equal to 1 square (1 ounce) of unsweetened baking chocolate. It may be found in the baking section of any grocery store, requires no melting, and comes in easy-to-open packets that pour right into the batter.

LABOR DAY

Labor Day Ice Cream

What could be more perfect for a Labor Day picnic than fresh fruit ice cream? The days of the old-fashioned hand-cranked ice cream freezers are over now that the market is full of "instant" ice cream makers, either electric models or the brilliantly simple ones you freeze by turning a handle every few minutes.

My dear friend Toni Burks, food editor for the *Roanoke Times & World-News* in Virginia, has converted her old-fashioned southern boiled custard into the base for the most delicious ice cream imaginable. Toni tells me that she used to spend a long time standing over her stove, constantly stirring her custard, only to have it scorch more times than not. The microwave version is the best.

OLD SOUTHERN CUSTARD BASE

MAKES 2½ QUARTS

EQUIPMENT:	deep 4-quart round casserole dish or bowl, small mixing bowl, electric mixer, large mixing bowl or pan
COOKING TIME:	9 to 11 minutes (Low wattage ovens 10¼ to 13 minutes)
STANDING TIME:	overnight

2 cups milk
1 cup sugar
¼ teaspoon salt
6 eggs
2 pounds fruit of choice, such as blackberry, peach, etc., chopped or pureed
2 cups whipping cream
2 teaspoons flavoring, such as vanilla or almond extract

Place milk in deep casserole dish or bowl. (If dish is flat-bottomed, **elevate** it on an inverted saucer.) Place on turntable if available and microwave on HIGH for 2 to 3 minutes (LW 2¼ to 3½ minutes) or until hot and steamy. Add ½ cup sugar and salt, **stirring** until well blended; set aside.

Whisk eggs in small bowl until light and well blended. Slowly add beaten eggs to scalded milk mixture, **whisking** constantly to blend well. Microwave on 70 percent power or MEDIUM-HIGH for 7 to 8 minutes (LW 8 to 9½ minutes) or until thickened, **beating** twice with electric mixer during cooking. (Egg will soft-set around the edge of the bowl, and beating will incorporate it into the milk.)

Cool mixture quickly by placing in a large bowl or pan of ice water and stirring regularly. **Cover** and chill overnight. Combine fruit with remaining ½ cup of sugar, **stir** well, and refrigerate overnight.

When you're ready to make ice cream, **stir** whipping cream and flavoring into chilled custard. Pour to fill line in canister of ice cream maker and freeze according to manufacturer's directions. When partially frozen, **stir** in fruit. Continue to freeze.

Suggestions: This recipe can easily be scaled down for smaller ice cream freezers—or prepare the entire recipe and use any leftover custard as a topping for fresh fruit, pound cake, or puddings.

HOMEMADE ICE CREAM TIPS

Always follow directions for your particular ice cream maker. Use enough fruit and sugar along with a pinch of salt to improve the taste. The mix should be strongly flavored, because cold chills the taste buds.

Mix chunks of fruit with sugar before adding to the mixture to keep them from freezing hard. Use fruit in season to flavor the ice cream—apricots, peaches, nectarines, blueberries, strawberries, raspberries, blackberries, and bananas are all worth a try.

Add more zip to the flavor with liqueur. However, keep in mind that alcohol will slow down the freezing process. Flavoring extracts lose their potency when added to hot mixtures, so add them to the chilled custard base.

ROSH HASHANAH: JEWISH NEW YEAR

The culinary customs that Jewish people observe during their New Year holiday of Rosh Hashanah have been traced back to early biblical times. On the New Year it is customary to serve apple slices dipped in a bowl of honey, signifying the heartfelt yearning for a sweet and happy year.

Fruited Holiday Brisket

SERVES 4 TO 8

EQUIPMENT: 1-quart round casserole dish, long-tined meat fork, large roasting bag with casserole dish to hold it or deep 3-quart casserole dish with cover, small mixing bowl

COOKING TIME: Fruit—5 to 7 minutes (Low wattage ovens 6 to 8 minutes)

2-pound roast—60 to 70 minutes (LW ovens 72 to 84 minutes)

4-pound roast—1 hour and 50 minutes to 2 hours and 10 minutes (LW ovens 2 hours and 12 minutes to 2 hours and 36 minutes)

STANDING TIME: 10 minutes

1   **bag (12 ounces) assorted dried fruits**
2   **lemon slices**
3   **tablespoons dark brown sugar**
1   **2- to 4-pound flat-cut brisket**
½   **cup ketchup**
½   **cup water**
1   **envelope (1¼ ounces) dry onion soup mix**
½   **teaspoon ground ginger**
2   **whole bay leaves**
     fresh parsley sprigs for garnish

Place dried fruits, lemon slices, and brown sugar in 1-quart casserole dish. Add enough water to cover fruit and **cover** with lid or plastic wrap, pulling back one corner to vent the steam. (If dish is flat-bottomed, **elevate** it on an inverted saucer.) Microwave on HIGH for 5 to 7 minutes (LW 6 to 8 minutes), **stirring** and **rotating** dish ½ turn after 4 minutes until fruit is soft and plump. Let **stand, covered,** while preparing brisket.

Pierce both sides of meat deeply with tines of fork. Place meat in lightly floured oven roasting bag or casserole dish with cover. In small bowl, mix remaining ingredients and pour over meat. If top of meat is not covered with liquid, add additional water. Close bag with a string, dental floss, or a rubber band, leaving a small opening to vent the steam, and place in glass baking dish to catch any drippings. If you're using a casserole dish with a vented cover, place a piece of wax paper between the dish and cover to form a tight seal (see box on page 228). (If dish is flat-bottomed, **elevate** it on an inverted saucer.)

Microwave on HIGH for 10 minutes (LW 12 minutes), reduce power to 50 percent or MEDIUM, and microwave for 25 to 30 minutes (LW 30 to 36 minutes) per pound until fork-tender, **rotating** dish ½ turn every 15 minutes. (When you're using a roasting bag, turn entire bag over halfway through cooking time; if you're using a casserole dish, turn meat over halfway through cooking time.)

Once meat is tender, let **stand, covered,** for 10 minutes. After standing, remove bay leaves, slice brisket across the grain, place on serving platter, and **cover** with foil to keep warm. Drain plumped dried fruits and place around the brisket platter. Mix equal parts of brisket gravy and remaining fruit juices and baste over platter of meat and fruits. Garnish with parsley.

Troubleshooting: Be sure to leave a small space when you're closing the roasting bag to let the steam escape so that the bag doesn't melt. Be sure not to use a metal twist tie but substitute string, dental floss, or a rubber band.

Using a thick-cut piece of brisket won't be as tender and won't cook as evenly as the flat-cut brisket.

Suggestions: Assorted dried fruit is attractive, but if you prefer, use a single dried fruit variety of your choice.

TIGHTLY COVERED CONTAINERS

When you're covering cooking containers with plastic wrap, you must always pull back one corner to allow the steam an avenue of escape. However, when a recipe calls for a tightly covered container, just vented plastic wrap won't do—but that doesn't mean you should eliminate the venting step. Use a casserole dish with its own lid or cover. Should this cover have a spoon grove, a small opening that allows you to leave a plastic utensil in the container while it's covered, or a vent hole, place a piece of wax paper between the dish and the cover to form a tight seal that will heavily steam the contents of the dish.

Honeyed Carrots with Matzo Balls

Carrots in one form or another are served to signify a wish for prosperity in the coming year. Combined with honey, carrots are said to contain "sugar and spice and everything nice."

SERVES 6 TO 8

EQUIPMENT:	small mixing bowl, deep 2- and 3-quart round casserole dishes, 1-cup glass measure
COOKING TIME:	28 to 33¾ minutes (Low wattage ovens 34¼ to 40 minutes)
STANDING TIME:	3 minutes

2 **eggs**
2 **tablespoons vegetable oil**
1 **packet (2½ ounces) matzo ball mix**
1½ **quarts hot water**
1 **pound carrots, peeled and sliced ¼-inch thick**
6 **tablespoons parve margarine, sliced**
6 **tablespoons orange juice**
1 **teaspoon salt**
½ **teaspoon ground cinnamon**
½ **cup honey**
2 **tablespoons flour**

Blend eggs and oil in small bowl and add matzo ball mix. **Stir** with a fork until evenly mixed. **Cover** bowl and refrigerate for 15 minutes.

Place hot water in a deep 3-quart casserole dish and microwave on HIGH for 5 minutes (LW 6 minutes) or until a rolling boil begins. With wet hands, using a ½-teaspoon measure, form about 40 small balls. Drop balls into boiling water, **cover** with lid or plastic wrap, pulling back one corner to vent the steam, and microwave on HIGH for 3 minutes (LW 3½ minutes) or until water comes to a boil again.

Reduce power to 50 percent or MEDIUM and microwave for 5 to 7 minutes (LW 6 to 8 minutes), **stirring** after 3 minutes. Remove balls from water, place in a dish, **cover** with aluminum foil, shiny side toward the dish, and let **stand** while preparing honeyed carrots.

Place sliced carrots in deep 2-quart casserole dish and set aside. Add sliced margarine to glass measure and microwave on HIGH for 1 to 1¼ minutes (LW 1¼ to 1½ minutes), then **stir** in orange juice, salt, cinnamon, and honey, blending well. Add honey mixture to sliced carrots, **stirring** until well combined. **Cover** with lid or plastic wrap, pulling back one corner to vent the steam. (If dish is flat-bottomed, **elevate** it on an inverted saucer.) Place on turntable if available and microwave on HIGH for 9 minutes (LW 11 minutes), **stirring** twice during cooking. (**Rotate** dish ½ turn when stirring if not using turntable.)

Remove ⅓ of honey syrup and mix with the flour until smooth. **Stir** into carrots, **cover** again, and microwave on HIGH for 4 to 7 minutes (LW 5 to 8 minutes) or until carrots are tender, **stirring** once during cooking. (**Rotate** dish ½ turn when stirring if not using turntable.)

Add warm matzo balls to carrots and **stir** very carefully to coat balls with the thickened, honeyed syrup. **Cover** again and microwave on HIGH for 1 to 1½ minutes (LW 1½ to 2 minutes) to heat through. Let **stand, covered,** for 3 minutes and serve.

Troubleshooting: By slicing the carrots into uniformly sized pieces they will all cook in the same length of time.

If you find some carrots cooked and others hard, you used a container with square corners. If that is the only container available, move the carrots out of the square corners frequently.

Pineapple Kugel— Pineapple Yogurt Noodle Pudding

Every Jewish cook has her own favorite kugel recipe, many being passed down from generation to generation. On a kosher table, when made with any milk product, this dish can be served only as a main course, side dish, or dessert in a dairy, or fish meal. In the case of a nonkosher dinner noodle pudding can be served as a side dish with meat, chicken, or fish or as a dessert.

Noodle pudding makes a special addition to any buffet table, and even if you're not celebrating the Jewish New Year, try this welcome change from potatoes or plain pasta.

SERVES 8 TO 10

> EQUIPMENT: small, medium, and large mixing bowls, 2-quart round casserole dish, custard cup
> COOKING TIME: 21¾ to 27½ (Low wattage ovens 26¼ to 33½ minutes)
> STANDING TIME: 5 minutes

½ **cup (¼ pound) butter or margarine, sliced**
1 **cup hot cooked medium noodles, drained**
1 **8-ounce container pineapple yogurt**
1 **cup small-curd cottage cheese**
4 **eggs**
⅔ **cup sugar**
1 **8-ounce can crushed pineapple, drained**
½ **cup golden raisins**
1 **teaspoon ground cinnamon**
1 **teaspoon vanilla extract**
¼ **teaspoon salt**
2 **tablespoons butter or margarine, sliced**
½ **cup cinnamon graham cracker crumbs**

Place ½ cup margarine in small bowl and microwave on HIGH for 1 to 1½ minutes (LW 1¼ to 1¾ minutes) or until melted. In large bowl, combine noodles and melted butter. **Stir** in yogurt and cottage cheese and set aside.

In medium bowl, beat eggs and mix in sugar, pineapple, raisins, cinnamon, vanilla, and salt. Add to noodle mixture and blend gently but thoroughly.

Pour noodle mixture into casserole dish and set aside. Place 2 tablespoons butter in custard cup and microwave on HIGH for 45 to 55 seconds (LW 1 to 1½ minutes) or until melted. **Stir** cracker crumbs into melted butter and sprinkle over noodles. (If dish is flat-bottomed, **elevate** it on an inverted saucer.) Place on turntable if available and microwave, **uncovered,** on HIGH for 20 to 25 minutes (LW 24 to 30 minutes), until just set. (**Rotate** dish ¼ turn every 4 minutes if not using turntable.) Let **stand** on a hard heat-proof surface for 5 minutes. Cut into squares and serve warm.

Troubleshooting: When baked in a conventional oven, noodle pudding becomes very brown, crusty, and dry on top. When microwaving, the top of the dish will not brown but will be soft and moist. Be careful not to overcook trying to get a crusty dry top, as it will ruin the recipe.

Suggestion: May be frozen in individual servings. When ready to serve, defrost on 30 percent power or LOW for 1 to 2 minutes, then heat on HIGH for 45 seconds to 1 minute.

Sweet Noodle Kugel

SERVES 8 TO 10

EQUIPMENT:	small, medium, and large mixing bowls, custard cup, 2-quart round casserole dish
COOKING TIME:	22 to 27¾ minutes (Low wattage ovens 27¾ to 33 minutes)
STANDING TIME:	5 minutes

1　**8-ounce package medium noodles**
3　**tablespoons butter or margarine, sliced**
1　**3-ounce package cream cheese**
3　**eggs**
1　**cup sour cream**
½　**cup small-curd cottage cheese**
½　**cup sugar**
1　**teaspoon ground cinnamon**
⅛　**teaspoon salt**
1　**teaspoon vanilla extract**
1　**6-ounce package Sun-Maid fruit bits**

TOPPING
2　**tablespoons butter or margarine, sliced**
1　**tablespoon dark brown sugar**
½　**teaspoon ground cinnamon**
½　**cup graham cracker crumbs**

Cook and drain noodles, but do not rinse with cold water. Place noodles in medium bowl. Place 3 tablespoons butter in custard cup, **cover** with a paper towel, and microwave on HIGH for 45 to 60 seconds (LW 55 to 65 seconds) or until melted. **Stir** into noodles and set aside.

Remove cream cheese from wrapper and place in small bowl. Microwave on HIGH for 30 to 60 seconds (LW 45 to 65 seconds) or until softened.

Place eggs in large bowl and beat slightly with a fork. Blend in softened cream cheese, sour cream, cottage cheese, sugar, cinnamon, salt, and vanilla, **stirring** in fruit bits last. Add buttered noodles and combine gently. Spoon mixture into a round casserole dish.

For topping, place 2 tablespoons butter in custard cup, **cover** with a paper towel and microwave on HIGH for 40 to 50 seconds (LW 50 to 60 seconds) or until melted. **Stir** in brown sugar until dissolved. Add cinnamon and crumbs, **stirring** to combine. Sprinkle topping over noodle mixture. (If dish is flat-bottomed, **elevate** it on an inverted saucer.) Place on turntable if available and microwave, **uncovered,** on HIGH for 20 to 25 minutes (LW 25 to 30 minutes) or until set. (**Rotate** dish ¼ turn every 4 minutes if not using turntable.) Let **stand** on a hard heat-proof surface for 5 minutes before cutting into squares. Serve warm.

Troubleshooting: Do not overbake, trying to get a crusty brown top; it will not happen in the microwave. The top will remain soft and moist.

Suggestions: Freeze leftovers cut into individual servings wrapped in plastic wrap. When ready to use, defrost on 30 percent power or LOW for 1 to 2 minutes, then heat on HIGH for 45 seconds to 1 minute.

SLICING BUTTER AND MARGARINE

Many people complain that when they're melting butter or margarine it pops and spatters the inside of the microwave. Part of the problem can be trying to melt large chunks. Always slice butter or margarine when you're melting it or adding it to recipes; it will melt faster.

The popping sound occurs as the fat melts and boils. It won't hurt anything, but it will spatter if the container is not covered with a paper towel, wax paper, or vented plastic wrap. The melting process starts on the outside of the piece of butter and melts to the center. It takes much longer for one large piece to melt from the outside to the center, whereas small pieces melt individually and much faster.

HALLOWEEN

Halloween Caramel Apples

Halloween is really for the kids and those of us that are still kids at heart. The microwave is a great cooking tool for the children, because they can't get burned as long as they use microwave-safe utensils. I always think of caramel apples at Halloween, and the microwave avoids all the mess of caramel sticking to the pot.

SERVES 4

EQUIPMENT:	4 wooden sticks, deep 1-quart bowl or 6-cup glass measure
COOKING TIME:	2½ to 3½ minutes (Low wattage ovens 3 to 4 minutes)
STANDING TIME:	until set

4   chilled medium apples
1   14-ounce bag Kraft caramels
2   tablespoons water

Wash and pat dry 4 well-chilled apples and insert a wooden stick through the stem end into the core of each one. Place caramels and water in deep bowl or measure and microwave on HIGH for 2½ to 3½ minutes (LW 3 to 4 minutes), **stirring** caramel mixture well every minute until smooth. Carefully coat the apples completely with the hot caramel mixture and place on a sheet of buttered wax paper to set. Once cool, refrigerate until ready to serve. Allow to **stand** at room temperature for 15 minutes before serving.

Troubleshooting: Chill your apples first to help the caramel stick better.

Melt the caramel in a small, deep micro-safe container so that you will have enough room to turn the apples and completely cover them with the hot mixture.

To keep the cooled apples from sticking to the plate, place a piece of buttered wax paper over a dinner plate and place the dipped apples on the buttered surface. Let them cool and harden slightly, then refrigerate.

THANKSGIVING

Oyster Stuffing

What you stuff in that turkey doesn't have to be just plain bread stuffing.

MAKES ENOUGH FOR A 16- TO 18-POUND TURKEY

EQUIPMENT:	deep 3-quart round casserole dish
COOKING TIME:	11 to 15 minutes (Low wattage ovens 15 to 20 minutes)
STANDING TIME:	5 minutes

> 1 **12-ounce container shucked fresh oysters**
> 1 **cup diced onion**
> 1 **cup chopped celery**
> 1 **cup chopped fresh mushrooms**
> 1 **heaped tablespoon finely minced garlic**
> 4 **scallions, chopped**
> ¼ **cup snipped fresh parsley**
> 1 **teaspoon poultry seasoning**
> ½ **teaspoon seasoned salt**
> ½ **cup (¼ pound) butter or margarine, sliced**
> 2 **cups chicken broth**
> 8 **to 10 cups dry bread cubes or packaged stuffing mix**

Drain and chop oysters, reserving them along with their liquid. Place onions, celery, mushrooms, garlic, scallions, parsley, seasonings, and butter in deep casserole dish. **Cover** with lid or plastic wrap, pulling back one corner to vent the steam. (If dish is flat-bottomed, **elevate** it on an inverted saucer.)

Microwave on HIGH for 7 to 9 minutes (LW 9½ to 12 minutes) or until vegetables are crisp-tender. Add broth and reserved oyster liquid to vegetables, **cover,** and microwave for 4 to 6 minutes (LW 5½ to 8 minutes) or until the liquid is boiling.

Add oysters to hot liquid and carefully fold in bread cubes, mixing to moisten completely. Stuff turkey just before ready to bake.

Suggestions: To use as a side dish, place stuffing in a 12 x 8-inch casserole dish and **cover** with plastic wrap, pulling back one corner to vent the steam. (If dish is flat-bottomed, **elevate** it on an inverted saucer.) Microwave on HIGH for 6 to 8 minutes (LW 7½ to 10 minutes) or until hot. (If dish has been made ahead of time and refrigerated, it may take longer to heat through.) Let **stand, covered,** for 5 minutes and fluff with a fork before serving.

OYSTERS

There was a time when oysters were avoided during the months without an *R* in their name (like November), but thanks to modern refrigeration and expanded harvesting techniques, they can be enjoyed whether fresh or frozen all year and make a wonderful Thanksgiving stuffing.

You may notice when buying oysters that they are often labeled as either select or standard. This label refers to their size, not their quality. Select oysters are large, while standard oysters are medium to small in size. If you purchase frozen oysters, thaw them in the refrigerator or in an airtight container under cold running water. Once thawed, they should be used quickly and not refrozen.

Pumpkin Caramel Cake

SERVES 8 TO 10

EQUIPMENT:	12-cup bundt or tube pan, large mixing bowl, electric mixer
COOKING TIME:	16 to 17 minutes (Low wattage ovens 17 to 18 minutes)
STANDING TIME:	10 minutes

2 teaspoons sugar mixed with 1 teaspoon ground cinnamon for dusting pan
1 box Pillsbury Plus yellow cake mix
¼ cup orange juice
3 eggs
1 cup canned pumpkin
1 teaspoon baking soda
1 teaspoon ground cinnamon
½ teaspoon ground nutmeg
Whipped Caramel Frosting (recipe follows)
½ cup finely chopped nuts

Grease bundt or tube pan, dust with cinnamon sugar, and set aside. Combine all ingredients except frosting and nuts in large bowl and blend at low speed. Increase speed to medium and beat for 5 minutes. Pour batter into prepared dish. (If dish is flat-bottomed, **elevate** it on an inverted saucer.) Place on turntable if available and microwave on 30 percent power or LOW for 11 minutes (LW 13 minutes). (**Rotate** dish ¼ turn every 3 minutes if not using turntable.)

Increase power to HIGH and microwave for 5 to 6 minutes (LW 6 to 7 minutes) or until top appears almost dry. (**Rotate** dish ¼ turn every 3 minutes if not using turntable.) Let **stand** on a hard heat-proof surface for 10 minutes, then turn out onto a serving dish. When completely cool, frost with whipped caramel frosting and sprinkle with nuts. Refrigerate until ready to serve.

WHIPPED CARAMEL FROSTING

EQUIPMENT: deep medium mixing bowl (stainless steel if available)

1   pint whipping cream
⅓   cup packed light brown sugar
½   teaspoon vanilla extract
½   cup finely chopped nuts

Beat cream, brown sugar, and vanilla in a chilled deep mixing bowl until stiff.

Troubleshooting: Whipping cream whips better and faster if you use a stainless-steel bowl. Place bowl in freezer for 5 to 10 minutes to chill or, if you're using glass, place it in the refrigerator for 10 to 15 minutes to chill.

FOREFATHERS DAY

My grandfather had an old friend named Running Horse who was a true blooded Indian. Running Horse would always tell the youngsters in their town about his forefathers, how they lived and how their ways were so different from ours. The Indian people would eat some form of corn three times a day. Succotash was one dish that New Englanders easily adopted and enjoyed. Today "Forefathers Day" is celebrated each year on December 2 in Plymouth, Massachusetts, and succotash is one of the featured dishes on the buffet table.

Running Horse's contribution to my grandparents' Thanksgiving table was always homemade succotash. I know Running Horse spent hours removing his corn kernels from the cob, but my version is much quicker and easier.

Succotash

SERVES 4 TO 6

EQUIPMENT:	2-quart round casserole dish
COOKING TIME:	16 to 19 minutes (Low wattage ovens 19 to 22¾ minutes)
STANDING TIME:	2 minutes

1   **10-ounce paper-covered box frozen corn kernels**
1   **10-ounce paper-covered box frozen baby lima beans**
4   **tablespoons butter or margarine, sliced**
⅔   **cup light cream**
½   **teaspoon salt**
¼   **teaspoon pepper**
2   **tablespoons chopped pimiento**
1   **teaspoon snipped fresh parsley**

Place both paper-covered boxes of vegetables on 2 layers of paper towel on oven floor and microwave on HIGH for 6 minutes (LW 7¼ minutes). Shake boxes, turn over, and microwave on HIGH for 6 to 8 minutes (LW 7¼ to 9½ minutes) or until tender. Let boxes **stand** for 2 minutes.

Empty both boxes into casserole dish and add remaining ingredients. **Stir** to combine and **cover** with lid or plastic wrap, pulling back one corner to vent the steam. (If dish is flat-bottomed, **elevate** it on an inverted saucer.) Microwave on HIGH for 4 to 5 minutes (LW 4½ to 6 minutes) or until heated through, **stirring** and **rotating** dish ½ turn once. Let **stand, covered,** for 2 minutes and serve.

Troubleshooting: Be sure both boxes of frozen vegetables are covered with paper wrappers. If covered with aluminum foil, remove wrappers completely before microwaving, or the foil will arc and may cause the paper towels to ignite.

HANUKKAH

Blintz Cupcakes

You will be pleased to know that each cupcake is an excellent source of protein and vitamins A, B, D, E, and K.

MAKES 12 CUPCAKES

EQUIPMENT:	6-cup muffin dish or 6 custard cups, medium mixing bowl, electric mixer, small mixing bowl
COOKING TIME:	3 to 3½ minutes (Low wattage ovens 3¼ to 3¾ minutes)
STANDING TIME:	3 minutes

1 **cup small curd cottage cheese**
3 **tablespoons sour cream**
3 **eggs**
3 **tablespoons sugar**

1 **teaspoon vanilla extract**
1 **cup Bisquick**
½ **teaspoon ground cinnamon**

TOPPING
2 **teaspoons dark brown sugar**
½ **teaspoon ground cinnamon**
1 **tablespoon chopped nuts**

Line each muffin cup or custard cup with 2 paper cupcake liners; set aside.

In mixing bowl, blend together cottage cheese, sour cream, eggs, sugar, and vanilla using an electric mixer. Combine biscuit mix and cinnamon in a small bowl and add to the cheese mixture, mixing well. Spoon batter into prepared muffin papers, filling the cups ⅔ full.

Mix topping ingredients together and sprinkle over batter. Microwave on HIGH for 3 to 3½ minutes (LW 3¼ to 3¾ minutes) or until toothpick inserted in center comes out clean. Place muffin dish on hard heat-proof surface and immediately remove cupcakes to cooling rack. Discard outer paper liner and allow cupcakes to **stand** for 3 minutes.

Suggestions: Serve them warm with sour cream and strawberries. Or try cherry pie filling or fresh blueberries and whipped topping.

LINING MUFFIN CUPS

If you use only one paper cupcake liner when lining muffin dishes or custard cups, the excess moisture that forms in the cups will be absorbed into the baking muffin or cupcake. To absorb this excess moisture, always line each opening with 2 paper liners; one will absorb the moisture, and the other will hold the baking muffin or cupcake.

CHRISTMAS

Fruitcake Ring

'Tis the season to bake fruitcakes! You will notice I have left out the citron found in many old-fashioned fruitcakes: I find a lot of people don't care for it. Of course you can pour rum over the cake, but I've used an orange glaze that seeps into the cake, making it very moist and full of flavor.

SERVES 8 TO 10

EQUIPMENT:	2-quart ring mold or bundt pan, large mixing bowl, sifter, small mixing bowl, custard cup
COOKING TIME:	15½ to 19 minutes (Low wattage ovens 19¼ to 22¾ minutes)
STANDING TIME:	10 minutes

½ **cup butter-flavored Crisco**
1 **cup dark brown sugar**
2 **eggs**
1 **tablespoon grated orange or lemon zest**
1 **teaspoon vanilla extract**
3 **tablespoons orange or lemon juice**
2 **cups flour**
1 **teaspoon baking soda**
½ **teaspoon salt**
½ **cup golden raisins**
½ **cup maraschino cherries, cut into thirds**
1 **cup chopped dates**
1 **cup buttermilk**
½ **cup chopped nuts**

GLAZE
⅓ **cup sugar**
6 **tablespoons orange juice**
maraschino cherries and white almonds for garnish

Grease ring mold or bundt pan and sprinkle with chopped nuts if desired.

In large bowl, cream Crisco and brown sugar together. Beat in eggs; add orange or lemon zest, vanilla, and orange or lemon juice. Sift together flour, baking soda, and salt.

Place raisins, cherries, and dates in a small bowl and add 3 tablespoons of the flour mixture, tossing until well coated. Add the balance of the flour mixture to the creamed mixture, alternately with the buttermilk. Stir in fruits and nuts and spoon into prepared dish. (If dish is flat-bottomed, **elevate** it on an inverted saucer.) Place on a turntable if available and microwave on 50 percent power or MEDIUM for 9 minutes (LW 10¾ minutes). (**Rotate** dish ¼ turn every 3 minutes if not using turntable.)

Increase power to HIGH and cook for 6 to 9 minutes (LW 7½ to 10¾ minutes) or until cake pulls away from the sides of the dish and there are no visible moist spots on top. (**Rotate** dish ¼ turn every 3 minutes.) Let **stand** on a hard heat-proof surface for 10 minutes. Invert onto serving plate. Pierce top of cake (while still warm) several times with a long wooden pick or meat fork.

In custard cup, combine sugar and orange juice. Microwave on HIGH for 30 to 60 seconds (LW 1 to 1¼ minutes) or until very warm, stirring until sugar is dissolved. Drizzle over cake, allowing orange juice mixture to drip down into the holes. For decoration, place whole maraschino cherries and white almonds along the top to form flowers. When cake is completely cool, **cover** tightly and let **stand** overnight.

Troubleshooting: Instead of buying buttermilk especially to use in this recipe, make your own by combining 1 cup regular milk and 1 tablespoon vinegar or lemon juice. Another method of making buttermilk is to mix equal parts of milk and sour cream together.

Be sure to coat fruit with a small amount of the flour mixture to ensure that the fruit stays suspended in the cake and doesn't collect at the bottom.

Suggestions: Packed in colorful tins, this fruitcake makes a wonderful holiday gift from your kitchen.

Cheesecake Dreamers

I use this recipe all year long, but for my holiday table it makes an instant centerpiece. I use cherry pie filling to top each little cheesecake and place the cakes all along the outside edge of a doily-covered footed cake dish. I fill the center of the dish with artificial holly and berries, and it looks so festive! I have even fashioned a Christmas tree by covering a Styrofoam cone with red foil and pushing the holly and berry stems into the cone to cover it completely. What you use in the center of the dish won't matter, as long as you have plenty of cheesecake dreamers to keep refilling the dish.

MAKES 12 INDIVIDUAL DESSERTS

EQUIPMENT:	plastic muffin pan or 6 glass custard cups, small mixing bowl, cooling rack
COOKING TIME:	6 to 7½ minutes (Low wattage ovens 7¼ to 9½ minutes)
STANDING TIME:	until cool

- **12 vanilla wafers**
- **1 8-ounce package cream cheese**
- **¼ cup sugar**
- **1 egg**
- **1 tablespoon milk**
- **1 teaspoon vanilla extract**
- **1 teaspoon lemon juice**
- **1 teaspoon grated lemon zest**
- **1 can (21 ounces) cherry or blueberry pie filling**

Place 2 paper cupcake liners in each cup of a plastic muffin pan or 6 custard cups. Place one vanilla wafer in the bottom of each double cupcake liner. Set aside.

Remove cream cheese from foil wrapper and place in small bowl. Microwave on 50 percent power or MEDIUM for 60 to 90 seconds (LW 1¼ to 2 minutes) or until softened. Add sugar, egg, milk, vanilla, lemon juice, and lemon zest and blend together well. Fill each liner ⅔ full with cream cheese mixture. Place muffin pan in microwave or, if you're using custard cups, place in a circle on a turntable if available.

Microwave on 50 percent power or MEDIUM for 5 to 6 minutes (LW 6 to 7½ minutes) or until set, **rotating** dish or cups ½ turn every 2 minutes if not using a turntable.

Remove tarts to cooling rack, immediately discarding wet second cupcake paper. Cool completely and top with pie filling of your choice. Follow directions for remaining wafers and filling. Refrigerate until ready to serve.

Troubleshooting: You must reduce the power to 50 percent or MEDIUM for this recipe. Microwaving the cream cheese filling on HIGH will cause it to rise too quickly, and it may flow over the sides of the cup.

Suggestions: This recipe can easily be doubled, and you can also top it with fresh strawberries, raspberries, blueberries, or peaches.

CHRISTMAS GIFTS TO MAKE IN THE MICROWAVE

Homemade Christmas gifts can mean so much more to the recipient than something store-bought. Grandparents, aunts, uncles, teachers, and even the family pet will really enjoy receiving something made especially for them. You might want to include a recipe card giving them the instructions on how to duplicate your gift.

Homemade Dog Biscuits

There is one member of your family that this Christmas gift would mean more to than words can express. By making your own dog biscuits, you produce a healthy snack, free of the additives, chemicals, and preservatives found in commercial dog biscuits. I consulted with veterinarian Dr. Gerald Fishbeck of Fairhaven, Connecticut, for his comments on my recipe. Dr. Fishbeck notes that he sees more digestive problems in dogs from people overfeeding them table food at holiday time than at any other time of the year. He feels your pet would be far healthier given a homemade treat than a large dish of table scraps. You can cut the biscuits with a dog bone–shaped cookie cutter or make your own pattern from cardboard. Fashion a wreath out of cardboard and tie the bones onto it with pretty red and green ribbons or fill Fido's stocking to the top, but please, don't let him or her eat the entire batch at one sitting.

MAKES 15 TO 20 PIECES, DEPENDING ON SHAPE AND SIZE

EQUIPMENT:	medium mixing bowl, pastry blender or 2 table knives, rolling pin, cookie cutter
COOKING TIME:	6 to 10 minutes (Low wattage ovens 7½ to 12 minutes)
STANDING TIME:	10 to 15 minutes to cool

1   **cup whole wheat flour**
¼   **cup flour**
½   **cup yellow cornmeal**
¾   **cup instant nonfat dry milk**
½   **cup uncooked oatmeal**
½   **teaspoon garlic powder**
½   **teaspoon onion powder**
¼   **teaspoon seasoned salt**
3   **tablespoons liver powder (available at health food stores; optional)**
1   **teaspoon sugar**
⅓   **cup butter, margarine, or solid shortening**
1   **egg**
1   **tablespoon powdered beef or chicken flavor gravy mix**
½   **cup beef or chicken broth**

Combine flour, cornmeal, powdered milk, oatmeal, garlic and onion powders, salt, liver powder, and sugar in medium bowl. Cut shortening into dry ingredients with a pastry blender or table knives until mixture resembles coarse crumbs (as in making a pie crust).

Stir in egg. **Stir** gravy mix into broth until combined. Slowly pour broth mixture into dry ingredients and mix with a fork to blend. Form dough into a ball and knead on a floured board for 3 to 4 minutes. Divide dough in ½ and roll the dough ½-inch thick as you would cookie dough. Using a cute cookie cutter, cut out as you would cookies.

Arrange 6 to 8 pieces like the spokes of a wheel on 2 layers of paper towel on the floor of the microwave. Prick the center of each biscuit twice with the tines of a fork to keep the biscuits flat. Microwave on 50 percent power or MEDIUM for 6 to 10 minutes (LW 7½ to 12 minutes), **rotating** the paper towel every 3 minutes and turning the biscuits over after 4 minutes, until dry and firm to the touch. Once biscuits feel firm and before they begin to burn, remove them to a cooling rack and watch them crisp as they cool.

Troubleshooting: Because the size of the cut-out biscuits varies, microwave the first batch with great care and watch them closely to be sure they don't begin to burn. They will feel firm to the touch when done but will crisp up quite hard as they cool.

Suggestions: Place cooled biscuits in a tightly covered tin or plastic container to keep them fresh.

Fragrant Citrus Potpourri

Whether we like it or not, most of our homes are closed up tight for the winter, trapping all kinds of stale odors. A lovely way to add a fresh fragrance to the otherwise familiar winter smells is to simmer a potpourri mixture in your microwave, on your wood or coal stove, or in a potpourri burner. Prepackaged potpourri mixtures can be expensive, but homemade mixtures make wonderful gifts. You might want to purchase a potpourri burner as part of the gift or line the inside of a coffee mug or handled ceramic soup dish with an oversized piece of plastic wrap. Fill the container with your potpourri mixture, bring the sides of the plastic wrap up and over the mixture, and tie the top with a colored ribbon or yarn. An especially nice touch is to include a card giving the recipient the recipe as well as instructions for its use.

Whether you use all the fruits recommended or just your favorites, this mixture will add a splash of heavenly flavors to any room. The mixture is best when boiled in water, as the boiling releases the oils in the spices.

MAKES 1¼ CUPS

EQUIPMENT:	sharp paring knife, 1-cup glass measure
COOKING TIME:	5 to 7 minutes (Low wattage ovens 6 to 8 minutes)
STANDING TIME:	24 to 36 hours

1 lemon
1 orange
1 lime
1 tangerine
¼ cup water
2 tablespoons apple pie spice
¼ cup whole cloves
4 whole cinnamon sticks, broken into chunks
4 or 5 whole nutmegs
1 teaspoon ground ginger
2 bay leaves, crumbled
1 teaspoon cardamom seeds

Using a sharp paring knife, carefully cut strips of only the colored skin (zest) from each fruit, being careful not to cut into the white membrane underneath the skin. (It isn't necessary to cut the skin from the tangerine, as it should peel off very easily.) Once the skins have been removed from the fruit, cut them into 1½-inch lengths, refrigerating the fruit for other uses.

Line a paper plate with 2 layers of paper towel and cover with a single layer of fruit skin strips. Place the paper plate in the microwave on top of an inverted saucer. Add water to glass measure and place next to the paper plate. Microwave on HIGH for

5 to 7 minutes (LW 6 to 8 minutes), **rearranging** the strips every minute, until they just begin to dry. Repeat process with any remaining undried strips. Place the dried strips on a fresh paper plate lined with paper towels and allow to air-dry for 24 to 36 hours.

Combine the air-dried fruit strips in a plastic bag with all the remaining spices. Secure bag tightly and shake well to mix the ingredients.

To freshen the air, place 1 cup water in small bowl and add 1 heaped tablespoon potpourri mixture. Microwave on HIGH for 3 to 4 minutes (LW 4 to 5 minutes) or until boiling. Remove the container from the microwave and let **stand** until cool. If fragrance isn't strong enough, repeat above instructions once or twice more.

Troubleshooting: Cut fruit strips as uniformly in size as possible, because things of the same size microwave in the same length of time.

Suggestions: To use on top of a wood or coal stove, mix 2 heaped tablespoons to a quart of water.

Jams and Condiments

MICROWAVING JAM

The most important things to remember when you're microwaving jam are that batches should be small and large containers need to be used to contain the boiling. If you plan to can your jam, use a water bath canner on your conventional stove.

Microwave energy will not penetrate paraffin, which must be melted on your stove top; it just won't melt properly in the microwave. You want to make jam but don't have canning equipment? No problem: cool the jam and ladle into plastic freezer containers. Mark the container with its contents and date of freezing, and you'll find your jam will hold its color and flavor beautifully in the freezer until it's needed. Be sure not to use glass containers for freezing unless they are freezer-safe.

Always use a metal spoon when stirring and removing the foam from the top of the jam pot. To test the doneness of the jam, dip the metal spoon into the jam and hold the spoon vertically. When you are able to see 2 drops of jam run together on the edge of the spoon to form one single drop, the jam is done.

Blueberry Jam

MAKES 3 PINTS OF JAM

EQUIPMENT: deep 3- or 4-quart round casserole dish, potato masher

COOKING TIME: 15 to 19 minutes (Low wattage ovens 17¾ to 22 minutes)

STANDING TIME: none required

1½ pints fresh blueberries, washed and stemmed
1 tablespoon fresh lemon juice
½ 1¾-ounce box powdered fruit pectin
2¼ cups sugar

In deep casserole dish, completely mash blueberries with potato masher. **Stir** in the lemon juice and pectin. **Cover** dish with wax paper. (If dish is flat-bottomed, **elevate** it on an inverted saucer.) Place on turntable if available and microwave on HIGH for 9 to 11 minutes (LW 10¾ to 13 minutes) or until the mixture comes to a full rolling boil all around the dish and in the center, **stirring** well every 3 minutes. (**Rotate** dish ½ turn when stirring if not using turntable.)

Stir in sugar and microwave on HIGH for 5 to 7 minutes (LW 6 to 8 minutes) or until mixture comes to another full boil, **stirring** every 2 minutes. (**Rotate** dish ½ turn when stirring if not using turntable.) Boil for 1 full minute on HIGH. Skim off any foam using a metal spoon and place in sterilized canning jars, decorative glasses, or freezer containers. If you're using plastic, be sure to cool jam first so as not to melt the container.

Troubleshooting: Be sure to measure pectin carefully and label leftover for next batch.

Suggestions: If you're using frozen blueberries, be sure you start with 2 cups of mashed berries.

Fresh Cherry Jam

MAKES 3½ CUPS

EQUIPMENT: deep 3-quart round casserole dish
COOKING TIME: 14 to 21 minutes (Low wattage ovens 16½ to 24 minutes)
STANDING TIME: none required

3 cups finely chopped fresh sweet cherries, stems and pits removed
1 tablespoon fresh lemon juice
½ 1¾-ounce box powdered fruit pectin
3 cups sugar

Grind or finely chop prepared cherries and place in deep casserole dish. Sprinkle cherries with lemon juice and pectin, mixing to combine completely. (If dish is flat-bottomed, **elevate** it on an inverted saucer.) Place on turntable if available and microwave, **uncovered,** on HIGH for 8 to 12 minutes (LW 9½ to 14 minutes) or until mixture is rapidly boiling all around dish and in the center, **stirring** every 4 minutes. (**Rotate** dish ½ turn when stirring if not using turntable.)

Add sugar and **stir** to combine. Microwave, **uncovered,** on HIGH for 6 to 9 minutes (LW 7 to 10 minutes), **stirring** once after 3 minutes and then every minute to prevent boiling over, until mixture is at a full rolling boil. (**Rotate** dish ½ turn when stirring if not using turntable.)

Boil hard for 1 minute on HIGH and then, using pot holders, carefully remove the hot dish from the microwave. Using a metal spoon, skim off any foam and place hot jam in sterilized jars for canning. If not canning, cool jam before placing in freezer containers or in a large jar to store in the refrigerator.

Troubleshooting: Measure pectin carefully and reserve the balance for jams later in the season.

Do not place hot jam in plastic containers; they may melt.

Peach Jam

MAKES 3½ CUPS

EQUIPMENT: deep 3- or 4-quart round casserole dish, potato masher

COOKING TIME: 11 to 17 minutes (Low wattage ovens 14 to 20 minutes)

STANDING TIME: none required

1   pound peaches, skinned, pitted, and mashed with a potato masher (2 cups prepared fruit)
1   tablespoon fresh lemon juice
½   1¾-ounce box powdered fruit pectin
2¾   cups sugar

Place mashed fruit in deep casserole dish and mix in lemon juice. Completely **stir** in powdered pectin and **cover** with wax paper. (If dish is flat-bottomed, **elevate** it on an inverted saucer.) Place on turntable if available and microwave on HIGH for 7 to 10 minutes (LW 8½ to 12 minutes) or until mixture comes to a full rolling boil all around the sides of the container and in the center, **stirring** once. (**Rotate** dish ½ turn when stirring if not using turntable.)

Immediately add sugar and **stir.** Microwave on HIGH for 3 to 6 minutes (LW 4½ to 7 minutes) or until mixture comes to a full rolling boil again. **Stir** after 3 minutes and then every minute to prevent the jam from boiling over. (**Rotate** dish ½ turn when stirring if not using turntable.)

Once mixture is completely boiling, boil for 1 minute more on HIGH. Skim off any foam with a metal spoon and place in sterilized canning jars, decorative glasses, or completely cool and place in plastic freezer containers.

Troubleshooting: Measure pectin carefully, labeling leftover for next batch.

Strawberry Jam

MAKES 3½ CUPS

EQUIPMENT: deep 3- or 4-quart round casserole dish, potato masher

COOKING TIME: 10 to 17 minutes (Low wattage ovens 12 to 19½ minutes)

STANDING TIME: none required

1 quart fresh strawberries, cleaned and hulled, to make 2½ cups mashed berries

½ 1¾-ounce box powdered fruit pectin

3 cups sugar

Mash strawberries in deep casserole dish. Add pectin and **stir** thoroughly. **Cover** with wax paper. (If dish is flat-bottomed, **elevate** it on an inverted saucer.) Place on turntable if available and microwave on HIGH for 5 to 9 minutes (LW 6 to 10½ minutes) or until mixture comes to a full boil all around the edges and center of dish, **stirring** twice during cooking. (**Rotate** dish ½ turn when stirring if not using turntable.)

Completely **mix** in sugar and microwave, **uncovered,** on HIGH for 4 to 7 minutes (LW 5 to 8 minutes) or until mixture comes to a full rolling boil, **stirring** every minute to prevent mixture from boiling over. After mixture comes to a full boil, boil for 1 minute on HIGH. Using a metal spoon, skim off foam and let jam cool slightly. Pour into sterilized canning jars, decorative glasses, or freezer containers. If you're using plastic, be sure to cool first to avoid melting containers.

Suggestions: Be sure to measure pectin carefully and label leftover for next batch. You may substitute 20 ounces of frozen strawberries for fresh.

Some canning jars can be used in the freezer, but be sure to check that they are freezer-safe before using.

Raspberry Jam

MAKES 3½ CUPS

EQUIPMENT:	deep 3- or 4-quart round casserole dish, potato masher
COOKING TIME:	15 to 19 minutes (Low wattage ovens 17¾ to 22¾ minutes)
STANDING TIME:	none required

1   quart fresh raspberries
½   1¾-ounce box powdered pectin
3   cups sugar

Carefully pick over the berries and use only firm, fully ripe, blemish-free fruit. In deep casserole dish, thoroughly crush the berries with potato masher. Thoroughly **stir** pectin into the fruit and **cover** dish with wax paper. (If dish is flat-bottomed, **elevate** it on an inverted saucer.) Microwave on HIGH for 9 to 11 minutes (LW 10¾ to 13¼ minutes) or until the mixture comes to a full rolling boil all around the dish and in the center, **stirring** twice.

   Stir in the sugar and microwave, **uncovered,** on HIGH for 5 to 7 minutes (LW 6 to 8 minutes) or until mixture comes to another full boil, **stirring** twice. Once boiling, boil for 1 full minute on HIGH. Remove dish from microwave and, using a metal spoon, skim off any foam on top of the jam.

Troubleshooting: Be sure to cool the very hot jam before placing in plastic freezer containers. If canning, place hot jam in sterilized jars and process in water bath canner.

Suggestions: If you don't like all the seeds in your jam, sieve part of the pulp to remove some of the seeds. Be sure to measure pectin carefully and label leftover for next batch.

Good Morning Raspberry Butter

Besides using plain jam on your morning toast, try turning it into raspberry butter. It will keep fresh in your fridge for 10 to 12 days if it lasts that long.

MAKES ¾ CUP

> EQUIPMENT: small mixing bowl
> COOKING TIME: 35 to 45 seconds (Low wattage ovens 40 to 50 seconds)
> STANDING TIME: 1 to 2 minutes

½ cup butter or margarine
¾ cup confectioners' sugar
2 tablespoons raspberry jam (see preceding recipe)

Remove butter from its wrapper and place in small bowl. Microwave on 30 percent power or LOW for 35 to 45 seconds (LW 40 to 50 seconds) or until softened. Watch carefully, if butter begins to melt around the edges, stop microwaving immediately and let the dish **stand** for 1 to 2 minutes to soften.

Add confectioners' sugar to soften butter and blend until smooth and creamy. Completely fold in jam and serve on toast, muffins, pancakes, waffles, or fresh bread. Refrigerate any leftovers.

CRANBERRIES

You should purchase cranberries that are firm, plump, and red to reddish black in color. Fresh from the bag, cranberries can be chopped and up to 1 cup can be added to basic muffin or quick bread mixes before baking. They can be added to fresh fruit pies along with blueberries, apples, raisins, or your mincemeat mixture.

Cranberry Wine Relish

MAKES 4 CUPS

EQUIPMENT:	deep 3- or 4-quart round casserole dish or bowl
COOKING TIME:	12 to 18 minutes (Low wattage ovens 14 to 21 minutes)
STANDING TIME:	none required

1 12-ounce bag fresh cranberries
1 cup red wine
1½ cups sugar
**   grated zest of 1 orange**
1 cinnamon stick

Combine all ingredients in deep casserole dish or bowl and **cover** with wax paper. (If dish is flat-bottomed, **elevate** it on an inverted saucer.) Place on turntable if available and microwave on HIGH for 12 to 18 minutes (LW 14 to 21 minutes) or until cranberries burst open, are soft, and sauce is slightly thickened, **stirring** every 4 minutes. (**Rotate** dish ¼ turn when stirring if not using turntable.)

Skim foam from surface with metal spoon and place in a decorative serving dish. Remove cinnamon stick. Cool, then refrigerate until ready to serve.

Troubleshooting: Prepare relish several days before serving to allow flavors to blend.

Suggestions: To enhance meat platters, mound relish in orange shells or fill pear or peach halves and place around the outside of the platter.

PICKLES

The only drawback to pickling in the microwave is that you can't make as large a batch as you could on a conventional stove. On the positive side, if you're not equipped with all the necessary tools for canning, the small batches will be perfect to keep in your refrigerator.

The best pickles are made from just-ripe cucumbers free from deformities, bruises, and blemishes. For best results, prepare pickles within 2 days of picking cukes. If immediate preparation isn't possible, store unwashed cucumbers in the refrigerator, as they deteriorate at room temperature. The only way to keep the pickles for an indefinite period of time is to can them. For this process you will need a water bath canner and canning jars. At this time there is no safe method for microwave-canning multiple jars, and this process must be done on a conventional stove.

If canning equipment is not available, you can pack the hot pickles into glass jars or cool them first and pack into plastic containers and keep them in your refrigerator until eaten. I don't suggest freezing, but they will keep for an indefinite period under refrigeration.

Bread-and-Butter Pickles

When we moved out into the country, our new neighbors had been farmers all their lives and preserving for the winter months was just routine for them. I was very lucky to be able to learn how to can, make jams, and especially these delicious bread-and-butter pickles from that patient neighbor. For years I had the time to make big batches of bread-and-butter pickles every year and can them. Time has been at a premium for me recently, but I just couldn't give up homemade pickles. After cutting down the original recipe to fit into the microwave, I found the finished pickles were exactly the same but took much less time to prepare. These pickles are just as good as, if not better than, store-bought pickles. Now you can take advantage of cucumbers when they are on sale all during the year, whenever your pickle container is empty.

MAKES 3 PINTS

EQUIPMENT:	large mixing bowl or small roasting pan, colander, deep 3- or 4-quart round casserole dish
COOKING TIME:	9 to 13 minutes (Low wattage ovens 11 to 15½ minutes)
SOAKING TIME:	3 hours
STANDING TIME:	none required

about 4 to 6 medium cucumbers (enough to make 6 cups, sliced)
2 **medium onions, peeled and cut into thin slices**
¼ **cup salt**
2 **cups cider vinegar**
1½ **cups sugar**
2 **tablespoons mustard seeds**
½ **teaspoon celery seeds**
dash of cayenne pepper

Gently wash and cut ends off cucumbers. Slice unpeeled cucumbers into ⅛-inch-thick slices. In a large bowl or small roasting pan, place cucumber and onion slices and sprinkle with salt. Cover the slices with a layer of ice cubes and lay a terry towel over the entire container. Let the **covered** container **stand** and soak for 3 hours.

Pour contents of container into colander and rinse with cold water until all traces of a salty taste are gone. Set vegetables aside to drain.

Place vinegar, sugar, mustard seed, celery seed, and cayenne pepper in deep casserole dish. **Stir** to blend and microwave, **uncovered,** on HIGH for 5 to 7 minutes (LW 6 to 8 minutes) or until rapidly boiling, **stirring** every 2 minutes.

Once liquid is boiling, gradually add the drained cucumbers and onions, **stirring** gently to distribute the brine. Microwave, **uncovered,** on HIGH for 4 to 6 minutes (LW 5 to 7½ minutes) or just until liquid boils, then immediately remove container from the microwave.

At this point you can pack hot pickles into sterilized canning jars, leaving ½-inch headspace, seal with lids, and process for 5 minutes in a hot water bath canner. If you're not canning, place hot pickles in tightly covered glass containers or cool and place in tightly covered plastic containers and keep refrigerated until all are gone. For best flavor, allow pickles to sit in brine for several days before eating.

Troubleshooting: The hardest part of this recipe is rinsing the salted cucumbers and onions until all the salty taste is gone. This may take several minutes, but do not underrinse, or the pickles will be too salty.

Suggestions: These make wonderful holiday gifts packed into a nice refrigerator container. Tie with a pretty ribbon and include the recipe, as I'm sure the recipient will want to make them again.

Index